GCSE
Spanish

Spice up your Spanish revision with this brilliant CGP book!
It's packed with the finest ingredients, including all the study notes and
practice questions you'll need for success in the Grade 9-1 exams.

We've also included free audio files to go with the listening questions.
You'll find them on the CD-ROM — or you can download them from this page:

www.cgpbooks.co.uk/GCSESpanishAudio

How to access your free Online Edition

You can read this entire book on your PC, Mac or tablet, with handy links to all the
online audio files. Just go to **cgpbooks.co.uk/extras** and enter this code:

1753 2347 4915 6351

By the way, this code only works for one person. If somebody else has used
this book before you, they might have already claimed the Online Edition.

D1439557

Complete
Revision & Practice
Everything you need to pass the exams!

Contents

Contents

Published by CGP

Editors:
Chloe Anderson
Rose Jones
Matt Topping
Jennifer Underwood

Contributors:
Matthew Parkinson
Jacqui Richards
Clare Swayne

With thanks to Karen Wells for the proofreading.

With thanks to Ana Pungartnik for the copyright research.

Acknowledgements:

Audio produced by Naomi Laredo of Small Print.

Recorded, edited and mastered by Graham Williams of The Speech Recording Studio,
with the assistance of Andy Le Vien at RMS Studios.

Voice Artists:

Jessica Gonzalez Campos

Daniel Martel Santana

Ángela Lobato del Castillo

Daniel Franco

CD-ROM edited and mastered by Neil Hastings.

AQA material is reproduced by permission of AQA.

Edexcel material is reproduced by permission of Edexcel.

With thanks to iStock.com for permission to use the images on pages 48, 53, 56, 68, 76, 79, 98, 105 and 175.

Abridged and adapted extract from 'Las inquietudes de Shanti Andía', on page 24, by Pío Baroja.

Abridged and adapted extract from 'Pepita Jiménez', on page 61, by Juan Valera.

Abridged and adapted extract from 'El paraíso de las mujeres', on page 185, by Vicente Blasco Ibáñez.

Abridged and adapted extract from 'Doña Perfecta', on page 188, by Benito Pérez Galdós.

Abridged and adapted extract from 'Viajes por Europa y América', on page 224 and audio tracks, by Gorgonio Petano y Mazariegos.

Abridged and adapted extract from 'Dos días en Salamanca', on page 226 and audio tracks, by Pedro Antonio de Alarcón.

ISBN: 978 1 78294 545 1
Printed by Elanders Ltd, Newcastle upon Tyne.
Clipart from Corel®

Numbers

Knowing the numbers in Spanish is really important — make sure you can understand, say and spell them.

Uno, dos, tres — One, two, three

0	cero	20	veinte
1	uno (un), una	21	veintiuno
2	dos	22	veintidós
3	tres	23	veintitrés
4	cuatro		
5	cinco	30	treinta
6	seis	31	treinta y uno
7	siete	40	cuarenta
8	ocho	50	cincuenta
9	nueve	60	sesenta
10	diez	70	setenta
11	once	80	ochenta
12	doce	90	noventa
13	trece		
14	catorce		
15	quince		
16	dieciséis		
17	diecisiete		
18	dieciocho		
19	diecinueve		

All twenty-something numbers are rolled into one — like 'veintiuno' (*twenty-one*).

After 30, numbers are joined by 'y' (*and*), but written separately — like 'treinta y uno' (*thirty-one*).

Grammar — using 'one' with masculine nouns

When you put '<u>one</u>' in front of a <u>masculine</u> word, uno becomes '<u>un</u>'.

veinti<u>ún</u> caballos	*21 horses*
treinta y <u>un</u> caballos	*31 horses*

Before a <u>feminine</u> word, the '<u>o</u>' changes to '<u>a</u>':

veinti<u>una</u> galletas	*21 biscuits*

See p.116 for more on masculine and feminine nouns.

100	cien(to)		700	setecientos/as
101	ciento uno		900	novecientos/as
200	doscientos/as		1000	mil
500	quinientos/as		1 000 000	un millón

'Cien' becomes 'ciento' when used in front of another number (except 'mil').

1826	mil ochocientos veintiséis	2000	dos mil
1984	mil novecientos ochenta y cuatro	2005	dos mil cinco

Primero, segundo, tercero — First, second, third

These words always end in '<u>o</u>' for <u>masculine</u> things and '<u>a</u>' for <u>feminine</u> things.

1st	primero/primera (1°/1ª)	6th	sexto/a
2nd	segundo/a (2°/2ª)	7th	séptimo/a
3rd	tercero/a (3°/3ª)	8th	octavo/a
4th	cuarto/a	9th	noveno/a
5th	quinto/a	10th	décimo/a

Grammar — 'primero', 'tercero' + masculine nouns

When '<u>primero</u>' or '<u>tercero</u>' appear in front of a masculine word, they <u>drop</u> the '<u>o</u>'.

el **<u>primer</u>** baile	*the <u>first</u> dance*
el <u>**tercer**</u> cantante	*the <u>third</u> singer*

Other useful number phrases

el número = number

una docena	*a dozen*	un par	*a couple / pair*	unos/as	*some / a few / about*

unas diez peras
about ten pears

First things first — learn your numbers...

Lee el texto y contesta a las preguntas en **español**.

'Tener' is a radical-changing verb. See p.138.

Marta tiene veintidós años. Su hermana solo tiene diecisiete años, pero su abuelo tiene ochenta y ocho años. Marta vive muy cerca de aquí — en la segunda calle a la derecha.

e.g. ¿Cuántos años tiene Marta? *Tiene veintidós años.*

1. ¿Cuántos años tiene su hermana? Tiene diecisiete años [1]
2. ¿Cuántos años tiene su abuelo? ochenta y ocho años [1]
3. ¿Dónde vive Marta? [1]

Times and Dates

Time to learn some really useful phrases which are sure to get you good marks in your Spanish GCSE.

¿Qué hora es? — What time is it?

1) You'll need to know how to <u>tell the time</u> for lots of topics. It's bound to come up in your exams...

See p.1 for more numbers.

Es la una.	*It's one o'clock.*
Son las dos.	*It's two o'clock.*
Son las cinco y cuarto.	*It's quarter past five.*
Son las dos menos cuarto.	*It's quarter to two.*
Son las siete y media.	*It's half past seven.*
Son las ocho y cinco.	*It's five past eight.*
Son las tres menos veinte.	*It's twenty to three.*

Grammar — at / it's X o'clock

To say '<u>at X o'clock</u>', you need '<u>a</u>':

a la una   at **one o'clock**
a las ocho   at **eight o'clock**

('La' changes to 'las' for anything other than 'one o'clock'.)

To say '<u>it's X o'clock</u>', use '<u>es</u>' or '<u>son</u>':

<u>**es**</u> la una   *it's one o'clock*
<u>**son**</u> las ocho   *it's eight o'clock*

('Es changes to 'son' for anything other than 'one o'clock'.)

2) The <u>24-hour clock</u> is also used in many Spanish-speaking countries, so make sure you can tell the time <u>both</u> ways.

The 24-hour clock

(Son) las veintiuna horas treinta minutos.	*(It's) 21.30.*
(Son) las tres horas catorce minutos.	*(It's) 03.14.*
(Son) las diecinueve horas cincuenta y cinco minutos.	*(It's) 19.55.*

Los días de la semana — The days of the week

la semana	*the week*	hoy	*today*	
el fin de semana	*(at) the weekend*	mañana	*tomorrow*	
lunes	*Monday*	ayer	*yesterday*	
martes	*Tuesday*	anoche	*last night*	
miércoles	*Wednesday*	pasado mañana	*the day after tomorrow*	
jueves	*Thursday*	anteayer	*the day before yesterday*	
viernes	*Friday*	el lunes	*on Monday*	
sábado	*Saturday*	los lunes	*on Mondays*	
domingo	*Sunday*	todos los días	*every day*	
		quince días	*a fortnight*	
		cada quince días	*every fortnight*	
		cada tres días	*every three days*	

In English, a fortnight is fourteen days, but if you're talking about a fortnight in Spanish, you actually say fifteen days.

Days of the week are always masculine and lower case.

Fui de compras ayer.	*I went shopping yesterday.*	*the day before yesterday* — anteayer
Tengo un examen pasado mañana.	*I have an exam the day after tomorrow.*	*tomorrow* — mañana
Voy al cine los sábados.	*I go to the cinema on Saturdays.*	*every six days* — cada seis días

Times and Dates

Here's some more essential vocabulary for times and dates — it's definitely worth learning.

More useful time phrases

≡ See p.2 for more time phrases. ≡

esta mañana	*this morning*
esta tarde	*this afternoon/evening*
esta noche	*tonight*
mañana por la mañana	*tomorrow morning*
la semana que viene	*next week*
la semana pasada	*last week*

To say '<u>in</u> the evening', you add '<u>por</u>':

> Juego al tenis por la mañana.
> *I play tennis in the morning.*

You don't translate 'at' here — you literally say 'I play tennis the weekend'.

in the afternoon —
por la tarde

at the weekend —
el fin de semana

Los meses del año — The months of the year

Just like the days of the week, the months of the year are all <u>masculine</u> and <u>shouldn't have capital letters</u>.

enero	*January*	julio	*July*	la estación	*season*
febrero	*February*	agosto	*August*	la primavera	*spring*
marzo	*March*	septiembre	*September*	el verano	*summer*
abril	*April*	octubre	*October*	el otoño	*autumn*
mayo	*May*	noviembre	*November*	el invierno	*winter*
junio	*June*	diciembre	*December*		

> Voy a la playa todos los años en agosto. *I go to the beach every year in August.*

> En invierno, iremos a esquiar. *In winter, we will go skiing.*

¿Qué fecha es? — What's the date?

In English, you say '<u>the third</u> of May' or '<u>the twentieth</u> of December'. In Spanish, you can say either '<u>el primero de</u>' or '<u>el uno de</u>' for the <u>first</u> of the month, but for all the other dates, you say '<u>the three</u> of May' or '<u>the twenty</u> of December'...

el tres de mayo	*(on) the third of May*
el veinte de diciembre	*(on) the twentieth of December*
Es el uno de / el primero de febrero.	*It's the first of February.*
Es el dos de marzo de dos mil dieciocho.	*It's the second of March 2018.*

You don't translate 'on' at the start of dates in Spanish, so both 'the third of May' and 'on the third of May' are written 'el tres de mayo'.

TRACK
LISTENING
01

Remember — Spanish days and months <u>don't</u> need capitals...

Listen to what Carlos, Anabel and Julia have to say, and then answer the questions in **English**.

e.g.   How often does Carlos go to the gym?   **Every day.**

1.   When was Anabel's birthday meal? [1]

2.   Where did Anabel go yesterday? [1]

3.   When is Julia going to the theatre? [1]

Questions

Knowing about questions will come in handy in your speaking test — you'll have to understand what you're being asked, and in the role-play you'll have to ask your teacher a question too. Best to be prepared.

Question marks and tone of voice

1) To turn a statement into a question, put an <u>upside down question mark</u> at the <u>beginning</u> and a <u>normal one</u> at the <u>end</u>.

2) When speaking, <u>raise your voice</u> at the <u>end</u> of the sentence to show you're asking a question.

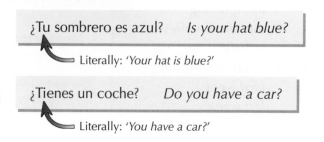

¿Tu sombrero es azul?   *Is your hat blue?*

Literally: *'Your hat is blue?'*

¿Tienes un coche?   *Do you have a car?*

Literally: *'You have a car?'*

¿Qué... — What...?

If your question starts with '<u>What...</u>', you normally need to start it with '<u>¿Qué...</u>' in Spanish.

¿Qué comes por la mañana?   *What do you eat in the morning?*

¿Qué quieres hacer el fin de semana?   *What do you want to do at the weekend?*

Go back to p.2-3 for more time phrases.

¿Cuál... — Which one..? What...?

1) '<u>¿Cuál...</u>' normally means '<u>Which...</u>' or '<u>Which one...</u>':

¿Cuál quieres?   *Which (one) do you want?*

2) However, sometimes you might need to use '<u>¿Cuál...</u>' even if you'd use '<u>What...</u>' in English. This is usually when you use the verb '<u>ser</u>' and you're asking for a <u>piece of information</u>, rather than a definition.

¿Cuál es tu problema?   *What is your problem?*

¿Cuál es tu dirección?   *What is your address?*

¿Cuándo? ¿Por qué? ¿Dónde? — When? Why? Where?

Question words like this are known as interrogatives. See p.131.

There are <u>loads of other words</u> you can use to <u>begin a question</u> — get them <u>all</u> learnt.

¿Cuándo?	*When?*
¿Por qué?	*Why?*
¿Dónde?	*Where?*
¿Cómo?	*How?*
¿Cuánto/a?	*How much?*
¿Cuántos/as?	*How many?*
¿Quién(es)?	*Who?*
¿Cuál?	*Which?*
¿Es...?	*Is it...?*

Remember that question words need accents.

¿Cuántos/as tienes?	*How many do you have?*
¿Por qué haces eso?	*Why are you doing that?*
¿De dónde eres?	*Where are you from?*
¿Cuál prefieres?	*Which do you prefer?*
¿Es muy difícil?	*Is it very difficult?*

Questions

Now you know how to form questions, you need to get practising them in conversations. If you're asking loads of questions, you might need to be able to say 'please', too — there's more about being polite on p.6.

Tengo una pregunta — I have a question

Here are some of the <u>most common ways</u> you can use the <u>question words</u> from p.4.

¿Qué fecha?	*What date?*
¿Qué día?	*What day?*
¿Cuándo es tu cumpleaños?	*When is your birthday?*
¿Cuántos años tienes?	*How old are you?*
¿A qué hora...?	*At what time...?*
¿Qué hora es?	*What time is it?*
¿Por cuánto tiempo?	*For how long?*
¿Cuánto cuesta(n)?	*How much does it / do they cost?*
¿Cuánto vale(n)?	*How much does it / do they cost?*
¿Cuánto es?	*How much is it?*
¿De qué color (es)?	*What colour (is it)?*

Question	**Simple Answer**	**Extended Answer**
¿Cuánto cuesta ir al cine?	Cuesta siete euros.	Cuesta siete euros, cincuenta céntimos. Es muy caro.
How much does it cost to go to the cinema?	*It costs seven euros.*	*It costs seven euros, fifty cents. It's very expensive.*

SPEAKING

To learn Spanish or not to learn Spanish, that is the question...

Have a look at the role-play that Carla did with her teacher.

Grade 8-9

Teacher: ¿A qué hora vas al gimnasio, Carla?

Carla: Voy al gimnasio a las cuatro de la tarde.

Teacher: ¿Cuánto cuesta ir al gimnasio?

Carla: Cuesta tres euros cada vez.

Teacher: ¿Vas al gimnasio todos los días?

Carla: No, solo los fines de semana, pero los jueves, juego al **baloncesto**[1] porque me gusta mucho.

Teacher: Ah, **vale**[2], muy bien.

Carla: Y tú, ¿cuándo practicas **deporte**[3]?

Teacher: Juego al fútbol los sábados.

[1]basketball
[2]OK
[3]sport

Tick list:
✓ tenses: present
✓ opinion phrase
✓ correct time phrases e.g. los jueves
✓ correctly formed question

To improve:
+ add a few more complex structures, e.g. cada tres días

Use the instructions on the role-play card to prepare your own role-play. Address your friend as 'tú' and speak for about two minutes. [15 marks]

'!' means you'll need to answer a question you haven't prepared. You can have a good guess at what you might be asked though — here, the question is likely to still be on the topic of tennis as the questions before and after the '!' are about tennis too.

Estás hablando con tu amiga española sobre el deporte.
* *la hora cuando juegas al tenis*
* *la frecuencia con que juegas al tenis*
* *!*
* *el precio de jugar al tenis*
* *? deporte preferido*

When you see '?', you need to ask your teacher a question.

Being Polite

Being polite is an important part of the speaking test — so mind your manners with these tips.

Los saludos — Greetings

If you're writing these greetings as exclamations, you need an upside down exclamation mark at the start and a normal one at the end, for example: ¡Hola!

hola	*hello*
buenos días	*good day / good morning*
buenas tardes	*good afternoon / good evening*
buenas noches	*good night*
hasta luego	*see you later*
hasta el lunes	*see you on Monday*
hasta mañana	*see you tomorrow*
hasta pronto	*see you soon*
adiós	*goodbye*

¿Qué tal?	*How are you? (informal)*
¿Cómo estás?	*How are you? (informal)*
¿Cómo está?	*How are you? (formal)*

muy bien	*very well*	great — fenomenal
bien	*well*	so-so — así así
no muy bien	*not very well*	terrible — fatal

Question	**Simple Answer**	**Extended Answer**
¿Qué tal?	Bien, gracias.	Estoy fatal. Me duele la cabeza.
How are you?	*Well, thanks.*	*I feel terrible. I've got a headache.*

See p.85 for more illnesses.

Por favor y gracias — Please and thank you

You don't want to sound <u>rude</u> in the exam, so learn these <u>charming</u> little words and phrases.

por favor	*please*	Eres muy amable.	*That's very nice of you. (informal)*
gracias	*thank you*	Es muy amable.	*That's very nice of you. (formal)*
muchas gracias	*thank you very much*	De nada.	*You're welcome.*
Lo siento.	*I'm sorry.*	vale	*OK*
Lo siento mucho.	*I'm really sorry.*	¡Claro!	*Of course!*

¡Por favor! / ¡Perdone!	*Excuse me!* (E.g. for asking someone the way)
¡Con permiso!	*Excuse me!* (E.g. for wanting to get past someone)

Le presento a... — May I introduce... ?

If you're male, you say 'encantado', and if you're female, it's 'encantada'.

Use 'Esta es...' for introducing someone female.

Le presento a ...	*May I introduce ... ?*	Encantado/a.	*Pleased to meet you.*
Este es ...	*This is ...*	Mucho gusto.	*Pleased to meet you.*

Here's how a conversation might go if you wanted to introduce someone:

Señora Valls:	Hola Ana, ¿qué tal?	*Hello Ana, how are you?*
Ana:	Muy bien. ¿Cómo está?	*Very well. How are you?*
Señora Valls:	Así así.	*So-so.*
Ana:	Le presento a Arturo.	*May I introduce Arturo?*
Señora Valls:	Encantada.	*Pleased to meet you.*

Ana uses the formal way to ask how Señora Valls is because Señora Valls is older than her. See p.7 for more information.

If you're talking to someone you call 'tú', you say 'Te presento a...' — it's informal.

Being Polite

And the politeness doesn't end there — here are some more ways to charm the examiner...

Quisiera — I would like

1) Don't just say 'I want' — make sure you <u>ask politely</u> for what you would like:

> Quisiera un café. *I would like a coffee.*

2) And this is how to say that you <u>would like to do</u> something:

> Quisiera hablar. *I would like to talk.*
> ¿Puedo sentarme? *May I sit down?*

go to the toilet — ir al baño
have a drink — beber algo

'Poder' is a radical-changing verb. See p.138.

Tú y usted — Informal and Formal 'you'

Grammar — 'tú' and 'usted'

In Spanish, there are <u>four</u> different ways of saying '<u>you</u>'.

Informal 'you':

① '**Tú**' — for <u>one person</u> who's your <u>friend</u>, a <u>family member</u> or of a <u>similar age</u>.

② '**Vosotros/as**' — for a group of <u>two or more people</u> that you <u>know</u>.
Only use '<u>vosotras</u>' if all the people in the group are <u>female</u>.

Formal 'you':

③ '**Usted**' — for <u>one person</u> that is <u>older than you</u> or someone you <u>don't know</u>.

④ '**Ustedes**' — for a group of <u>two or more people</u> that you <u>don't know</u>.

'Usted' and 'ustedes' <u>don't use the same 'you' part of the verb</u> as 'tú' and 'vosotros'.

* For '<u>usted</u>', use the '<u>he/she/it</u>' part of the verb (see p.137-150).
* For '<u>ustedes</u>', use the '<u>they</u>' part of the verb.

'Tú', 'vosotros/as', 'usted' and 'ustedes' are all pronouns — see p.129.

So, here are the <u>four</u> different ways of asking where someone is from:

Tú	**Vosotros/as**	**Usted**	**Ustedes**
¿De dónde eres?	¿De dónde sois?	¿De dónde es?	¿De dónde son?

WRITING

Tú, vosotros, usted, ustedes — check you know them all...

Here, Andrés is introducing his two friends Mateo and Lucía to each other.

Andrés:	¡Buenos días, Mateo! ¿Qué tal?
Mateo:	Muy bien, gracias, ¿y tú?
Andrés:	Sí, bien. Esta es mi amiga, Lucía.
Mateo:	¡Hola Lucía! Encantado.
Lucía:	Mucho gusto.
Mateo:	¿Cómo estás, Lucía?
Lucía:	No muy bien, estoy enferma.
Mateo:	**Ay, ¡qué lástima!**[1]
Lucía:	Sí, es **una pena**[2].
Andrés:	**Pues**[3], hasta luego, Mateo.
Mateo:	¡Adiós!

Grade 4-5

[1] Oh, what a shame!
[2] a pity
[3] Well

Tick list:
✓ variety of phrases
✓ correct Spanish punctuation
✓ gender agreement

To improve:
+ develop each idea a bit further
+ different tenses (add a past or future)
+ use more varied adjectives, e.g. 'fatal' instead of 'no muy bien'

Now have a go yourself:

Escribe tu propio diálogo en el que te presentas.
*Escribe aproximadamente **40** palabras en **español**.*

[8 marks]

Opinions

Having opinions stops you sounding dull — but more importantly, it gets you marks, and lots of them.

¿Qué piensas de...? — What do you think of...?

¿Qué piensas?	*What do you think?*	Pienso que / Creo que...	*I think that...*
¿Qué piensas de... ?	*What do you think of... ?*	...me parece...	*I think... is...*
¿Qué te parece... ?	*What do you think of... ?*	Estoy de acuerdo.	*I agree.*
¿Cuál es tu opinión de... ?	*What's your opinion of... ?*	No estoy de acuerdo.	*I disagree.*
¿Le encuentras simpático/a?	*Do you find him/her nice?*	(No) es verdad.	*That's (not) true.*

> If you're talking about more than one thing, you need 'me parecen'.

¿Qué piensas de mi novio? — What do you think of my boyfriend?

Pienso que es amable. — I think he's kind.

> *What's your opinion of...? — ¿Cuál es tu opinión de...?*
>
> *I think — Creo que*

> See p.19 for more useful describing words.

Las opiniones — Opinions

Me gusta... (sing.)	*I like... (singular)*
Me gustan... (pl.)	*I like... (plural)*
Me gusta(n) mucho...	*I really like...*
Me encanta... (sing.)	*I love... (singular)*
Me encantan... (pl.)	*I love... (plural)*
Me interesa(n)...	*I'm interested in...*
Encuentro... fantástico.	*I find... fantastic.*

No me gusta(n)...	*I don't like...*
No me gusta(n)... para nada.	*I don't like... at all.*
... no me interesa(n).	*... doesn't / don't interest me.*
Encuentro... horrible.	*I find... awful.*
Odio...	*I hate...*

Grammar — 'gustar' and 'encantar'

Use '<u>me gusta</u>' and '<u>me encanta</u>' when you want to say you like or love a <u>singular</u> thing.

If you want to say you like or love a <u>plural</u> thing, <u>add</u> an '<u>n</u>' to the end.

Me gustan las uvas.   *I like grapes.*
Me encantan las películas.   *I love films.*

To say you <u>like doing an activity</u>, use an <u>infinitive</u> (see p.137) after the correct form of 'gustar' or 'encantar'.

e.g. **Me gusta bailar.**   *I like dancing.*

infinitive

Prefiero... — I prefer...

If you <u>don't like</u> something, always try to say what you <u>prefer</u>:

Prefiero...   *I prefer...*

Grammar — 'preferir' is a radical-changing verb

'<u>Preferir</u>' (*to prefer*) is a <u>radical-changing verb</u> (see p.138 for more). With 'preferir', the second '<u>e</u>' changes to '<u>ie</u>':

prefiero	*I prefer*
prefieres	*you prefer*
prefiere	*he/she/it prefers*
prefieren	*they prefer*

> The stem of the 'we' and 'you inf., pl.' forms doesn't change:
> 'preferimos' = 'we prefer'
> 'preferís' = 'you (inf., pl.) prefer'

Me gusta el té, pero prefiero el café.
I like tea, but I prefer coffee.

No me gusta cantar — prefiero bailar.
I don't like singing — I prefer dancing.

Opinions

As well as being able to give an opinion, you've got to be able to justify it. That's where adjectives come in...

Porque — Because

To start justifying your opinion, you need 'porque' (*because*). Look out, though — 'porque' and '¿por qué?' sound very similar, but they're written differently and mean different things.

¿Por qué te gusta ir al cine?	*Why do you like going to the cinema?*
Me gusta ir al cine porque...	*I like going to the cinema because...*

(No) me gusta porque es... — I (don't) like it because it's...

Here's a nice long list of adjectives you can use to justify your opinions and collect some good marks too.

bueno/a	*good*	agradable	*nice, kind*	interesante	*interesting*
estupendo/a	*fantastic*	amable	*friendly*	divertido/a	*amusing, entertaining, fun*
fenomenal	*great*	fabuloso/a	*fabulous*	malo/a	*bad*
genial	*brilliant*	increíble	*incredible*	desagradable	*unpleasant*
guay	*cool*	maravilloso/a	*marvellous*	aburrido/a	*boring*
emocionante	*exciting*	precioso/a	*beautiful*	ridículo/a	*ridiculous*
perfecto/a	*perfect*	bonito/a	*pretty*	decepcionante	*disappointing*
impresionante	*impressive*	entretenido/a	*entertaining*	raro/a	*strange*

These useful phrases could also help you out:

Me fastidia.	*It annoys me.*
Me aburre.	*It bores me.*
Me hace llorar.	*It makes me cry.*
Me hace reír.	*It makes me laugh.*

Adjectives change to agree with plural nouns too — see p.118 for more on agreement.

Grammar — nouns and adjectives agree

The ending of the adjective must agree with the noun (p.118).

'el cine' is masculine so 'bueno' must end in 'o'.

El cine es bueno.	*The cinema is good.*
La película es buena.	*The film is good.*

'la película' is feminine so the adjective ends in 'a'.

Adjectives that end with other letters like 'interesante' stay the same for both masculine and feminine nouns.

Make sure you can back your opinions up...

Luis and Elena are discussing the cinema. Read the dialogue and answer the questions in **English**.

Luis: ¿Te gusta ir al cine, Elena?

Elena: Sí, me encanta ir al cine porque es divertido. Me gustan las películas de acción. Y tú, ¿qué piensas del cine?

Luis: No me gusta ir al cine. Prefiero ver las películas en casa. Me encantan las comedias pero odio las películas románticas porque me parecen aburridas. ¿Qué piensas, Elena?

Elena: Sí, estoy de acuerdo. A veces son ridículas.

e.g. Why does Elena like going to the cinema? Because it's fun.

1. Does Luis prefer going to the cinema or watching films at home? [1]
2. Does Luis like romantic films? Why / Why not? [2]
3. What does Elena think of romantic films? [1]

Putting it All Together

Now you know all the ingredients that go into giving and justifying opinions, you need to be able to put them all together. This is really useful — you'll have something to say about any of the GCSE topics.

Putting your opinions together

este equipo	*this team*
esta revista	*this magazine*
esta música	*this music*
este grupo	*this band*
esta novela	*this novel*
este actor	*this actor*
esta actriz	*this actress*
esta película	*this film*
este periódico	*this newspaper*
esta canción	*this song*
esta tienda	*this shop*

Grammar — 'este' and 'esta'

'<u>Este</u>' means '<u>this</u>', but it has to agree with the noun it comes before — see p.120 for more information.

	masculine	feminine
singular	este	esta
plural	estos	estas

¿Qué te parece este grupo?	*What do you think of this band?*
Esta música es fenomenal.	*This music is great.*
¿Qué piensas de estos actores?	*What do you think of these actors?*

Question	**Simple Answer**	**Extended Answer**
¿Cuál es tu opinión de esta revista?	Me gusta mucho esta revista.	Me gusta mucho esta revista porque es muy interesante.
What's your opinion of this magazine?	*I really like this magazine.*	*I really like this magazine because it's very interesting.*

Remember to always back up your opinions

¿Qué piensas de este grupo?	*What do you think of this band?*	this team — este equipo
Me encanta este grupo porque me gusta la música rock.	*I love this band because I like rock music.*	their music is brilliant — su música es genial
¿Estás de acuerdo?	*Do you agree?*	And you, what do you think? — Y tú, ¿qué piensas?
No, odio la música rock — prefiero la música pop.	*No, I hate rock music — I prefer pop music.*	I find rock music awful — encuentro la música rock horrible

Don't keep your opinions to yourself — share them.

Listen to Antonio and Carolina talking about what they like doing. Decide whether the statements are true (T) or false (F), and write T or F next to them. The first one has been done for you.

e.g. Carolina likes going to the swimming pool. T

1. Antonio likes listening to music. [1]
2. Antonio thinks the shops in his city are fantastic. [1]
3. Antonio doesn't like reading newspapers. [1]
4. Carolina likes both reading and listening to music. [1]
5. Carolina thinks pop bands are awful. [1]

Listening Questions

Having a go at some exam-style questions is a great way to make sure you're ready for the real exams. The next four pages give you some practice in the sorts of things you'll have to do in your GCSE.

1   Listen to Rosa and Carmen talking about travelling.
Complete the sentences in **English**.

(TRACK LISTENING 03)

Example: Rosa has been to Madrid .... 6 times ....

1 a   Carmen first visited Ireland in ....   *[1 mark]*

1 b   To get to Madrid, Rosa drives .... kilometres.   *[1 mark]*

1 c   Carmen hopes to go back to Ireland when she turns ....   *[1 mark]*

2   Listen to Farah being asked about various foods and drinks. For each food or drink, put a tick in the appropriate box to indicate her opinion.

(TRACK LISTENING 04)

		Loves	Likes	Doesn't like	Hates
2 a	coffee				
2 b	breakfast cereals				
2 c	potatoes				
2 d	pears				
2 e	chocolate				

[1 mark]

[1 mark]

[1 mark]

[1 mark]

[1 mark]

Speaking Question

For the Speaking Question pages, you'll need to get a friend or a parent to read the teacher's role, so you can pretend it's a real assessment. Before the role-play starts, give yourself a few minutes to read through the candidate's role, and think about what you're going to say. You can make notes if you like.

Candidate's Role

- Your teacher will play the role of your Spanish friend. They will speak first.

- You should use *tú* to address your friend.

- – ! – means you will have to respond to something you have not prepared.

- – ? – means you will have to ask your friend a question.

> Estás hablando con tu amigo/a español/a sobre tu cumpleaños y tu tiempo libre.
>
> - Tu fecha de cumpleaños.
>
> - Tus regalos el año pasado (**dos** detalles).
>
> - !
>
> - ? Actividades preferidas en invierno.
>
> - Tus planes para el fin de semana que viene (**dos** detalles).

Teacher's Role

- You begin the role-play using the introductory text below.

- You should address the candidate as *tú*.

- You may alter the wording of the questions in response to the candidate's previous answers.

- Do not supply the candidate with key vocabulary.

> Introductory text: *Estás hablando con tu amigo/a español/a sobre tu cumpleaños y tu tiempo libre. Yo soy tu amigo/a.*
>
> - ¿Cuándo es tu cumpleaños?
>
> - ¿Qué recibiste para tu cumpleaños el año pasado?
>
> - ! ¿Cuál es la estación del año que más te gusta?
>
> - ? Allow the candidate to ask you a question.
>
> - ¿Tienes planes para el fin de semana que viene?

Reading Questions

1   Read these texts about Gloria, David and Salma's classes.

Gloria	En mi clase, hay treinta y dos alumnos. Soy la alumna más joven porque solo tengo quince años. Todos los demás tienen dieciséis años.
David	La semana pasada, nuestro profesor de biología nos dijo que tiene cuarenta y ocho años. En mi instituto, el aula de biología está en la segunda planta.
Salma	Prefiero las clases que tienen pocos alumnos. Es mejor que haya menos gente porque es más fácil escuchar al profesor. En mi clase ideal habría diez personas en vez de veinticinco como hay en realidad.

Answer the following questions.

Example: How many people are in Gloria's class? ....*32*........

1 a   How old did David's teacher say he is? ....   *[1 mark]*

1 b   What floor is David's biology class on? ....   *[1 mark]*

1 c   How many people are actually in Salma's classes? ....   *[1 mark]*

2   Omar has written an essay about the seasons for homework.

Prefiero visitar otros países en invierno. Me encanta viajar a climas tropicales cuando hace frío en mi país. En el verano, mi padre y yo jugamos al bádminton casi todos los fines de semana. Nos gusta pasar tiempo juntos. Si tuviera que elegir la estación que más me gusta, sería el otoño. Me gusta admirar los colores maravillosos de los árboles. Es relajante pasar tiempo en el jardín en primavera también.

Which two statements are **true**? Write the letters in the boxes.

A	Omar likes being outside in the spring.
B	Omar plays badminton in the winter.
C	Omar likes going on holiday in the summer.
D	Omar's favourite season is autumn.

☐ ☐

[2 marks]

Writing Questions

1 Rellena los espacios blancos en **español**.

1 a Voy al colegio .... (at nine o'clock).   *[1 mark]*

1 b Mi clase preferida es inglés .... (at half past ten).   *[1 mark]*

1 c La hora de comer es .... (at quarter to one).   *[1 mark]*

1 d La última clase empieza .... (at twenty to three).   *[1 mark]*

1 e Vuelvo a casa .... (at ten to four).   *[1 mark]*

2 Translate this dialogue into **Spanish**.

> — What do you think about this article in the newspaper?
> — I think that the journalist has some good ideas.
> — I disagree. I think the other article is better.
> — What's your opinion of the book he has read?
> — I find it fantastic.

....

....

....

....

....

....

[9 marks]

Revision Summary for Section One

You can use these questions to see what you already know and find out which bits you need to work on. Put a tick by each question you can answer, and then have another read through the section to crack the ones you weren't sure of the first time round. Tick the box by each page title once you've done all the questions in that bit. Soon you'll have a whole page of ticks — what could be more pleasing than that?

Numbers (p.1) ☑

1) Count out loud from 0 to 20 in Spanish. ☑

2) How do you say these numbers in Spanish?
   a) 25 b) 37 c) 60 d) 104 e) 2003 ☑

3) What's 'mil setecientos cuarenta y nueve' in English? ☑

4) How would you say 'the third book' in Spanish? ☑

Times and Dates (p.2-3) ☑

5) Diego's next lesson starts at 'las diez y cuarto'. What time is this in English? ☑

6) Say all the days of the week in Spanish, from Monday to Sunday. ☑

7) How do you say these in Spanish?
   a) today b) the weekend c) last night d) yesterday ☑

8) How do you say 'I go to the park in the summer' in Spanish? ☑

9) Say all the months of the year in Spanish. ☑

10) ¿Cuándo es tu cumpleaños? ☑

Questions (p.4-5) ☑

11) How would you turn the sentence 'Tiene dos hermanas' into a question? ☑

12) You overhear someone say '¿Cuánto cuestan?'. What are they asking? ☑

Being Polite (p.6-7) ☑

13) How would you introduce Fátima to your head teacher in Spanish? ☑

14) How would you ask politely for an ice cream in Spanish? ☑

15) Which form of 'you' would you use with these people?
   a) your little sister's classmates b) your new boss c) two guests you've never met before ☑

Opinions (p.8-9) ☑

16) Think of three different ways of asking someone for their opinion in Spanish. ☑

17) How would you say that you love dogs in Spanish? ☑

18) Pepe says: 'Me gusta jugar al baloncesto porque es emocionante.' What's he saying? ☑

Putting it All Together (p.10) ☑

19) How would you say 'I find this film disappointing' in Spanish? ☑

20) Gonzalo asks '¿Estás de acuerdo?'. What does he want to know? ☑

21) How would you say 'I hate this newspaper because it's ridiculous' in Spanish? ☑

22) Pick your favourite band or novel and say why you like it in Spanish. ☑

About Yourself

Being able to talk about yourself is really important — you just can't get by without it.

Preséntate — Introduce yourself

el nombre	*name*	el cumpleaños	*birthday*	
el apellido	*surname*	cumplir años	*to have a birthday*	
llamarse	*to be called*	la edad	*age*	
nacer	*to be born*	tener ... años	*to be ... years old*	
el nacimiento	*birth*	la nacionalidad	*nationality*	

Grammar — saying your age

In Spanish, you 'have' an age, so you need the verb '<u>tener</u>' to say <u>how old you are</u>. 'Tener' is a <u>radical-changing</u> verb — see p.138.
Tengo 16 años. *I'm 16 years old.*

¡Hola! Me llamo Juan.

Hello! I'm called Juan.

My name is Juan. — Mi nombre es Juan.
I'm Juan. — Soy Juan.

Tengo quince años.

I'm 15 years old.

Check p.3 for a reminder of how to say dates.

Mi cumpleaños es el dos de abril.

My birthday is the 2nd of April.

Nací en (el año) dos mil dos.

I was born in (the year) 2002.

English — inglés / inglesa
Scottish — escocés / escocesa
Welsh — galés / galesa
Irish — irlandés / irlandesa

Soy británico/a. Nací en Surrey.

I'm British. I was born in Surrey.

the north — el norte
the east — el este
the west — el oeste

See p.91 for more countries and nationalities.

Vivo en Málaga, en el sur de España.

I live in Málaga, in the south of Spain.

¿Cómo se escribe? — How do you spell it?

You might have to <u>spell</u> something out, so learn how to <u>pronounce</u> the letters of the <u>Spanish alphabet</u>.

A — ah	F — effay	K — ka	O — oh	U — ooh
B — bay	G — hay	L — elay	P — pay	V — oohbay
C — thay	H — atchay	M — emay	Q — coo	W — oohbay doblay
D — day	I — ee	N — enay	R — eray	X — ekis
E — ay	J — hota	Ñ — enyay	S — essay	Y — yay
			T — tay	Z — thayta

'h' like 'loch'   Double 'l' makes a 'y' sound.

Some Spanish words like 'adiós' have an accent to show which vowel you need to emphasise. Remember to write the accent too.

Practise your pronunciation for the speaking exam...

Read the question and then look at how Estefanía has answered it.
Háblame un poco de ti.

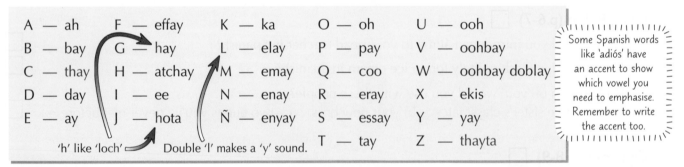

¡Hola! Me llamo Estefanía y soy de Venezuela.
Vivo en el norte del país, cerca de la ciudad de Caracas.
Mi cumpleaños es el veinticuatro de diciembre. Es un día muy especial, porque celebramos mi cumpleaños y la Navidad al mismo tiempo. Nací en el año dos mil.

Grade 6-7

Tick list:
✓ tenses: present, preterite
✓ correctly formed dates and years
✓ justifying opinions with 'porque'

To improve:
+ include an opinion about where you live

*Now try to answer the same question. Mention your name, where you're from and your birthday.
Try to speak for about two minutes. [10 marks]*

My Family

Learning to talk about who's in your family is an absolute must — examiners seem to love asking about it.

Mi familia — My family

los parientes	*relatives*	los hijos	*children*	el abuelo	*grandfather*
el padre	*father*	el marido	*husband*	la abuela	*grandmother*
la madre	*mother*	la mujer	*wife*	los nietos	*grandchildren*
los padres	*parents*	el hermanastro	*stepbrother*	el/la tío/a	*uncle/aunt*
el padrastro	*stepfather*	la hermanastra	*stepsister*	el/la primo/a	*cousin*
la madrastra	*stepmother*	el/la gemelo/a	*twin*	el/la sobrino/a	*nephew/niece*

Háblame de tu familia — Tell me about your family

Grammar — saying 'my' and 'your'

Possessive adjectives like '<u>my</u>' and '<u>your</u>' have to <u>agree</u> with the noun they come before (see p.120). Remember — '<u>su(s)</u>' could also mean '<u>your</u>' if you're being <u>formal</u> — see p.120.

mi padre	*my father*	**tu hermana**	*your sister*	**su tía**	*his / her / their aunt*
mis padres	*my parents*	**tus hermanas**	*your sisters*	**sus tías**	*his / her / their aunts*

Tengo una hermana mayor. Ella se llama Ramona.

I have an older sister. She is called Ramona.

an older brother — un hermano mayor
a younger sister — una hermana menor
a younger brother — un hermano menor

Hay cinco personas en mi familia — mi madre, mi padrastro, mis dos hermanastros menores y yo. Mis hermanastros se llaman David y Gabriel.

There are five people in my family — my mother, my stepfather, my two younger stepbrothers and me. My stepbrothers are called David and Gabriel.

Soy hijo único, pero me gustaría tener hermanos.

I'm an only child (male), but I would like to have brothers and sisters.

only child (female) — hija única

I like not having brothers and sisters — me gusta no tener hermanos

Question

¿Cómo es tu familia?

What's your family like?

Simple Answer

Soy hijo único, pero tengo muchos primos.

I'm an only child, but I have a lot of cousins.

Extended Answer

Soy hijo único, pero mi padre tiene cinco hermanos, así que en realidad, tengo muchos parientes. Mis primos viven cerca de aquí y siempre lo pasamos bien juntos.

I'm an only child, but my father has five brothers and sisters, so really, I have lots of relatives. My cousins live near here and we always have a good time together.

Examiners are fans of families — don't forget to revise them...

Translate this text into **English**. *[9 marks]*

Vivo con mi madre, mi hermana mayor y mis dos hermanas menores. Son gemelas. Para mí, es importante tener hermanos porque siempre tienes alguien con quien puedes salir. Los fines de semana, visito a mi padre, su mujer y mi hermanastro. Nació el año pasado y solo tiene seis meses. Me gustaría pasar más tiempo allí con ellos porque es muy divertido.

Describing People

You'll probably have to describe what people look like at some point in your exam — so carry on reading.

¿Cómo eres? — What are you like?

You'll need the verbs 'tener' (to have) and 'ser' (to be) for this page. They're irregular, so check p.138-139 to see how they work.

alto/a	tall	joven	young	negro	black
bajo/a	short	viejo/a	old	castaño	chestnut-brown
de altura mediana	medium height	marrón	brown	largo	long
gordo/a	fat	azul	blue	corto	short (hair)
delgado/a	slim	verde	green	liso	straight
guapo/a	good-looking	rubio/a	blonde	rizado	curly

'Marrón' loses its accent in the plural form.

El aspecto físico — Physical appearance

Question

¿Cómo eres?
What are you like?

Simple Answer

Soy alta. Tengo los ojos azules y tengo el pelo castaño.
I'm tall. I have blue eyes and I have brown hair.

Grammar — adjectives agree

Adjectives must agree with the noun they describe.
'Los ojos' are masculine plural, so adjectives like 'blue' must be in the masculine plural form — azules.
'El pelo' is masculine singular, so adjectives like 'curly' need to be in the masculine singular form — rizado — even if you're a girl.

Extended Answer

Soy bastante alta. No soy ni gorda ni delgada. Tengo los ojos azules y llevo gafas. Tengo el pelo corto y rizado, y no tengo pecas.
I'm quite tall. I'm neither fat nor slim. I have blue eyes and I wear glasses. I have short, curly hair, and I don't have freckles.

Soy muy bajo como mis padres. Sin embargo, mi hermano es mucho más alto que yo. Tengo el pelo rubio y tengo los ojos verdes.
I'm very short like my parents. However, my brother is much taller than me. I have blonde hair and I have green eyes.

Soy bajo y delgado. Tengo el pelo negro y tengo los ojos marrones. Tengo una barba también.

I'm short and slim. I have black hair and I have brown eyes. I also have a beard.

dark — moreno
a moustache — un bigote

Es altísima. Lleva gafas y tiene los ojos azules. Tiene el pelo castaño y liso.

She's really tall. She wears glasses and she has blue eyes. She has straight, chestnut-brown hair.

make-up — maquillaje
curly — rizado

Es de altura mediana y bastante gordo. Es pelirrojo y tiene los ojos verdes.

He's medium height and quite fat. He's red-haired and he has green eyes.

He's bald — Es calvo

Adjectives absolutely have to agree...

María y Jaime describen estas cuatro personas. Empareja las fotos con las descripciones.

 a)
 b)
 c)
 d)

Descripción 1 = foto .....
Descripción 2 = foto .....
Descripción 3 = foto .....
Descripción 4 = foto .....

[4 marks]

Personalities

Talking about personalities is a great way to show that you can use adjectives — but make sure they agree.

Mi personalidad — My personality

animado/a	*lively*	hablador/a	*chatty / talkative*	egoísta	*selfish*
alegre	*happy*	atrevido/a	*daring / cheeky*	maleducado/a	*rude*
cariñoso/a	*affectionate*	serio/a	*serious*	perezoso/a	*lazy*
comprensivo/a	*understanding*	sensible	*sensitive*	travieso/a	*naughty*
cortés	*polite*	callado/a	*quiet*	torpe	*clumsy*
gracioso/a	*funny*	valiente	*brave*	celoso/a	*jealous*

¿Cómo es... ? — What's... like?

Mi mejor amigo es gracioso y siempre alegre. Es sensible también. Sin embargo, a veces es un poco maleducado porque dice cosas sin pensar.

My best friend is funny and always happy. He's sensitive too. However, sometimes he's a bit rude because he says things without thinking.

My best friend (girl) — Mi mejor amiga

he always arrives late when we go to the cinema — siempre llega tarde cuando vamos al cine

Mis padres son comprensivos y amables. Mi madre es habladora pero mi padre es más callado.

My parents are understanding and kind. My mother is chatty but my father is quieter.

serious — serios

Mis profesoras son amables pero estrictas al mismo tiempo.

My teachers are friendly but strict at the same time.

kind — simpáticas

Grammar — making adjectives agree

Adjectives have to agree with the nouns they describe.

See the normal rules for adjective agreement on p.118.

But some adjectives work differently, like those ending in '-or' or '-ísta/-ista'.

1) '**Hablador**' — add an 'a' on the end for the feminine form and then 'es' and 'as' for the masculine and feminine plurals.

2) '**Egoísta**' stays the same in the singular and becomes 'egoístas' for both the masculine and feminine plurals.

Mis amigos son habladores.
My friends are chatty.

Mi primo es un poco egoísta.
My cousin is a bit selfish.

Don't forget to back up your opinions with reasons...

Benjamín has written you an email telling you about himself, and his family and friends.

A decir verdad[1], mis padres son muy cariñosos, **aunque**[2] pueden ser estrictos, sobre todo **si no arreglo mi dormitorio**[3]. En mi opinión, mis amigos son alegres y atrevidos, pero **según**[4] mis padres, son maleducados. **Cuando era pequeño**[5], era bastante travieso, pero ahora creo que soy comprensivo y gracioso. Me gustaría ser más valiente. Y tú, ¿cómo eres?

Grade 6-7

[1]To tell the truth

[2]although

[3]if I don't tidy my bedroom

[4]according to

[5]When I was little

Tick list:
✓ tenses: present, imperfect, conditional
✓ varied adjectives that agree correctly
✓ conjunctions e.g. aunque, pero

To improve:
+ complex structures, e.g. subjunctive
+ use a wider range of tenses, e.g. future

*Contesta a Benjamín y describe a tu familia. Escribe aproximadamente **90 palabras en español**. [16 marks]*

Pets

Time to learn to talk about your pets — some of the vocabulary from the last two pages might be useful here.

¿Tienes mascotas en casa? — Do you have pets at home?

el animal doméstico / la mascota	*pet*
el hámster	*hamster*
el conejo	*rabbit*
el cobayo / el conejillo de Indias	*guinea pig*
el pez tropical	*tropical fish*
el pez de colores	*goldfish*
la tortuga	*tortoise*

Sí, tengo un perro. Lo mejor de las mascotas es que no te juzgan.

Yes, I have a dog. The best thing about pets is that they don't judge you.

No tenemos ningún animal doméstico porque no podríamos pasar mucho tiempo con él, lo que sería cruel.

We don't have a pet because we wouldn't be able to spend much time with it, which would be cruel.

¿Cómo es tu mascota? — What's your pet like?

Me gustan los peces tropicales porque es relajante verlos nadar.

I like tropical fish because it's relaxing to watch them swim.

Tengo un gato. Es muy encantador, sobre todo cuando tiene hambre.

I have a cat. He's very charming, especially when he's hungry.

Odio el olor de los perros.

I hate the smell of dogs.

but they don't live very long — pero no viven mucho tiempo

adventurous and intelligent — atrevido e inteligente

snakes because they scare me — las serpientes porque me dan miedo

Grammar — comparing things

Use '<u>más ... que</u>' to say that something's '<u>more ... than</u>' something else.
Use '<u>menos ... que</u>' to say that something's '<u>less ... than</u>' something else.

Pienso que los gatos son <u>más independientes que</u> los perros.
I think that cats are <u>more independent than</u> dogs.

Los hámsters parecen <u>menos atrevidos que</u> los cobayos.
Hamsters seem <u>less adventurous than</u> guinea pigs.

Question	**Simple Answer**	**Extended Answer**
¿Te gustaría tener algún animal doméstico en el futuro?	Sí, quiero un gato porque son muy inteligentes.	Cuando sea mayor, me gustaría tener un perro. Creo que los perros son más fieles que los gatos.
Would you like to have any pets in the future?	*Yes, I want a cat because they're very intelligent.*	*When I'm older, I'd like to have a dog. I think dogs are more loyal than cats.*

 Try to give different points of view in your answers...

Translate this text into **English**. *[9 marks]*

Tengo un pájaro como mascota. Siempre ha sido muy hablador — repite lo que dices y es muy divertido cuando dice cosas ofensivas. Lo bueno de los pájaros es que comen frutas, verduras y cereales, así que su comida no cuesta mucho. Sin embargo, el fin de semana que viene, tengo que llevarlo al veterinario y creo que costará mucho dinero.

Style and Fashion

Fashion might come up in your exams — be ready to talk about how you like to dress.

La moda — Fashion

estar de moda	*to be in fashion*	la marca	*brand*	el tatuaje	*tattoo*
pasado de moda	*out of fashion*	de rayas / rayado	*striped*	el maquillaje	*make-up*
de estilo retro	*vintage style*	de lunares	*spotty*	el/la famoso/a	*celebrity*

Question

¿Cómo te vistes normalmente?
How do you dress normally?

Simple Answer

Normalmente llevo vaqueros y una camiseta. Prefiero la ropa cómoda.

I normally wear jeans and a t-shirt. I prefer comfortable clothes.

Extended Answer

Normalmente me visto de negro. No me importa ir vestido/a a la moda. Me gustan los tatuajes, así que cuando tenga dieciocho años, me tatuaré.

I normally dress in black. I'm not bothered about dressing fashionably. I like tattoos, so when I'm 18, I'll get a tattoo.

Grammar — it suits me

To say that something <u>suits you</u>, use the verb '<u>quedar</u>', followed by '<u>bien</u>'. To say something <u>doesn't suit you</u>, use '<u>quedar</u>' followed by '<u>mal</u>'. '<u>Quedar</u>' is like '<u>gustar</u>', so you need to add an <u>indirect object pronoun</u> (see p.130).

Esta blusa <u>me queda bien</u>.
This blouse <u>suits me</u>.

Estas botas <u>me quedan mal</u>.
These boots <u>don't suit me</u>.

Gasto mucho dinero en las joyas — tengo cientos de pendientes, anillos y collares.

I spend a lot of money on jewellery — I've got hundreds of earrings, rings and necklaces.

trainers, because it's important to wear certain brands — las zapatillas de deporte, porque es importante llevar ciertas marcas

No me importa estar en la onda. Prefiero vestirme de estilo retro. El fin de semana pasado compré un vestido de lunares de los años cincuenta. Creo que me queda bien.

Being fashionable doesn't matter to me. I prefer to dress in a vintage style. Last weekend I bought a spotty dress from the fifties. I think it suits me.

a velvet jacket — una chaqueta de terciopelo
a straw hat — un sombrero de paja

A mí me gusta vestirme como los famosos que admiro. Su manera de vestirse me inspira mucho.

I like to dress like the celebrities I admire. The way they dress inspires me a lot.

I don't care what celebrities wear. I think many of them are conceited. — Me da igual cómo se visten los famosos. Creo que muchos de ellos son engreídos.

Use a range of topical vocab to show you know your stuff...

Read Akemi's blog post about fashion and then use the text to complete the sentences.

Después de mucha investigación, creo que en los años ochenta había un estilo muy parecido a lo que se puede ver actualmente. Sin embargo, lo que ha cambiado desde entonces es la abundancia de tiendas. En el pasado existía una verdadera falta de tiendas.

Pienso que el Internet ha transformado todo. Puedes elegir algo y si te queda mal, no pasa nada, y lo puedes devolver fácilmente. Otro cambio es que hay más oportunidades para los **diseñadores**[1] jóvenes porque pueden usar la red como una tienda sin pagar los gastos altos de una tienda verdadera.

[1]designers

1. In the 1980s...
 A. fashion was similar to now.
 B. fashion was different to now.
 C. fashion was more important. *[1]*

2. The Internet has...
 A. made things harder for people in the fashion industry.
 B. made people spend more.
 C. made things easier for people in the fashion industry. *[1]*

Relationships

Saying whether you get on with people is a good way of showing you can use some more complex verbs.

Las relaciones — Relationships

aguantar	*to put up with*	conocer	*to know (a person)*
confiar	*to trust*	hacer amigos	*to make friends*
fastidiar	*to annoy*	la amistad	*friendship*
pelearse	*to fight*	llevarse bien / mal (con)	*to get on well / badly (with)*
enamorarse	*to fall in love*	relacionarse (con)	*to be in contact (with)*
la discusión	*argument*	el modelo de conducta	*role model*

> You need the personal 'a' with 'conocer' and 'aguantar'. Have a look at p.134 for more information.

Grammar — 'confiar'

'Confiar' is an irregular verb.
In the present tense, the 'i' has an accent on it in every form except the 'we' and 'you inf., plural' forms.

Confío en él. **I trust him.**

To say you trust someone, you need to use 'en'.

Grammar — reflexive verbs

'Llevarse', 'relacionarse' and 'pelearse' are reflexive verbs. Take off the 'se' and add the correct ending to the stem like a normal verb (see p.137). Then choose the right pronoun (see p.149) and put it in front of the verb.

Me llevo bien con mi hermana.   *I get on well with my sister.*

¿Te relacionas con ella?   *Are you in contact with her?*

Nos peleamos mucho.   *We fight a lot.*

Mis padres tienen una buena relación pero yo no me llevo bien con ellos debido a la barrera generacional entre nosotros.

My parents get on very well, but I don't get on well with them due to the generation gap between us.

I get on badly with them — me llevo mal con ellos

Me llevo mejor con mi hermano porque me ayuda mucho. Tiene un buen sentido del humor.

I get on better with my brother because he helps me a lot. He has a good sense of humour.

He's a good role model. — Es un buen modelo de conducta.

Mi hermana y yo nos peleamos mucho porque me fastidia.

My sister and I fight a lot because she annoys me.

I can't stand my sister — No aguanto a mi hermana

Conozco muy bien a mi novio y confío en él. Nos enamoramos hace dos años y no discutimos nunca.

I know my boyfriend really well and I trust him. We fell in love two years ago and we never argue.

'Conozco' (I know) is the only irregular bit of the verb 'conocer'.

To step up your Spanish, use a wide variety of verbs...

Read the questions and Víctor's responses below.

¿Qué hay en la foto? ¿Te llevas bien con tu familia?

En esta foto, hay dos chicos — **quizás**[1] son hermanos, pero se llevan bien porque no se pelean.

Generalmente, sí. Confío en mi madre, así que hablo con ella cuando tengo **dificultades**[2] con **amistades**[3], por ejemplo. Mi padre es muy simpático y me conoce bien. No aguanto a mi hermana porque es muy maleducada y estúpida a veces.

Grade 6-7

[1]perhaps
[2]difficulties
[3]friendships

Tick list:
✓ range of adjectives which agree
✓ complex verbs e.g. 'confiar en'
✓ extended reasons given

To improve:
+ a few more complex structures
+ try to use another tense

*Now answer these questions in **Spanish**. Try to speak for about two minutes. ¿Te llevas bien con tus padres? ¿Tienes una buena relación con tus hermanos / tus primos? ¿Confías en tus amigos? [12 marks]*

Socialising with Friends and Family

Cast your mind back into the past and remember those pre-revision days when you had a social life...

¿Eres un(a) buen(a) amigo/a? — Are you a good friend?

pasarlo bien	*to have a good time*	el/la conocido/a	*acquaintance*	optimista	*optimistic*
de buen humor	*in a good mood*	el/la compañero/a	*friend, colleague*	mimado	*spoilt*

Question

Para ti, ¿cómo es un(a) buen(a) amigo/a?

In your opinion, what's a good friend like?

Simple Answer

Un buen amigo es generoso y te escucha.

A good friend is generous and listens to you.

Extended Answer

Para mi la cualidad más importante en un amigo es que te hace reír. Soy una persona optimista y necesito que mis amigos sean alegres también.

For me, the most important quality in a friend is that they make you laugh. I'm an optimistic person and I need my friends to be cheerful too.

En mi tiempo libre... — In my free time...

Cuando no estoy en el colegio, me gusta socializar con mis amigos. Para mí es importante mantener las amistades.

When I'm not in school, I like to socialise with my friends. For me it's important to keep up my friendships.

Los domingos comemos en casa de mis abuelos. A veces preferiría estar con mis amigos, pero no quiero causar problemas.

On Sundays we have lunch at my grandparents' house. Sometimes I'd prefer to be with my friends, but I don't want to cause problems.

Cuando era pequeño, me gustaba jugar con mis primos menores, pero ahora me fastidian mucho. Creo que están un poco mimados.

When I was little, I liked playing with my younger cousins, but now they annoy me a lot. I think they're a bit spoilt.

Grammar — When I was little...

Use the imperfect tense (p.142) to say what you used to do when you were little.

Cuando era pequeño/a, me gustaba jugar con mi hermano.

When I was little, I liked playing with my brother.

Remember you'll need to use 'pequeño' if you're male and 'pequeña' if you're female.

Use the imperfect to say what you used to do...

Guillermo ha escrito un blog sobre lo que hace con sus amigos.

Cuando tengo tiempo libre, salgo con mis amigos **en pandilla**[1]. Normalmente somos un grupo de doce o trece jóvenes. Algunos son **mis amigos verdaderos**[2] porque son alegres y comprensivos. Sin embargo, otros son simplemente conocidos. Nos gusta ir al parque o al club de jóvenes en nuestro barrio. Cuando era pequeño, mis padres no me dejaban salir mucho por la tarde, pero ahora me dan más **libertad**[3].

Grade 6-7

[1] in a gang
[2] my true friends
[3] freedom

Tick list:
✓ tenses: present and imperfect.
✓ varied sentence structures

To improve:
+ add a future tense
+ give a few more opinions

Escribe tu propio blog sobre tu familia y tus amigos. Debes incluir los puntos siguientes:

- *si te gusta pasar tiempo con tu familia*
- *lo que te gustaba hacer con tu familia en el pasado*
- *si eres un(a) buen(a) amigo/a y por qué (no)*
- *lo que vas a hacer el fin de semana que viene.*

*Escribe aproximadamente **90** palabras en **español**.*

[16 marks]

Partnership

Getting married might seem a long way off, but think of a few opinions now so you've got something to say.

En el futuro... — In the future...

estar enamorado/a de	to be in love with
comprometerse	to get engaged
el casamiento / la boda	wedding
el matrimonio	marriage, married couple
el anillo	ring
el esposo / el marido	husband
la esposa / la mujer	wife
ser soltero/a	to be single
el estado civil	marital status

en mi opinión	in my opinion
a mi modo de ver	the way I see it
desde mi punto de vista	from my point of view
debo admitir que...	I must admit that...

Grammar — When I'm X years old...

To say 'when I'm 30' (or to say 'when' with a future event), use the subjunctive. See p.153.

Cuando tenga 60 años... **When I'm 60 years old...**

Question	**Simple Answer**	**Extended Answer**
¿Te gustaría casarte y tener hijos en el futuro?	No sé si quiero casarme, pero me gustaría tener hijos.	No sé si me casaré porque no me importa mucho. Me gustaría tener hijos cuando tenga treinta años, pero no sé cuántos hijos quiero tener.
Would you like to get married and have children in the future?	*I don't know if I want to get married, but I'd like to have children.*	*I don't know if I'll get married because it's not very important to me. I'd like to have children when I'm 30, but I don't know how many I want to have.*

¿El matrimonio es importante? — Is marriage important?

Quiero casarme porque estoy enamorado de mi novia, y desde mi punto de vista, las bodas son muy románticas.

I want to get married because I'm in love with my girlfriend, and from my point of view, weddings are very romantic.

I want to celebrate with my family — quiero celebrar con mi familia

Debo admitir que preferiría no casarme, porque una boda es bastante cara.

I must admit that I would prefer not to get married, because a wedding is quite expensive.

I never want to get married — no quiero casarme nunca

I'd prefer to buy myself a house — preferiría comprarme una casa

A mi modo de ver, no es necesario casarse antes de tener hijos, pero me gustaría hacerlo de todos modos.

The way I see it, it's not necessary to get married before having children, but I'd like to do it anyway.

marriage is important because it gives you stability — el matrimonio es importante porque te da estabilidad

READING Here's a literary text — take your time and read it carefully...

Read this extract from 'Las inquietudes de Shanti Andía' by Pío Baroja, and answer the questions.

Dolorcitas parecía **decidirse por**[1] mí; pero, al mismo tiempo, todo el mundo decía que iba a casarse con el hijo del **marqués**[2] de Vernay, un señor de Jerez, no muy rico, pero de familia aristocrática. Le escribí a Dolorcitas y le hablé varias veces **por la reja**[3].

[1]decide on
[2]marquis
[3]through the window bars

1. Decide whether these statements are true or false.
   a) Nobody thought Dolorcitas was going to get married.
   b) The Marquis of Vernay's son didn't have much money.
   c) The narrator never spoke to Dolorcitas.

2. Use the information in the text to fill in the gap.
   The Marquis of Vernay's son came from ....

[4 marks]

Listening Questions

Here's another opportunity to sharpen up your skills. Don't be tempted to miss these pages out — the time you spend getting used to the sorts of questions you'll get will be worth it in the end.

1 Four young people are describing what they look like.
Mark each **true** aspect of their current appearance with a tick.

TRACK
LISTENING
06

		brown eyes	short hair	black hair	curly hair	glasses	beard
Example:	Luca	✓			✓		✓
1 a	Beatriz						
1 b	Faisal						
1 c	Pilar						

[6 marks]

2 Listen to Inés and Saúl talking about marriage.

TRACK
LISTENING
07

2 a Which two statements are **true**? Write the letters in the boxes.

A	Saúl's wedding will be on the 22nd of June.
B	Saúl will get married in a church.
C	Saúl and Alba are going to invite lots of people to their wedding.
D	There will be four bridesmaids.

[2 marks]

2 b Which two statements are **true**? Write the letters in the boxes.

A	Inés has clear views on whether she wants to get married or not.
B	Inés thinks weddings are romantic.
C	Inés has a boyfriend who wants to get married.
D	Inés has based some of her views on her parents' experiences.

[2 marks]

Speaking Question

Candidate's Role

- Your teacher will play the role of your Spanish friend. They will speak first.

- You should use *tú* to address your friend.

- – ! – means you will have to respond to something you have not prepared.

- – ? – means you will have to ask your friend a question.

> Estás hablando de tus amigos con tu amigo/a español/a.
>
> - Tu mejor amigo/a (**dos** detalles).
>
> - Una actividad reciente con tu amigo/a.
>
> - !
>
> - ? Hermanos.
>
> - Hijos en el futuro y **una** razón.

Teacher's Role

- You begin the role-play using the introductory text below.

- You should address the candidate as *tú*.

- You may alter the wording of the questions in response to the candidate's previous answers.

- Do not supply the candidate with key vocabulary.

> Introductory text: *Estás hablando de tus amigos con tu amigo/a español/a.*
> *Yo soy tu amigo/a.*
>
> - ¿Cómo es tu mejor amigo o tu mejor amiga?
>
> - ¿Qué has hecho recientemente con tu amigo/a?
>
> - ! ¿Te llevas mejor con tus amigos o con tu familia?
>
> - ? Allow the candidate to ask you a question.
>
> - ¿Te gustaría tener hijos en el futuro?

Reading Questions

1   Translate this text into **English**.

> Tengo un hámster negro que se llama Elvis. Lo compré hace dos años. Elvis me hace reír mucho porque es un poco tonto. Duerme en su casa durante el día y sale por la noche para comer y jugar. A veces hace mucho ruido y no me deja dormir. En un mundo ideal, tendría varios hámsters, pero de momento no tengo suficiente espacio.

....

....

....

....

....

....

[9 marks]

2   Ravi ha escrito sobre su deportista preferido para un concurso.
Lee lo que dice y contesta a las preguntas en **español**.

> Si pudiera conocer a cualquier deportista, sería mi héroe de toda la vida, el futbolista Pau Rodríguez. No sólo es fuerte físicamente, sino también es inteligente, una cualidad que le permite jugar tácticamente y con mucho éxito. En los periódicos se lee con mucha frecuencia artículos que critican a los jugadores por su mal comportamiento en los momentos más estresantes de los partidos. A veces se ponen a pelear con el equipo rival y reciben tarjetas amarillas e incluso rojas como castigo. Rodríguez, sin embargo, no es así. Siempre piensa antes de actuar, lo que le ha convertido en un modelo a seguir para los jóvenes y sus compañeros de equipo también.

2 a   ¿Cuánto tiempo lleva Ravi admirando a su ídolo?

....   *[1 mark]*

2 b   ¿Qué opinan algunos periodistas sobre los jugadores de fútbol?

....   *[1 mark]*

2 c   ¿Por qué es Pau Rodríguez un buen ejemplo para otra gente?

....   *[1 mark]*

Writing Questions

1   Escribes una carta a tu amigo chileno para contarle sobre tu vida.

Menciona:

• las personas que hay en tu familia

• tu personalidad cuando eras pequeño/a

• las actividades que te gusta hacer con tu familia

• tu novio/a ideal.

Escribe aproximadamente **90** palabras en **español**.
Responde a todos los aspectos de la pregunta.   *[16 marks]*

2   Translate this text into **Spanish**.

> When I was little, I got on well with my parents but now I prefer to talk to my grandparents.
> They are more understanding. Therefore, I would prefer to live with them. I think I'll get on
> better with my parents in the future. We will not fight as much and they will be more sensitive.

....

....

....

....

....

....

....

[12 marks]

Revision Summary for Section Two

You've probably known how to say your name and whether you have brothers and sisters for ages now, but don't get lulled into a false sense of security — to impress at GCSE, you need to know the trickier stuff too. Use these questions to check your progress and see where the gaps in your knowledge are. Then you can revisit the tougher stuff and figure out anything that you weren't sure about.

About Yourself (p.16) ☑

1) You've just met a Spanish person. Tell them your age and when your birthday is in Spanish. ☑
2) Spell your name and surname out loud in Spanish. ☑

My Family (p.17) ☑

3) Say 'my grandmother has eight grandchildren' in Spanish. ☑
4) ¿Tienes hermanos? Contesta en español, con frases completas. ☑

Describing People (p.18) ☑

5) What's the Spanish for...?   a) medium height   b) old   c) green   d) curly ☑
6) Describe tu aspecto físico en español, con frases completas. ☑

Personalities (p.19) ☑

7) Translate these adjectives into Spanish in the form given in brackets.
   a) happy (masculine singular)   b) lively (feminine plural)   c) rude (feminine singular) ☑
8) Lucía is understanding and funny but sometimes she's jealous. Describe her in Spanish. ☑

Pets (p.20) ☑

9) What are the two ways of saying 'pet' in Spanish? ☑
10) How would you say that you'd like a goldfish in Spanish? ☑

Style and Fashion (p.21) ☑

11) Fiona says: 'Creo que estos vaqueros me quedan mal.' Translate this into English. ☑
12) ¿Te gusta vestirte como los famosos? Contesta en español, con frases completas. ☑

Relationships (p.22) ☑

13) Julio says: 'Normalmente me llevo bien con mi hermano pero a veces nos peleamos.'
    What's his relationship with his brother like? ☑
14) How would you say that your parents annoy you in Spanish? ☑

Socialising with Friends and Family (p.23) ☑

15) ¿Crees que eres un(a) buen(a) amigo/a? ¿Por qué (no)? ☑
16) Steve liked visiting his grandparents when he was younger. How would he say this in Spanish? ☑

Partnership (p.24) ☑

17) Translate into English: 'Mi estado civil cambiará el año que viene porque voy a casarme.' ☑
18) ¿Te gustaría casarte en el futuro? ¿Por qué (no)? Contesta en español, con frases completas. ☑

Technology

Mobile phones, computers, the Internet... you need to know how to talk about all of these for your GCSE.

La tecnología en la vida diaria — Technology in everyday life

el ordenador	*computer*
el portátil	*laptop*
el móvil	*mobile phone*
el mensaje (de texto)	*(text) message*
mandar / enviar	*to send*
recibir	*to receive*
usar / utilizar	*to use*

Grammar — I could / couldn't ...

To imagine what you '<u>could do</u>' or '<u>couldn't do</u>', use the <u>conditional</u> tense of '<u>poder</u>' (see p.146) followed by the <u>infinitive</u>.

Sin mi móvil, <u>no podría hablar</u> con mis amigos.
Without my mobile phone, <u>I couldn't talk</u> to my friends.

<u>No podría hacer</u> mis deberes sin un portátil.
<u>I couldn't do</u> my homework without a laptop.

Question

¿Para qué usas tu móvil?
What do you use your mobile phone for?

Simple Answer

Uso mi móvil para mandar mensajes.
I use my mobile phone to send messages.

Extended Answer

Tener un móvil es muy importante para mí. Sin mi móvil, no podría ni mandar ni recibir mensajes.

Having a mobile phone is very important for me. Without my mobile phone, I couldn't send or receive messages.

Navegando por la red — Surfing the Internet

la red	*the Internet*	el usuario	*user*	el videojuego	*video game*
el internauta	*Internet user*	el correo electrónico	*email*	el buscador	*search engine*
el navegador	*browser*	descargar	*to download*	la herramienta	*tool*

Me encanta descargar canciones.	*I love downloading songs.*
Me gustan los videojuegos porque puedes comunicarte con otros usuarios.	*I like video games because you can communicate with other users.*

La red es una herramienta muy útil porque puedes usar un buscador para encontrar información.

The Internet is a very useful tool because you can use a search engine to find information.

→ crucial for modern life —
crucial para la vida moderna

Mis padres usan la red para sus cuentas bancarias porque es más fácil que ir al banco.

My parents use the web for their bank accounts because it's easier than going to the bank.

Many Internet users —
Muchos internautas

Gracias a la red, es más cómodo hacer las compras. Hace unos días, compré unos regalos por Internet y ya están aquí.

Thanks to the Internet, it's more convenient to do your shopping. A few days ago, I bought some presents online and they're already here.

However, it's difficult to know if you like the product or not because you buy it without seeing it in reality. — Sin embargo, es difícil saber si te gusta el producto o no porque lo compras sin verlo en realidad.

Technology

Singing technology's praises isn't enough — you also need to be able to talk about its disadvantages.

Lo malo de la tecnología... — The bad thing about technology...

Grammar — the ... thing is that...

In Spanish, you can say 'the good thing' or 'the bad thing' by using 'lo' followed by 'bueno' or 'malo'.

Lo bueno / malo es que...   *The good / bad thing is that...*

You can do this with any adjective:

Lo mejor / peor es que...   *The best / worst thing is that...*

Lo peligroso es que...   *The dangerous thing is that...*

To say 'the most... thing', just add 'más' before the adjective:

Lo más útil es que...   *The most useful thing is that...*

acceder	*to access*
el archivo	*file*
borrar	*to erase / delete*
el buzón	*inbox, mailbox*
adjuntar	*to attach*
el correo basura	*spam*
la contraseña	*password*
el servidor de seguridad	*firewall*
el disco duro	*hard disk/drive*

Lo peor de los móviles es que la gente puede grabar videos sin informarte.

The worst thing about mobiles is that people can record videos without telling you.

Es importante tener una contraseña para proteger tu identidad. Si alguien averigua tu contraseña, puede acceder a tus archivos. Por eso no se debe utilizar nunca la red sin un buen servidor de seguridad.

It's important to have a password to protect your identity. If someone finds out your password, they can access your files. Therefore you should never use the Internet without a good firewall.

Me molesta cuando recibo correo basura porque tengo que borrar todos los mensajes de mi buzón para encontrar los que me importan.

It annoys me when I receive spam because I have to delete all the messages from my inbox to find the ones that matter to me.

share your photos with other people you don't know — compartir tus fotos con otra gente a la que no conoces

ruin your hard disk — estropear tu disco duro

sometimes it harms your computer and causes you problems — a veces daña tu ordenador y te causa problemas

Question	**Simple Answer**	**Extended Answer**
Dame una desventaja de la tecnología. *Give me one disadvantage of technology.*	Una desventaja es que no puedes escapar de la tecnología. *One disadvantage is that you can't escape from technology.*	Una desventaja es que siempre tienes que estar conectado. Lo más irritante es cuando mis amigos se enfadan cuando no contesto a sus mensajes enseguida. *One disadvantage is that you always have to be connected. The most irritating thing is when my friends get angry when I don't reply to their messages straightaway.*

The good thing, the bad thing — lo bueno, lo malo...

Translate this text into **Spanish**. *[12 marks]*

I couldn't live without technology because it is very useful. I like playing video games online with my brother. We speak to Internet users in other countries. Yesterday, I played with a boy in Chile, but in order to protect my identity, I never use my name. The best thing about mobile phones is that you don't have to be at home to use the Internet. In the future, I think children will have mobile phones when they are 2 or 3 years old.

Social Media

Another chance to talk about technology. Watch out for any radical-changing verbs, though.

Las redes sociales — Social networks

la red social	*social network*
el sitio web	*website*
la sala de chat	*chat room*
el blog	*blog*
la cuenta	*account*
desactivar	*to deactivate / block*
charlar	*to chat*
colgar	*to post (online)*

Grammar — colgar (to post)

'Colgar' (*to post*) is a radical-changing verb (see p.138) that changes in the present tense:

Mis amigos cuelgan fotos en mi muro.
My friends post photos on my wall.

Question

¿Usas las redes sociales?
Do you use social networks?

Simple Answer

Sí, me gusta charlar con mis amigos en las redes sociales.
Yes, I like chatting with my friends on social networks.

Extended Answer

Sí, comparto fotos con mis amigos. Mis padres tienen miedo de las redes sociales porque no las entienden.
Yes, I share photos with my friends. My parents are scared of social networks because they don't understand them.

Uso los medios sociales para... — I use social media to...

Me encanta usar las redes sociales para hablar con mis amigos que viven lejos de mí.

I love using social networks to talk to my friends who live far away from me. ← my cousins who live in Canada — mis primos que viven en Canadá

Diría que los jóvenes pasan demasiado tiempo en las redes sociales.

I would say that young people spend too much time on social networks. ← should spend more time outside — deberían pasar más tiempo al aire libre

Uso las redes sociales todos los días para charlar con la gente que comparte mis intereses. Me gusta cocinar, así que cuelgo recetas y fotos de la comida en unos sitios web.

I use social networks every day to chat to people who share my interests. I like cooking, so I post recipes and photos of food on some websites. ← I watch videos to learn more about cooking — veo vídeos para aprender más sobre la cocina

Extend your answers by giving reasons...

Lee lo que dice Belén sobre las redes sociales y decide si las frases son verdaderas (V) o falsas (F).

Uso las redes sociales después del colegio. Es relajante charlar sobre cosas estúpidas. Sin embargo, a veces, mis amigos se pelean si alguien ha colgado una foto sin permiso. No podría vivir sin las redes sociales, pero me molesta cuando salgo con mi novio y pasa todo el tiempo viendo cosas ridículas en su móvil en lugar de charlar conmigo.

e.g. Belén sólo usa las redes sociales los sábados. **F**

1. Belén charla sobre cosas no muy serias. *[1]*

2. Las redes sociales causan problemas entre sus amigos. *[1]*

3. Según ella, la vida sería mejor sin las redes sociales. *[1]*

4. El novio de Belén cree que la red es estúpida. *[1]*

The Problems with Social Media

To seriously impress the examiners, give balanced opinions. Here's how to get started...

Las ventajas y desventajas — Advantages and disadvantages

la ventaja	*advantage*	por una parte	*on one hand*	debido a	*due to*
la desventaja	*disadvantage*	por otra parte	*on the other hand*	gracias a	*thanks to*

Me encanta que siempre hay alguien con quien puedo charlar en las redes sociales.

I love it that there's always someone I can chat to on social networks.

Por una parte, es muy fácil mantenerte en contacto con los amigos, pero por otra parte, creo que es muy importante salir con los amigos y estar juntos en la vida real.

On the one hand, it's very easy to keep in contact with your friends, but on the other hand, I believe it's very important to go out with your friends and be together in real life.

Debido a las redes sociales, sé lo que está pasando en el mundo.

Due to social networks, I know what's happening in the world.

Chat rooms are useful but they can be dangerous. — Las salas de chat son útiles, pero pueden ser peligrosas.

often, the friends you have on social media aren't real friends — muchas veces, los amigos que tienes en las redes sociales no son amigos de verdad

I waste time looking at useless things — pierdo tiempo mirando cosas inútiles. 'Pierdo' comes from 'perder', which is a radical-changing verb. See p.138.

Question

¿Cuál es tu opinión de las redes sociales?

What's your opinion of social networks?

Simple Answer

Es divertido usar las redes sociales pero pueden ser peligrosas también.

It's fun to use social networks but they can be dangerous too.

Extended Answer

Una ventaja es que no te aburres nunca. Sin embargo, no me gustan las salas de chat porque la gente te puede mentir. Pienso que voy a desactivar mi cuenta.

An advantage is that you never get bored. However, I don't like chat rooms because people can lie to you. I think I'm going to deactivate my account.

Don't just say 'me gusta' — vary your language...

Have a look at Manuel's answer to this question.

¿Crees que los jóvenes deberían pasar menos tiempo en las redes sociales?

A mi modo de ver, las redes sociales tienen más ventajas que desventajas. Mucha gente dice que pasamos demasiado tiempo charlando con los amigos en el mundo virtual, pero yo no estoy de acuerdo. No puedo salir con mis amigos después del colegio, así que es conveniente usar las redes sociales para comunicarme con ellos. Además, las redes sociales te pueden **enseñar**[1] mucho sobre el mundo y lo que pasa en tu **barrio**[2]. Puede ser más barato navegar por Internet para aprender estas cosas que comprar un periódico.

Grade 8-9

[1]teach
[2]neighbourhood

Tick list:
✓ tenses: present
✓ comparatives
✓ connectives e.g. además
✓ opinions

To improve:
+ use more tenses, e.g. future, conditional
+ use intensifiers e.g. muy, bastante

Contesta a estas preguntas en **español** *— intenta hablar durante* **5** *minutos.*

- *¿Te gusta usar las redes sociales?*
- *¿Cuáles son las desventajas de las redes sociales?*
- *¿Crees que los jóvenes deberían pasar menos tiempo en las redes sociales?* [30 marks]

Listening Questions

Doing loads of practice is a sure-fire way to improve. That's why we've come up with these questions — they'll have you on your way to GCSE glory in no time at all.

1   José and Laura are preparing a presentation about what they use the Internet for. Listen to their presentation and then answer the questions below in **English**.

TRACK LISTENING 08

What does Laura use the Internet for? Give **three** things.

1 a   ....   *[1 mark]*

1 b   ....   *[1 mark]*

1 c   ....   *[1 mark]*

1 d   What, according to José, is the biggest problem with the Internet?

....   *[1 mark]*

1 e   What does Laura think is the biggest disadvantage of the Internet?

....   *[1 mark]*

2   Unos jóvenes están participando en un debate sobre las redes sociales. Para cada persona, decide si tiene una opinión positiva (**P**), negativa (**N**), o positiva y negativa (**P+N**).

TRACK LISTENING 09

2 a   Azucena   ☐   *[1 mark]*

2 b   Sharif   ☐   *[1 mark]*

2 c   Silvia   ☐   *[1 mark]*

Speaking Question

Candidate's Role

- Your teacher will play the role of a mobile phone salesperson. They will speak first.

- You should use *usted* to address the salesperson.

- – ! – means you will have to respond to something you have not prepared.

- – ? – means you will have to ask the salesperson a question.

> Estás hablando de la tecnología con un/a vendedor/a de móviles.
>
> - Usos de tu móvil (**dos** detalles).
>
> - !
>
> - Vivir sin tu móvil.
>
> - Ventajas de Internet (**dos** detalles).
>
> - **?** Lo malo de la red.

Teacher's Role

- You begin the role-play using the introductory text below.

- You should address the candidate as *usted*.

- You may alter the wording of the questions in response to the candidate's previous answers.

- Do not supply the candidate with key vocabulary.

> Introductory text: *Está hablando de la tecnología con un/a vendedor/a en una tienda de móviles. Yo soy el/la vendedor/a.*
>
> - ¿Para qué usa su móvil?
>
> - ! ¿Cuándo recibió el móvil que tiene ahora?
>
> - ¿Podría vivir sin su móvil?
>
> - ¿Cuáles son las ventajas de Internet?
>
> - **?** Allow the candidate to ask you a question.

Reading Questions

1   Translate this text into **English**.

> — ¿Has visto el muro de Luisa recientemente? — preguntó Naiara.
>
> — No, ¿por qué? dijo Sara.
>
> — Porque acaba de colgar unas fotos muy tontas y pienso que hay una foto de ti.
>
> — ¿De verdad? Tendré que llamarla ahora mismo para preguntarle por qué lo hizo.
>
> — Sí, claro. Luisa no piensa nunca antes de publicar cosas en las redes sociales.

....

....

....

....

....

....

[9 marks]

2   Translate this text into **English**.

> A mi amigo le encantan las redes sociales. Estoy harto de no verle, así que le dije:
>
> — ¿Por qué no vienes a tomar un café con nosotros? ¡Pasas todo el tiempo en tu portátil!
>
> ¡Es importante hacer otras cosas de vez en cuando, Fernando! Yo sé que las redes
>
> sociales tienen ventajas, pero ¡estás obsesionado!

....

....

....

....

....

....

[9 marks]

Writing Questions

1 Usted se interesa mucho por las redes sociales.
Escriba usted un reportaje sobre ellas.

Debe incluir los puntos siguientes:

- por qué las redes sociales son tan populares

- las desventajas de las redes sociales

- si usted ha tenido algún problema debido a las redes sociales

- cómo podríamos evitar los problemas causados por las redes sociales.

Justifique sus ideas y sus opiniones.
Escriba aproximadamente **150** palabras en **español**.   *[32 marks]*

2 Translate this text into **Spanish**.

> My parents hate technology. Last year they bought a computer, but they only use it to
> send emails. I think it is essential to know how to surf the web. I use the Internet to
> download music. I couldn't live without the Internet because it's a very big part of my life.

....

....

....

....

....

[12 marks]

Revision Summary for Section Three

Here's a question for you — how tech-savvy in Spanish are you? Have a read through these questions and see if there are any you're a bit unsure about. Try to use as much of the vocab on the pages in your answers as you can, and remember you can always flick back through the section once you're done.

Technology (p.30-31) ☑

1) ¿Para qué usas tu ordenador o tu portátil? Answer in Spanish in full sentences. ☑

2) How would you say in Spanish that you got a mobile phone for your birthday? ☑

3) Give three things you use your mobile phone for. Answer in Spanish. ☑

4) What's the Spanish for...?
   a) email   b) search engine   c) tool   d) video game   e) Internet user ☑

5) Translate Pau's comments about the Internet into English: 'Paso muchas horas navegando por la red. Diría que es mi pasatiempo preferido porque se puede aprender cosas y divertirse al mismo tiempo. Además, se puede utilizar la red para organizar la vida diaria.' ☑

6) How would you say that you use the Internet to download songs and films in Spanish? ☑

7) ¿Te gusta hacer las compras en la red? Contesta en español con frases completas. ☑

8) What's 'el disco duro' in English? ☑

9) Write down one potential disadvantage of the Internet in Spanish. ☑

10) Omar says: 'Lo peor de Internet es el riesgo de recibir un virus.' Translate this into English. ☑

11) Carlos asks you: '¿Recibes mucho correo basura?' What does he want to know? ☑

12) You read this advice in a chat room: 'Todo el mundo debe proteger su información personal. La mejor manera de hacer eso es elegir contraseñas seguras que incluyen números y letras y no compartirlas con nadie.' What does it mean in English? ☑

Social Media (p.32-33) ☑

13) How do you say these words in Spanish?
   a) website   b) account   c) to post (online)   d) to chat ☑

14) ¿Usas las redes sociales con mucha frecuencia? Contesta en español con frases completas. ☑

15) Jazmín says: 'Uso las redes sociales para charlar con mis amigos. Si vamos a algún sitio, saco fotos y las cuelgo en mi muro en seguida.' Translate this into English. ☑

16) Cara writes a blog about her favourite films. How could she say this in Spanish? ☑

17) You're preparing for a debate in class and you have to argue that social media is bad. Write down two things you could say in Spanish. ☑

18) How would you say 'I think that social networks have more advantages than disadvantages' in Spanish? ☑

Books and Reading

Time to think about your favourite book, whether it's a thriller, a fantasy or a detective novel.

¿Lees mucho? — Do you read a lot?

la lectura	*reading*	la revista	*magazine*
leer	*to read*	el periódico	*newspaper*
el libro	*book*	la prensa	*the press*
la novela	*novel*	el libro electrónico	*e-book*
el tebeo	*comic strip*	el lector de libros electrónicos	*e-reader*

Grammar — 'leer' in the preterite tense

The verb '<u>leer</u>' (*to read*) is <u>irregular</u> in the <u>preterite tense</u> (see p.141). In both of the '<u>you</u>' forms and the '<u>we</u>' form, there's an <u>accent</u> on the first '<u>i</u>'. The '<u>he/she/it</u>' and '<u>they</u>' forms have a '<u>y</u>' in them.

<u>Leíste</u> un buen libro ayer.   ***You (inf., sing.) read a good book yesterday.***

Ana <u>leyó</u> tres libros.   ***Ana read three books.***

A mí me encanta leer las novelas de suspense porque las tramas suelen ser emocionantes.

I love reading thrillers because the plots are usually exciting.

→ *detective novels — las novelas policíacas*

Desafortunadamente, no tengo mucho tiempo para leer novelas largas.

Unfortunately, I don't have much time to read long novels.

← *the newspaper every day — el periódico todos los días*

Los libros no me interesan mucho. Prefiero ver películas porque no tengo que concentrarme tanto.

Books don't interest me much. I prefer to watch films because I don't have to concentrate as much.

← *to read comic strips — leer los tebeos*

Question	**Simple Answer**	**Extended Answer**
¿Cuál es tu opinión de los lectores de libros electrónicos? *What's your opinion of e-readers?*	Son una buena idea porque puedes llevar varios libros contigo. *They are a good idea because you can take several books with you.*	Prefiero los libros en papel, pero debo admitir que los libros electrónicos son prácticos, sobre todo cuando vas de vacaciones. *I prefer paper books, but I must admit that e-books are practical, especially when you go on holiday.*

Practise doing role-plays just like this one...

Have a look at this example role-play. Javier is talking to a librarian.

Grade 6-7

Librarian: ¿Le gusta leer?

Javier: No leo mucho, pero me gustaría leer más.

Librarian: Hábleme de un libro que le ha gustado.

Javier: El año pasado leí una novela policíaca que se llama 'La noche oscura'. Me gustó mucho. ¿Tiene usted alguna recomendación?

Librarian: Sí, recomendaría 'El jardín misterioso'. ¿Le gustan los libros electrónicos?

Javier: Prefiero los libros electrónicos porque son más ligeros que los libros de papel. ¿Usted tiene un lector de libros electrónicos?

Librarian: Sí, pero no lo utilizo mucho.

To improve:
+ Use different opinion phrases to avoid repeating 'gustar'.

*Now prepare your own role play. Use 'usted' and speak for about **two** minutes. [15 marks]*

Usted está en una biblioteca. Habla con el/la empleado/a.

- leer — frecuencia
- !
- ? género preferido
- los periódicos — opinión
- ? lector de libros electrónicos — precio

Tick list:
✓ tenses: present, preterite, conditional
✓ correct use of 'usted'

Music

Music's definitely worth revising well — it often comes up in the exams and it's great for showing off your knowledge of tenses. Some of the vocab is a bit tricky, though, so make sure it doesn't trip you up.

La música — Music

la batería	drums
la canción	song
el / la cantante	singer
cantar	to sing
la letra	song lyrics
el grupo	band
el / la músico/a	musician
tocar	to play (an instrument)
la grabación	recording
en directo	live

Grammar — 'tocar' + instrument

Use the verb '<u>tocar</u>' to say you <u>play an instrument</u>.

When you're using the 'yo' form of 'tocar' in the <u>preterite</u> tense (see p.141), the '<u>c</u>' changes to '<u>qu</u>'.

Toco el violín.   ***I play the violin.***

Toqué el violín ayer.   ***I played the violin yesterday.***

Tocaba el violín.   ***I used to play the violin.***

Use the <u>imperfect</u> tense (p.142) to say what you <u>used to do</u>.

Question	**Simple Answer**	**Extended Answer**
¿Tocas algún instrumento?	Sí, toco la guitarra y el clarinete.	Sí, toco la guitarra en un grupo. Cuando era pequeño, tocaba el piano. Me gustaría aprender a tocar la batería, pero mis padres no me dejarán hacerlo.
Do you play an instrument?	*Yes, I play the guitar and the clarinet.*	*Yes, I play the guitar in a band. When I was little, I used to play the piano. I would like to learn to play the drums, but my parents won't let me do it.*

¿Te gusta escuchar música? — Do you like listening to music?

Me encanta escuchar música porque me hace sentir relajado/a. No me gusta la música pop. Diría que mi género de música preferido es el hip-hop.

I love listening to music because it makes me feel relaxed. I don't like pop music. I'd say that my favourite genre of music is hip-hop.

Puedo descargar muchos tipos de música instantáneamente, lo que me parece fenomenal.

I can download many types of music instantly, which seems great to me.

Adoro a DiskoBeetz e intento ir a todos sus conciertos. Sus videos musicales son siempre entretenidos y originales.

I adore DiskoBeetz and I try to go to all their concerts. Their music videos are always entertaining and original.

rap music — la música rap
rock music — la música rock
classical music — la música clásica

take my music with me and listen to it while I'm jogging or on the train — llevar la música conmigo y escucharla cuando salgo a correr o cuando estoy en el tren

Their song lyrics are interesting. — La letra de sus canciones es interesante.

I love live music. — Me encanta la música en directo.

Remember you 'tocar' an instrument...

Marisol is a Spanish singer. Listen to the interview and then answer the questions in **English**.

e.g. What kind of music is most important to Marisol's sister? *pop music*

1. Which instrument would Marisol like to learn to play?   [1]
2. What two advantages of listening to music on the Internet does Marisol mention?   [2]
3. Why does Marisol like going to concerts?   [1]

Cinema

Make sure you can talk about a film you saw recently — and remember to always back up your opinions.

En el cine — At the cinema

la película	*film*	el papel	*role*	la estrella	*star, celebrity*
el actor	*actor*	la trama	*plot*	la banda sonora	*soundtrack*
la actriz	*actress*	el reparto	*cast*	la entrada	*ticket*

Me encantan las películas policíacas porque son muy emocionantes.

I love detective films because they're very exciting.

Prefiero las películas de aventura porque me dan menos miedo que las películas de terror.

I prefer adventure films because they scare me less than horror films.

No me gustan las películas de ciencia ficción porque es difícil seguir la trama.

I don't like science fiction films because it's difficult to follow the plot.

science fiction — de ciencia ficción

often the special effects are great — muchas veces los efectos especiales son fenomenales

Romantic films annoy me — Las películas románticas me fastidian

you always know what's going to happen — siempre sabes lo que va a pasar

La última película que vi... — The last film I saw...

Question

Describe la última película que viste.

Describe the last film you saw.

Simple Answer

El sábado, vi una película de acción. Me gustó mucho.

On Saturday, I saw an action film. I really liked it.

Extended Answer

El fin de semana pasado, vi una película de acción. Se trataba de dos familias que luchaban durante cientos de años. Tengo ganas de ver la nueva película de Geoff Frank porque me gusta el reparto.

Last weekend, I saw an action film. It was about two families who were fighting for hundreds of years. I'm looking forward to seeing the new film by Geoff Frank because I like the cast.

Grammar — I saw...

To say 'I saw...' you need the preterite tense. Check how to form it on p.141.

El viernes, vi una comedia.

On Friday, I saw a comedy.

Unlike most verbs when they're in the 'yo' form of the preterite tense, 'vi' doesn't have an accent.

Grammar — 'se trata de'

Use 'se trata de' to say what a film is about:

Se trata de unos jóvenes muy ricos.

It's about some very rich young people.

And you can use it in the imperfect to say what a film was about:

Se trataba del amor. *It was about love.*

Remember — 'de' + 'el' = 'del' (p.133).

Check you know when to use each type of past tense...

Translate this text into **Spanish**. *[12 marks]*

I love films. In my opinion, detective films are the best. They are the most entertaining films because you have to think about the plot. Last week, I saw a really funny film. I like seeing films with my friends at the weekend. In the future, I would love to be an actress.

TV

Learn how to talk about your TV habits and those of other people with this handy page.

¿Qué hay en la tele? — What's on TV?

el programa	programme	las noticias	the news	los dibujos animados	cartoons
la cadena	channel	el documental	documentary	la telenovela	soap opera
el anuncio	advert	el concurso	game show, contest	el reality show	reality show

Question	**Simple Answer**	**Extended Answer**
¿Te gusta ver la tele?	Sí, me gusta ver la tele los fines de semana.	Sí, me gusta ver la tele los fines de semana. Mi cadena preferida es BBC1 porque no hay anuncios.
Do you like watching TV?	*Yes, I like watching TV at the weekend.*	*Yes, I like watching TV at the weekend. My favourite channel is BBC1 because there aren't any adverts.*

¿Qué te gusta ver? — What do you like watching?

Grammar — 'la gente' is singular

In English, 'people' is a plural noun. In Spanish, 'la gente' is singular, so you need the 'he/she/it' bit of the verb and the feminine singular form of 'many'.

Mucha gente **cree** que...   ***Many** people **believe** that...*

A mí me gusta ver las telenovelas. Mucha gente dice que son aburridas y ridículas pero me ayudan a relajarme. No me gusta ver las noticias, especialmente cuando hablan sobre política.

I like watching soap operas. Many people say that they're boring and ridiculous but they help me relax. I don't like watching the news, especially when they're talking about politics.

Some people think that — Alguna gente piensa que

I don't understand why people complain — no entiendo por qué la gente se queja

Suelo ver varios tipos de programas. Hoy en día hay tanta diversidad. Sin embargo, quisiera ver más documentales y menos dibujos animados.

I usually watch several types of programmes. These days there is so much diversity. However, I would like to see more documentaries and fewer cartoons.

See p.46 for how to use the verb 'soler'.

there's so much rubbish — hay tanta basura

Now there's something for everyone. — Ahora hay algo para todo el mundo.

Mi abuelo pasa todos los días viendo la tele porque no puede salir. A él le encantan los concursos porque puede participar desde el sofá.

My grandad spends every day watching TV because he can't go out. He loves game shows because he can join in from the sofa.

TV is very important for him. — La televisión es muy importante para él.

Don't just say what you watch — say why you like it too...

Read Eli's email about TV, then decide whether the statements are true or false.

¡Hola Melissa! ¡Lo pasé fenomenal durante el intercambio contigo! Lo que me sorprendió fue la cantidad de telenovelas en la televisión británica. Sin embargo, no había tantos anuncios como en España. En España preferimos los dramas, sobre todo los que se tratan de figuras históricas. Creo que son muy emocionantes y han tenido mucho éxito recientemente.

e.g. Eli enjoyed the exchange. **True.**

1. The number of soap operas didn't surprise Eli. [1]

2. British TV had more adverts than Spanish TV. [1]

3. Historical dramas are popular in Spain. [1]

4. Eli thinks historical dramas are exciting. [1]

Food

There's loads of tricky vocab on this page, but don't panic — just learn a few chunks at a time.

Los alimentos — Foods

la manzana	apple
el melocotón	peach
la fresa	strawberry
la naranja	orange
el plátano	banana
la pera	pear
las uvas	grapes
la piña	pineapple

las legumbres	vegetables, pulses
las verduras	vegetables
las judías verdes	string beans
los champiñones	mushrooms
los guisantes	peas

la zanahoria	carrot
la col	cabbage
la patata	potato
la cebolla	onion
la lechuga	lettuce

la carne	meat
la carne de vaca	beef
la carne de cordero	lamb
la carne de cerdo	pork
la carne de ternera	veal
el filete	steak
el jamón	ham
el pollo	chicken
la salchicha	sausage
el pescado	fish
el atún	tuna
las gambas	prawns
los mariscos	seafood

el aceite	oil
el ajo	garlic
el huevo	egg
la pimienta	ground pepper
la sal	salt
el azúcar	sugar
la nata	cream
el queso	cheese
la mantequilla	butter

los calamares	squid
el chorizo	Spanish sausage
el gazpacho	cold soup
la tortilla	omelette
las tapas	nibbles, bar snacks
los churros	long doughnuts

el arroz	rice
una barra de pan	a loaf of bread
la tostada	toast

el café	coffee
el té	tea
el zumo	juice
la leche	milk
el vino	wine
la cerveza	beer

el caramelo	boiled sweet
la mermelada	jam
la galleta	biscuit
el pastel	cake, pie
el helado	ice cream

¿Qué te gusta comer? — What do you like to eat?

Grammar — meal times

These are the <u>nouns</u> for Spanish meals:

el desayuno	**breakfast**	You can also
el almuerzo	**lunch**	say 'la comida'.
la merienda	**afternoon snack**	
la cena	**dinner**	

These nouns can be made into <u>verbs</u>:

desayunar	**to have breakfast**	You can say
almorzar	**to have lunch**	'comer' too.
merendar	**to have an afternoon snack**	
cenar	**to have dinner**	

Almuerzo a la una. Suelo comer un bocadillo.
I have lunch at one o'clock. I usually eat a sandwich.

'Almorzar' (to have lunch) is a radical-changing verb ('o' to 'ue'). See p.138.

Mis padres trabajan mucho, así que comemos mucha comida basura. Mi plato preferido es pollo al curry.
My parents work a lot, so we eat a lot of junk food. My favourite meal is chicken curry.

I love Chinese / Mediterranean food. — Me encanta la comida china / mediterránea.

Take a moment to digest all that by doing this question...

Listen to three people's opinions about food. Tick the statements that are true. *[3 marks]*

e.g. When he was younger, Joaquín ate lots of sweets. ✓

1. Joaquín likes eating junk food.
2. Alejandra doesn't think she eats enough fruit.
3. Raquel thinks it's difficult to find things she can eat in restaurants.

Eating Out

Restaurants often come up in the role-play section of the exam — so get learning your stuff.

¡Vamos al restaurante! — Let's go to the restaurant!

pedir	to order, ask for	el plato (combinado)	(set) dish
traer	to bring	el primer plato	starter
el camarero	waiter	el segundo plato	main course
la camarera	waitress	el postre	dessert
la carta	the menu	la bebida	drink
el tenedor	fork	la cuenta	bill
el cuchillo	knife	la propina	tip
la cuchara	spoon	a la plancha	grilled
el vaso	glass	tener hambre	to be hungry
incluido	included	tener sed	to be thirsty

Grammar — ordering politely

Use 'quisiera' to order what you'd like politely. 'Quisiera' comes from the imperfect subjunctive of 'querer' (to want). See p.146 and 154.

Quisiera un filete.
I'd like a steak.

You can also say 'me apetece', which means 'I fancy'.

Me apetece un café.
I fancy a coffee.

Question	Simple Answer	Extended Answer
¿Qué le gustaría tomar?	Quiero la sopa, por favor.	De primer plato, quisiera la sopa, y de segundo plato, el atún.
What would you like?	*I want the soup, please.*	*For the starter, I'd like the soup, and for main course, the tuna.*

Me encanta ir a restaurantes pero normalmente no puedo comer mucho. Sin embargo, siempre pido un postre porque me gustan las cosas dulces.

I love going to restaurants but normally I can't eat much. However, I always order a dessert because I like sweet things.

but sometimes it's hard to choose what you want to eat — pero a veces es difícil elegir lo que quieres comer

Comemos en restaurantes a menudo, especialmente cuando tenemos hambre y no tenemos tiempo para cocinar.

We often eat in restaurants, especially when we're hungry and we don't have time to cook.

To say you're hungry or thirsty, you need to use the verb 'tener' (to have). I'm thirsty — tengo sed

Una vez probé unas gambas a la plancha — estaban muy saladas.

Once I tried some grilled prawns — they were very salty.

fried — fritas
spicy — picantes

SPEAKING Charm waiters and examiners alike with 'usted' and 'quisiera'...

Here's an example of a role-play — Pedro is in a restaurant.

Pedro está hablando con un camarero en un restaurante. **Grade 8-9**

Camarero: Buenas tardes. ¿En qué puedo servirle?[1]

Pedro: Quisiera gambas a la plancha con verduras y arroz.

Camarero: De acuerdo.

Pedro: ¿Usted tiene algo para mi amigo? No le gustan los mariscos.

Camarero: Sí, le recomendaría una pizza margarita con ensalada.

Pedro: ¡Muy bien! Y, de postre, me apetece un helado grande con dos cucharas.

Camarero: Sí, muy bien. [1]How can I help you?

Tick list:
✓ tenses: present, imperfect subjunctive, conditional
✓ correct use of 'usted'

To improve:
+ use more varied conjunctions

Estás hablando con un camarero.
• *lo que quieres comer*
• *lo que no te gusta comer*
• *!*
• *? comida vegetariana*
• *lo que comiste durante tu última visita al restaurante*

*Prepare the role-play on the right. Address the waiter as 'usted', and try to speak in **Spanish** for about **two** minutes. [15 marks]*

Sport

Some sport vocab is easy because it's similar to English. To impress the examiners, use some harder stuff too.

¿Practicas algún deporte? — Do you play any sports?

el fútbol	*football*	el baloncesto	*basketball*	la pesca	*fishing*
el rugby	*rugby*	la equitación	*horse riding*	el atletismo	*athletics*
el tenis	*tennis*	la natación	*swimming*	el alpinismo	*mountain climbing*
el hockey	*hockey*	la vela	*sailing*	el patinaje	*skating*
el bádminton	*badminton*	el piragüismo	*canoeing*	los deportes de riesgo	*adventure sports*

jugar al fútbol / tenis	*to play football / tennis*	correr	*to run*	el polideportivo	*sports centre*
montar a caballo	*to ride a horse*	bailar	*to dance*	la piscina	*swimming pool*
montar en bici	*to ride a bike*	nadar	*to swim*	el estadio	*stadium*
ir en monopatín	*to go by skateboard*	patinar	*to skate*	la pista	*track, court, slope*
ser aficionado/a a...	*to be fond / a fan of...*	pescar	*to fish*	la pista de hielo	*ice rink*

Question

¿Te gusta practicar deporte?
Do you like doing sport?

Simple Answer

Me gusta montar en bici porque es divertido.
I like riding my bike because it's fun.

Extended Answer

Me gusta montar en bici después del colegio porque es divertido estar con mis amigos al aire libre.
I like riding my bike after school because it's fun to be with my friends in the fresh air.

Grammar — 'jugar' + 'a' + sport

Use 'jugar a' to say what sports you play. In Spanish, you can't say 'Juego a el fútbol'. So if the sport is a masculine noun (like 'el fútbol'), the 'a' and the article 'el' combine to form 'al' (see p.133).

Juego al netball.   ***I play netball.***

Juegas al tenis.   ***You play tennis.***

'jugar' is a radical-changing verb — its stem changes from 'u' to 'ue' in the present tense. See p.138.

Mi deporte preferido es... — My favourite sport is...

Me encanta montar a caballo varias veces por semana. Para mí, es crucial hacer deporte.

I love going horse riding a few times per week. For me, it's crucial to do sport.

I like going to the ice rink — Me gusta ir a la pista de hielo

Juego al rugby los lunes. Me gusta porque puedo divertirme con mis amigos y hacer deporte al mismo tiempo.

I play rugby on Mondays. I like it because I can have a good time with my friends and do sport at the same time.

the sports centre where we practise is near my house — el polideportivo donde practicamos está cerca de mi casa

See p.19 for how to make the adjective 'deportista' agree.

No soy exactamente deportista, pero el deporte es bastante importante para mí — voy al colegio en monopatín y los fines de semana, pesco con mi padre.

I'm not exactly sporty, but sport is quite important to me — I go to school on my skateboard and at the weekend, I fish with my father.

and sport isn't very important to me — y el deporte no es muy importante para mí

but in my spare time, I prefer to cook or read — pero en mi tiempo libre, prefiero cocinar o leer

Sport

A double sport session — aren't you lucky? It's really important that you can talk about sport in an interesting way, showing off your Spanish as you go, so — on your marks, get set, go!

El deporte en la tele — Sport on TV

el partido	*match*	marcar un gol	*to score a goal*
la carrera	*race*	el campeón	*champion*
ganar	*to win*	el campeonato	*championship*
perder	*to lose*	el torneo	*tournament*
el equipo	*team*	la copa	*trophy, cup*
el jugador	*player*	los Juegos Olímpicos	*the Olympic Games*

Grammar — 'usually' + infinitive

Use the verb '<u>soler</u>' plus the <u>infinitive</u> to say what you <u>usually do</u>. It's a <u>radical-changing verb</u> — its <u>stem</u> changes from '<u>o</u>' to '<u>ue</u>'. See p.138.

<u>Suelo</u> ver el tenis los viernes.
I usually watch tennis on Fridays.

Prefiero jugar al hockey que verlo en la tele. En vez de pasar mucho tiempo viendo la tele, los jóvenes deberían practicar deporte.

Suelo ver el fútbol en la tele los fines de semana. Me encantaría visitar un estadio. Me imagino que sería muy emocionante estar allí si tu equipo marca muchos goles y gana el partido.

Me encanta ver los Juegos Olímpicos porque es interesante ver los deportes menos populares como el piragüismo. Sueles aprender algo sobre ellos y son emocionantes también.

I prefer playing hockey to watching it on TV. Instead of spending a lot of time watching TV, young people should do sport.

I usually watch football on TV at the weekend. I would love to visit a stadium. I imagine that it would be very exciting to be there if your team scores a lot of goals and wins the match.

I love watching the Olympic Games because it's interesting to watch the less popular sports like canoeing. You usually learn something about them and they're exciting too.

I'm a fan of basketball. — Soy aficionado/a al baloncesto.

At primary school, I usually played football during break time. — En la escuela primaria, solía jugar al fútbol en el recreo.
'Solía' is the imperfect tense of 'soler'.

The verb 'imaginarse' means 'to imagine / suppose'.

the championship — el campeonato
the tournament — el torneo

it's exciting when someone from your country wins a medal — es emocionante cuando alguien de tu país gana una medalla

---

Be a good sport and try out this practice writing question...

Julia has written a blog about the sporting opportunities her school provides.

Mi colegio se llama Westwater College. Quisiera compartir unos **datos**[1] con vosotros **para que sepáis**[2] por qué es un colegio excepcional. **En cuanto a**[3] la educación física, se puede elegir entre varios deportes, entre ellos el tenis, el baloncesto y el hockey. **Tenemos mucha suerte**[4] porque nuestro profesor de hockey participó en los Juegos Olímpicos. Además, tenemos una piscina enorme. Después del colegio, se puede practicar deportes de riesgo, **incluso**[5] el piragüismo.

Grade 8-9

[1] information, facts
[2] so that you know
[3] With regard to
[4] We're very lucky
[5] even

To improve:
+ use another tense e.g. future

Escribe tu propio blog sobre el deporte en tu colegio. Menciona:

- *tu opinión sobre las oportunidades deportivas en tu colegio*
- *una actividad deportiva reciente en el colegio*

*Escribe aproximadamente **150** palabras en **español**.*
Responde a los dos aspectos de la pregunta. [32 marks]

Tick list:
✓ tenses: present, preterite, present and imperfect subjunctives
✓ connectives e.g. 'además'
✓ idiomatic phrases e.g. 'tenemos mucha suerte'
✓ complex sentences including opinions

Listening Questions

If you know what to expect in the exams, life'll seem a whole lot easier and more pleasant.
With that in mind, here's another batch of realistic questions for you to have a go at.

1 Escucha esta conversación entre un cliente y una camarera.
Contesta a las preguntas en **español**.

TRACK LISTENING 12

1 a ¿Qué tipo de bebida quiere el cliente? Da **dos** detalles.

.... *[2 marks]*

1 b ¿Qué plato recomendaría el cocinero?

.... *[1 mark]*

1 c ¿Qué pide el hombre por fin? Da **tres** detalles.

.... *[3 marks]*

1 d ¿Qué elige de postre?

.... *[1 mark]*

2 Escucha este diálogo entre Mireia, Rahim e Isabel.
Indica los deportes que les gusta ver en la televisión con (✓).

TRACK LISTENING 13

		el fútbol	el tenis	el rugby	el atletismo	la natación
2 a	Mireia					
2 b	Rahim					
2 c	Isabel					

[6 marks]

Speaking Question

Topic: Cultural Life

- Spend a couple of minutes looking at the photo and the prompts below it.

- You can make notes on a separate piece of paper.

Mira la foto y prepara las respuestas a los puntos siguientes:

- la descripción de la foto

- tu opinión sobre los conciertos

- tu género de música preferido hace cinco años

- si te gustaría aprender a tocar algún instrumento

- !

Teacher's Material

- Allow the student to develop his / her answers as much as possible.

- You need to ask the student the following questions **in order**:

- Describe esta foto. ... ¿Algo más?

- A mí no me gusta mucho ir a conciertos. Y tú, ¿qué opinas? ... ¿Por qué?

- ¿Cuál era tu género de música preferido hace cinco años? ... ¿Algo más?

- ¿Te gustaría aprender a tocar algún instrumento? ... ¿Por qué (no)? / ¿Algo más?

- ¿Te gustan los conciertos? ... ¿Por qué (no)? / ¿Algo más?

Reading Questions

1   Read this magazine article about a Spanish radio programme.

> Hay un nuevo programa de música en la radio española que se llama 'MúsicaZen'. En una entrevista, la presentadora, una mujer que trabaja en esta industria desde hace más de veinticinco años, charlaba con entusiasmo sobre el estilo que podemos esperar.
> — Tendrá muchos géneros de música, pero quiero que la gente pueda relajarse mientras escucha. ¡Será una experiencia totalmente única con poquísimos anuncios! Además vamos a charlar con músicos, cantantes y otras personas que trabajan en la industria musical. Creo que será muy interesante y original.

Which two statements are **true**? Write the letters in the boxes.

A	MúsicaZen is a long-running radio programme.
B	The programme will be presented by someone experienced.
C	MúsicaZen will specialise in one particular style of music.
D	There will be lots of interesting adverts on the programme.
E	Many different people will contribute to the programme.

[2 marks]

2   Translate this text into **English**.

> — ¿Por qué no te gustaría hacer piragüismo? Es un deporte emocionante y divertido.
> — Me parece un deporte muy difícil y peligroso.
> — Es verdad que te puedes hacer daño. Un amigo mío se rompió el brazo hace un año.
> Si prefieres, podrías ir al polideportivo para jugar al baloncesto o al bádminton.

....

....

....

....

....

....

[9 marks]

Writing Questions

1   Acabas de comer en un restaurante en tu barrio. Escribe un artículo sobre tu experiencia.

Menciona:

- lo que pediste

- tu opinión de la comida

- el estilo de comida que más te gusta

- si volverías al restaurante.

Escribe aproximadamente **90** palabras en **español**.
Responde a todos los aspectos de la pregunta.   *[16 marks]*

2   Translate this text into **Spanish**.

> I love detective novels. When I was younger, they scared me but
> now I like them a lot. When I am older, I would like to write novels. I
> think it would be fun to spend all day thinking about ideas for books.
> However, I am not very patient, so I would only write short books.

....

....

....

....

....

....

....

[12 marks]

Revision Summary for Section Four

There's loads of vocab in this section, so these questions give you the perfect opportunity to put what you've learned to the test. Don't worry if you've forgotten some of it — you can always have another gander at the section and then come back and tick the rest of the boxes.

Books and Reading (p.39) ☑

1) How would you say the following words in Spanish?
   a) novel   b) comic strip   c) newspaper

2) ¿Qué te gusta leer? Contesta en español, con frases completas.

Music (p.40) ☑

3) ¿Tocas algún instrumento? Answer this question in Spanish.

4) Renata says: 'Soy cantante. Ayer hice la grabación para mi nueva canción. El mes que viene, la voy a cantar en directo en la radio. A mí me encanta la canción porque la letra es fenomenal.' Translate what she says into English.

5) How would you say that you used to like rap music but now you like rock music?

Cinema (p.41) ☑

6) How would you say these types of film in Spanish?
   a) science fiction film   b) comedy   c) horror film

7) Julio says: 'Lo malo de ir al cine es que las entradas son caras.' What is his complaint?

8) Pick your favourite genre of film and say why you like it in Spanish.

TV (p.42) ☑

9) You're flicking through a Spanish TV guide and see these descriptions. What do they mean?
   a) un concurso   b) una telenovela   c) un documental   d) un programa sobre la historia

10) ¿Te gusta ver la tele? ¿Por qué (no)? Contesta en español, con frases completas.

Food (p.43) ☑

11) You're following a Spanish recipe. It says you need 'seis manzanas, dos peras, azúcar, leche, dos huevos y mermelada de melocotón.' What do you need in English?

12) ¿Qué comes normalmente para el desayuno? Da tres detalles.

13) Say what your favourite meal is in Spanish.

Eating Out (p.44) ☑

14) If you saw 'pollo a la plancha' on a menu, what would you expect?

15) Simón's rice is too spicy. How could he say this in Spanish?

16) You're about to leave the restaurant. Ask the waiter politely for the bill.

Sport (p.45-46) ☑

17) ¿Practicas algún deporte? Contesta en español, con frases completas.

18) How would you say that in the future, you would like to learn to ride a horse?

19) ¿Te gusta ver los deportes en la televisión? ¿Por qué (no)? Contesta con tres frases completas.

Customs and Festivals

Spanish-speaking countries have lots of different festivals that they celebrate throughout the year. You'll need a bit of background knowledge about them for your exams, so read on.

¡Celebremos! — Let's celebrate!

la fiesta	*festival, party*	¡Feliz cumpleaños!	*Happy Birthday!*
festejar	*to celebrate*	¡Felicitaciones!	*Congratulations!*
el día festivo	*public holiday*	¡Feliz año nuevo!	*Happy New Year!*
el santo	*saint's day*	Nochevieja	*New Year's Eve*
la fecha patria	*national independence day*	el Año Nuevo	*New Year*
		tener suerte	*to be lucky*

> **Grammar** — Let's...
>
> To say '<u>let's...</u>', use the '<u>we</u>' form of the <u>present subjunctive</u> (see p.153).
> **Hablemos** de las fiestas.
> *Let's talk about festivals.*

'La Tomatina' es una fiesta que tiene lugar en agosto en Buñol, Valencia. Los participantes se lanzan tomates los unos a los otros. Atrae a miles de turistas cada año.

'La Tomatina' is a festival that takes place in August in Buñol, Valencia. Participants throw tomatoes at each other. It attracts thousands of tourists each year.

En Nochevieja en España, es tradicional comer 12 uvas para traer buena suerte.

On New Year's Eve in Spain, it's traditional to eat 12 grapes to bring good luck.

San Fermín — The running of the bulls

One festival in Spain that causes some controversy is <u>San Fermín</u>, which takes place in <u>Pamplona</u> each July.

el toro	*bull*		la plaza de toros	*bullring*	polémico	*controversial*
la corrida	*bullfight*		el torero	*bullfighter*	la tradición	*tradition*

Muchas personas corren por las calles estrechas con los toros peligrosos hasta la plaza de toros.

Many people run through the narrow streets with the dangerous bulls to the bullring.

Durante la fiesta, los habitantes y los turistas llevan ropa blanca y pañuelos rojos.

During the festival, locals and tourists wear white clothes and red scarves.

La corrida de toros es una tradición común en España, pero es polémica porque alguna gente piensa que es cruel. Sin embargo, otros creen que es un arte.

Bullfighting is a common tradition in Spain, but it's controversial because some people think that it's cruel. However, others believe it's an art.

Festivals could well crop up in your exams...

Read the text on the right, and then decide whether the sentences below are true (T) or false (F).

1	The festival started because of an argument between a local man and a tourist.	
2	The argument was settled calmly.	
3	The streets are full of people.	
4	They grow the tomatoes in Extremadura.	

[4 marks]

[1]Tonnes

La fiesta que se llama 'La Tomatina' comenzó en 1945 a causa de una disputa entre los habitantes. La disputa se convirtió en una pelea con verduras. Hoy en día, mucha gente viaja a Buñol para participar en la fiesta. **Toneladas**[1] de tomates vuelan por el aire y las calles están llenas de gente. La fiesta tiene lugar en Valencia, pero los tomates se cultivan en Extremadura.

Customs and Festivals

Next up it's All Souls' Day and a day that's a bit like April Fools' Day. It's worth learning a bit about these ones too — and you might come across some really good vocab while you're at it.

El Día de los Muertos — All Souls' Day

El <u>Día de los Muertos</u> is a Mexican, Central American and Filipino tradition. According to <u>folklore</u>, heaven's gates open at midnight on <u>1st November</u> and the spirits of the dead <u>reunite</u> with their families for <u>24 hours</u>.

la Catrina	*popular female skeleton icon*	morir	*to die*
la calavera de azúcar	*skull made of sugar*	el muerto	*dead (person)*
el maquillaje	*make-up*	el mariachi	*Mexican musician*

'Muerto' is an irregular past participle — see p.144 for more.

En la tradición mexicana, la muerte no es espantosa.

In Mexican tradition, death isn't frightening.

> the lives of the dead are celebrated — se celebran las vidas de los muertos

El Día de los Muertos, las familias limpian y arreglan las tumbas de sus parientes y celebran fiestas.

On All Souls' Day, families clean and tidy the graves of their relatives and throw parties.

> friends — amigos

> share stories — comparten historias

Alguna gente se disfraza de 'la Catrina'. Honran a los muertos y lo demuestran con calaveras de azúcar, flores y música del mariachi.

Some people dress up as 'la Catrina'. They respect the dead and show it with sugar skulls, flowers and Mexican music.

> wear make-up like — lleva maquillaje como

An example of how some people dress to celebrate All Souls' Day.

El Día de los Inocentes — 28th December

El Día de los Inocentes is like <u>April Fools' Day</u>, but it takes place in December in the Spanish-speaking world.

Grammar — the personal 'a'

You need to add an '<u>a</u>' before the word for a <u>person</u> or <u>pet</u> <u>after all verbs</u> apart from '<u>tener</u>' and '<u>ser</u>'. This is called the <u>personal 'a'</u>. See p.134.

Gasté una broma <u>a</u> mi primo.
I played a trick on my cousin.

la broma *joke, trick*   los medios de comunicación *the media*

Es tradicional gastar una broma a alguien, por ejemplo sustituir el azúcar con la sal.

It's traditional to play a joke on someone, for example substitute sugar with salt.

Los medios de comunicación presentan noticias falsas como broma.

The media feature false news stories as a joke.

SPEAKING

Don't forget about other Spanish-speaking countries...

Laura has answered the following questions.

1. **¿Qué hiciste el año pasado para festejar tu cumpleaños?**
2. **¿Cuál es tu opinión de las fiestas en los países donde se habla español?**
3. **¿Cómo celebrarás la Nochevieja?**

Tick list:
✓ tenses: preterite, present, future
✓ good use of reflexive verbs

1. El año pasado fui a patinar sobre hielo para celebrar mi cumpleaños. Me lo pasé bien pero el único problema fue que me hice daño en el hielo.

2. Me fascinan las fiestas del mundo hispanohablante. Por ejemplo, las tradiciones y las costumbres del Día de los Muertos me interesan mucho.

3. No estoy segura, ¡pero quizás comeré uvas como se hace en España!

To improve:
+ more detailed answers
+ more adjectives

Now answer the same questions. Speak for about 3 minutes. [15 marks]

54

Customs and Festivals

Christmas and Easter sound familiar but they're celebrated differently in the Spanish-speaking world.

Semana Santa — Easter week

The Catholic festival <u>Semana Santa</u> is the biggest religious celebration in Spanish-speaking countries.

| la Pascua | *Easter* | la iglesia | *church* |
| el paso | *statue paraded at Easter* | la costumbre | *custom, way* |

La Pascua es un evento sombrío. Hay procesiones con música. Se llevan pasos por las calles y los participantes llevan ropa que esconde sus identidades.

Easter is a sombre event. There are processions with music. Statues are carried around the streets and the participants wear clothes that hide their identities.

Grammar — impersonal verbs

To say that something is done <u>without</u> saying <u>who</u> does it, use '<u>se</u>' and the <u>3rd person</u> part of the verb (p.153).

Se ven las procesiones.
The processions are watched.

¡Feliz Navidad! — Merry Christmas!

| Nochebuena | *Christmas Eve* | el Día de Reyes | *Epiphany, 6th January* | Papá Noel | *Father Christmas* |
| Navidad | *Christmas* | el villancico | *Christmas carol* | el turrón | *Spanish nougat* |

Muchas comunidades participan en la lotería el 22 de diciembre.

Many communities participate in the lottery draw on 22nd December.

because they want to win 'El Gordo', the big prize — porque quieren ganar 'El Gordo', el gran premio

Muchos españoles celebran el Día de Reyes. Los Reyes Magos traen regalos a los niños o, si no se han comportado bien, un trozo de carbón.

Many Spaniards celebrate Epiphany. The Three Kings bring the children presents or, if they haven't behaved well, a piece of coal.

I love to sing Christmas carols — me encanta cantar villancicos

En Navidad, me gusta comer turrón.

At Christmas, I like to eat nougat.

we usually eat turkey — solemos comer pavo

Otras fiestas religiosas — Other religious festivals

El Eid al-Fitr es una fiesta musulmana que marca el fin del mes de Ramadán.

Eid al-Fitr is a Muslim festival that marks the end of the month of Ramadan.

Muchos judíos celebran Hanukkah. Se encienden velas y se comen alimentos fritos.

Many Jews celebrate Hanukkah. Candles are lit and fried food is eaten.

Make sure you can discuss the festivals you celebrate...

Listen to these people talking about Christmas celebrations and complete the sentences below.

1. **The winning lottery number is...**
   A) ...80673.
   B) ...13773.
   C) ...80636. *[1]*

2. **Ana's going to...**
   A) ...travel the world using her winnings.
   B) ...buy a new car and an island.
   C) ...buy a luxury flat and go on holiday. *[1]*

3. **Carla's favourite food at Christmas was...**
   A) ...seafood.
   B) ...turkey.
   C) ...chocolate nougat. *[1]*

4. **For Christmas, Diego's brother got...**
   A) ...some toys.
   B) ...a bike.
   C) ...a mobile. *[1]*

Listening Questions

Just before you get out the balloons and bunting to celebrate the end of this section, try these questions for size. They're loaded with subject-specific vocab and tricky bits of grammar. Enjoy.

1 Durante una visita a México vas a un museo y haces una visita guiada.
Escucha la información y escribe la letra apropiada en cada casilla.

(TRACK LISTENING 15)

A	diciembre	C	seria	E	pantallas	G	maquillaje
B	izquierda	D	imágenes	F	noviembre	H	derecha

1 a En la pared, hay muchas ☐

[1 mark]

1 b Las fotos más recientes están a la ☐

[1 mark]

1 c Los mexicanos llevan ☐

[1 mark]

1 d La fiesta es divertida pero también es ☐

[1 mark]

1 e El evento se celebra a principios de ☐

[1 mark]

2 You overhear Clara and Tariq talking about the festivals they celebrate.
Listen to what they say and write the correct letter in each box.

(TRACK LISTENING 16)

2 a What does Clara say about Chinese New Year celebrations?

A	She prefers them to the Spanish New Year festivities.
B	She likes Chinese New Year and Spanish New Year equally.
C	She thinks the processions last too long.

☐

[1 mark]

2 b What does Clara say about the tradition of eating twelve grapes at midnight?

A	It's surprisingly difficult to do.
B	She thinks it's just a silly tradition.
C	People of all ages can take part.

☐

[1 mark]

2 c According to Tariq, what is the best part of the Eid al-Fitr festivities?

A	He can spend lots of time with his relatives.
B	He can eat food that he doesn't normally eat.
C	He can stop fasting during the day.

☐

[1 mark]

Speaking Question

Candidate's Material

- Spend a couple of minutes looking at the photo and the questions below it.

- You can make notes on a separate piece of paper.

You will be asked the following **three** questions, and **two** questions you haven't prepared:

- ¿Qué hay en la foto?

- ¿Qué hiciste el año pasado durante las vacaciones de Pascua?

- ¿Te gusta comer comida tradicional durante las fiestas? ¿Por qué (no)?

Teacher's Material

- Allow the student to develop his / her answers as much as possible.

- You need to ask the student the following questions **in order**:

  - ¿Qué hay en la foto?

  - ¿Qué hiciste el año pasado durante las vacaciones de Pascua?

  - ¿Te gusta comer comida tradicional durante las fiestas? ¿Por qué (no)?

  - ¿Pasas mucho tiempo con tu familia durante las fiestas? ¿Por qué (no)?

  - ¿Te gustaría celebrar la Nochevieja en otro país?

Reading Questions

1 Lee este texto sobre la Semana Santa y contesta a las preguntas en **español**.

> La Semana Santa es una semana muy tradicional ya que conmemora la muerte y la resurrección de Cristo. La fecha exacta cambia cada año. Para mucha gente, lo más importante es ver las procesiones que pasan por las calles. Las procesiones suelen ser solemnes pero también impresionantes, gracias a los pasos que llevan las figuras de Cristo y su madre. Pero, ¡cuidado si visitas España durante la Semana Santa! Habrá mucha gente por las calles, así que será más difícil hacer turismo.

1 a ¿Qué pasa con la fecha de la Semana Santa?

.... *[1 mark]*

1 b ¿Cómo son las procesiones? Da **dos** adjetivos.

.... *[2 marks]*

1 c ¿Por qué será más complicado para los turistas durante las celebraciones?

.... *[1 mark]*

2 Kieran has just stayed with a Spanish family for Christmas. He has emailed his exchange partner to thank him and to tell him what he thought of Christmas in Spain.

> Gracias por unos días tan fantásticos. Me lo he pasado fenomenal. Me gustaron mucho las preparaciones finales que hicisteis para la Navidad. Aunque nunca he conocido una Navidad sin Papá Noel, prefiero la idea de que los tres Reyes Magos traen regalos a los niños españoles. El aspecto religioso es más obvio y otra ventaja es que la fiesta dura más tiempo. Durante el tiempo que pasé en España, probé turrón, pero la verdad es que todavía no sé exactamente si me gusta o no. ¡Tendré que comer más! ¡Hasta pronto!

Which two statements are **true**? Write the letters in the boxes.

A	Kieran was fascinated by the Spanish Christmas preparations.
B	Father Christmas isn't important to Kieran's family.
C	Kieran likes the Spanish tradition of the Three Kings.
D	Kieran didn't have enough time to try nougat.
E	Kieran loved nougat.

☐ ☐

[2 marks]

Writing Questions

1 Has decidido escribir un blog sobre las celebraciones españolas y británicas.

Menciona:

• algunas festividades españolas que te interesan

• una celebración reciente con tu familia.

Escribe aproximadamente **150** palabras en **español**.
Responde a los dos aspectos de la pregunta.

[32 marks]

2 Translate the following passage into **Spanish**.

> Yesterday we learned about some Spanish festivals. El Día de los Inocentes
> takes place on 28th December in Spain. It is a religious event but it's fun too.
> I would love to go to Buñol with my friends to take part in the tomato festival.
> I think it would be really interesting but I don't have enough money to go this year.

....

....

....

....

....

....

....

[12 marks]

Revision Summary for Section Five

You've made it to the end of Section Five — that calls for a celebration, surely. To get you in a party mood, here's a set of questions to check what you know. Don't worry if you've forgotten bits and pieces along the way — just have another read through the pages and top up your knowledge.

Customs and Festivals (p.52-54) ☑

1) Laura's just passed her driving test. How would you congratulate her in Spanish?
2) What would you be celebrating on 'Nochevieja'?
3) 'Tengo mucha suerte porque mañana es mi cumpleaños.' Translate this into English.
4) 'El 25 de mayo es una fiesta patria en Argentina.' What's special about 25th May in Argentina?
5) What's the Spanish tomato-throwing festival called?
6) ¿Te gustaría ir a una corrida de toros? ¿Por qué (no)? Contesta en español.
7) 'El Día de los Muertos es una buena oportunidad para pensar en los muertos. Preparamos platos de comida para ellos y compramos juguetes para los niños que han muerto también.' Translate these comments into English.
8) Where is El Día de los Muertos celebrated?
9) What's a 'calavera de azúcar'?
10) How would you say that on El Día de los Inocentes, you will play a joke on your friends?
11) Tomás says: 'Mis amigos británicos me contaron que reciben huevos de chocolate en Pascua. En mi familia, decoramos los huevos en vez de comerlos.' Translate what he says into English.
12) How would you say: 'Easter week is important for me. We go to church twice and I see my grandparents and my cousins.'
13) Felipe says: 'Me encanta ver las procesiones de Semana Santa.' What does he love doing?
14) If you were celebrating 'Nochebuena', what date would it be?
15) How do you say...?   a) Christmas carol   b) Father Christmas   c) Spanish nougat
16) You read this advert in a Spanish newspaper: '¡Ya vienen los Reyes Magos! El paseo por el pueblo empezará a las seis en la Calle de Córdoba y terminará en la plaza mayor. Los Reyes lanzarán caramelos a los niños.'
    What will the procession be celebrating? What will the kings throw?
17) What's the Spanish for...?   a) religious   b) Ramadan
18) Esther says: 'El año nuevo judío se llama Rosh Hashaná. Pasamos tiempo juntos y encendemos velas.' What does Esther's family do to celebrate Rosh Hashanah?
19) Selin says: 'My family celebrates Muslim festivals, for example Eid al-Fitr.' How could she say this in Spanish?

Talking About Where You Live

For your Spanish GCSE, you'll need to be able to describe where you live and what's there.

En mi barrio... — In my neighbourhood...

el pueblo	*town*	el mercado	*market*	Correos	*Post Office*		
el centro	*centre*	el parque	*park*	la comisaría	*police station*		
las afueras	*outskirts*	la mezquita	*mosque*	la peluquería	*hairdresser's*		
el edificio	*building*	la biblioteca	*library*	la carnicería	*butcher's*		
el ayuntamiento	*town hall*	el museo	*museum*	el estanco	*tobacconist's*		
el aparcamiento	*parking*	la fábrica	*factory*	el puerto	*port / harbour*		

'Correos' doesn't have an article.

Question

¿Dónde vives?
Where do you live?

Simple Answer

Vivo en un pueblo en Cumbria.
I live in a town in Cumbria.

Grammar — adding 'ito'

In Spanish, you can <u>add bits</u> onto the ends of <u>nouns</u> and <u>adjectives</u> to <u>change</u> their <u>meanings</u>. Adding '<u>ito/a/os/as</u>' makes the word <u>smaller</u> or <u>cuter</u>. Find out more on p.127.

Extended Answer

Vivo en un pueblo pequeñito en el campo. Preferiría vivir más cerca de Londres porque hay más que hacer. Aquí no hay ni una tienda de ropa, lo que me fastidia mucho.

I live in a really small town in the countryside. I'd prefer to live closer to London because there's more to do. Here there's not a single clothes shop, which annoys me a lot.

Háblame de tu pueblo — Talk to me about your town

En mi barrio, hay mucho que hacer. Por ejemplo, el viernes fui al teatro. Sería casi perfecto si tuviera una bolera.

In my neighbourhood, there's a lot to do. For example, on Friday I went to the theatre. It would be almost perfect if it had a bowling alley.

Mi ciudad tiene varios edificios impresionantes. También hay una carnicería y una librería.

My city has various impressive buildings. There's also a butcher's and a bookshop.

Creo que es mejor vivir en el campo que en la ciudad. En un mundo ideal, viviría más lejos de las fábricas porque hacen mucho ruido.

I think it's better to live in the countryside than in the city. In an ideal world, I'd live further away from the factories because they make a lot of noise.

if it had a pedestrian zone — si tuviera una zona peatonal
'Tuviera' is the imperfect subjunctive of 'tener' — see p.154.

pretty — bonitos
modern — modernos

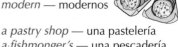

a pastry shop — una pastelería
a fishmonger's — una pescadería
a bakery — una panadería
a stationery shop — una papelería

from the shopping centre because there are so many people — del centro comercial porque hay tanta gente

---

Don't just list things — give your opinions too...

Tu amigo español te ha escrito para describir su pueblo.

¡Hola George! Voy a contarte todo sobre el pueblo que visitarás el mes que viene. En el centro, hay el ayuntamiento y varios edificios oficiales. Además, se puede visitar el museo del pueblo y hay **un montón de**[1] tiendas. Según mi padre, van a construir un polideportivo, lo que sería fenomenal, porque ahora hay poco que hacer por la tarde después del colegio y los jóvenes **acaban**[2] en la calle, molestando a la gente.

Grade 8-9

[1]loads of
[2]end up

To improve:
+ use a past tense
+ use a comparative

Tick list:
✓ tenses: present, future, conditional
✓ connectives
✓ use of 'se puede'
✓ well-explained opinion

Ahora describe tu barrio, y menciona:
- *cómo es tu pueblo;*
- *cómo cambiarías tu pueblo.*

*Escribe aproximadamente **150** palabras en **español**. Responde a los dos aspectos de la pregunta.*

[32 marks]

The Home

This is your chance to describe your home — and it's a good time to revise the conditional tense too...

Mi casa — My house

mudarse (de casa)	to move house	el salón	lounge
la casa (adosada)	(semi-detached) house	la cocina	kitchen
el piso	flat	el comedor	dining room
la planta baja	ground floor	la escalera	stairs
la segunda planta	second floor	el dormitorio	bedroom
la habitación	room	los muebles	furniture
el cuarto de baño	bathroom	la estantería	shelves
el aseo	toilet	la pared	wall
la ducha	shower	el sótano	basement

Grammar — there is / are

To say what <u>there is</u> in your house, use '<u>hay</u>'. It <u>stays the same</u> regardless of whether the thing you're talking about is <u>singular</u> or <u>plural</u>.

En mi casa, <u>hay</u> un salón.
In my house, <u>there is</u> a lounge.

<u>Hay</u> siete habitaciones.
***There are** seven rooms.*

Vivo en una casa adosada.
En mi dormitorio, hay una cama, un armario, una alfombra en el suelo, una mesita, y un espejo.

I live in a semi-detached house. In my bedroom, there's a bed, a wardrobe, a carpet on the floor, a little table, and a mirror.

In the kitchen, there's a sink, a fridge and an oven. — En la cocina, hay un fregadero, una nevera y un horno.

Vivimos en un piso pequeño.
La habitación que más me gusta es el salón porque es cómodo.

We live in a small flat. The room I like best is the lounge because it's comfortable.

there are armchairs — hay sillones

Me gustaría mudarme a una casa más grande.

I'd like to move to a bigger house.

to have more electrical appliances — tener más electrodomésticos

Question

¿Cómo sería tu casa ideal?

What would your ideal house be like?

Find out more about the conditional tense on p.146.

Simple Answer

Mi casa ideal tendría muchas habitaciones y un jardín grande.

My ideal house would have a lot of rooms and a big garden.

Extended Answer

La casa de mis sueños tendría un jardín enorme y una piscina de lujo. Además, sería mejor si no tuviera que compartir mi habitación.

The house of my dreams would have an enormous garden and a luxury pool. It would also be better if I didn't have to share my room.

Remember, 'hay' can mean 'there is' or 'there are'...

Read this passage from 'Pepita Jiménez' by Juan Valera.

Tiene la casa limpísima y todo en un orden perfecto. Los muebles no son artísticos ni elegantes; pero tampoco **se advierte**[1] en ellos nada pretencioso y de mal gusto. **Para poetizar su estancia**[2], tanto en el patio como en las salas y galerías, hay multitud de flores y plantas. No tiene, en verdad, ninguna planta rara ni ninguna flor exótica; pero sus plantas y sus flores, de lo más común que hay por aquí, están cuidadas con extraordinario **mimo**[3].

[1]is observed
[2]To make her surroundings more poetic
[3]care

Decide whether the following statements are true or false.

e.g. The house is very clean. **True**
1. The furniture is elegant.
2. The flowers are only in the kitchen.
3. There are many flowers and plants.
4. The flowers are mostly exotic.
5. The flowers are well looked after.

[5 marks]

What You Do at Home

Get your hands dirty with this page on daily routine and chores... and we've thrown in some reflexives too.

Un día típico — A typical day

despertarse	*to wake up*
levantarse	*to get up*
ducharse	*to have a shower*
lavarse la cara	*to wash your face*
vestirse	*to get dressed*
acostarse	*to go to bed*
dormirse	*to go to sleep*

Grammar — reflexive verbs

All of these verbs are <u>reflexive</u> — they help you say what you do <u>to yourself</u>. To use them, <u>remove</u> the <u>reflexive pronoun</u>, <u>conjugate the verb</u> as normal, and put the <u>reflexive pronoun</u> back <u>in front of the verb</u> in its <u>correct form</u> (see p.149).

Me despierto a las siete.   *I wake up at seven o'clock.*

¿A qué hora te levantas?   *What time do you get up?*

Se acuestan temprano.   *They go to bed early.*

Some of these verbs are radical-changing too. See p.138.

Question	**Simple Answer**	**Extended Answer**
¿Qué haces por la mañana?	Me despierto a las siete y luego me ducho.	Me despierto a las siete, pero no me levanto hasta las siete y media. Luego me ducho y me visto rápidamente.
What do you do in the morning?	*I wake up at seven o'clock and then I have a shower.*	*I wake up at seven o'clock, but I don't get up until half past seven. Then I have a shower and get dressed quickly.*

Las tareas domésticas — Chores

arreglar	*to tidy*	hacer la cama	*to make the bed*	pasar la aspiradora	*to do the vacuuming*
ayudar	*to help*	pasear al perro	*to walk the dog*	hacer las compras	*to do the shopping*
limpiar	*to clean*	cortar el césped	*to mow the lawn*	sacar la basura	*to take out the rubbish*

Hago mi cama y arreglo mi dormitorio antes de salir de casa. Es importante que todos ayuden en casa.

I make my bed and I tidy my bedroom before leaving the house. It's important that everyone helps at home.

'Es importante que' needs to be followed by the subjunctive form of 'ayudar' — 'ayuden'. See p.153-154.

Después de la cena, pongo todo en el lavaplatos y paseo al perro.

After dinner, I put everything in the dishwasher and I walk the dog.

I clear the table — quito la mesa
I take out the rubbish — saco la basura

En verano, corto el césped, pero mis padres no me dejan hacer las compras porque siempre compro cosas que no les gustan.

In the summer, I mow the lawn, but my parents don't let me do the shopping because I always buy things they don't like.

I lay the table because I break the glasses — poner la mesa porque rompo los vasos

Present, past, future — use as many tenses as you can...

Translate this text into **English**. *[9 marks]*

Creo que es importante ayudar en casa, pero no pienso que sea justo si yo hago mucho y mi hermano menor hace muy poco. Me encanta pasear al perro. Mi padre me da dinero si corto el césped, así que lo haré el domingo que viene. La semana pasada tuve que limpiar el cuarto de baño. ¡Qué asco!

Shopping

Time to indulge in some retail therapy and pick some marks up along the way.

¡Vamos al centro comercial! — Let's go to the shopping centre!

los grandes almacenes	*department store*
el/la dependiente/a	*sales assistant*
la talla / el número	*clothes size / shoe size*
el descuento	*discount*
las rebajas	*the sales*
el recibo	*receipt*
cambiar	*to change*
pagar	*to pay*
devolver	*to return (an item)*
reembolsar	*to refund*
quejarse	*to complain*
en efectivo	*(in) cash*
la tarjeta de crédito	*credit card*

Question

¿Te gusta ir de compras?

Do you like going shopping?

Simple Answer

Sí, me gusta ir de compras, sobre todo cuando hay rebajas.

Yes, I like going shopping, especially when there are sales.

Extended Answer

Sí, me gusta ir de compras pero a veces es estresante si no tienen la talla correcta o si tienes que cambiar algo.

Yes, I like going shopping but sometimes it's stressful if they don't have the right size or if you have to change something.

¿Me puede ayudar? — Can you help me?

You might have to pretend you're in a <u>shop</u> in the <u>role-play</u>.
Make sure you know how to ask a shop assistant for different <u>items</u>.

Grammar — I would like...

To say what you'd like, you can use '<u>quisiera</u>' as well as '<u>me gustaría</u>'.
'Quisiera' is the <u>imperfect subjunctive</u> form of the verb '<u>querer</u>'. See p.154.

   Quisiera un descuento, por favor.   *__I'd like a discount, please.__*

If you're telling <u>someone</u> what you'd like <u>them</u> to do, you need the <u>present subjunctive</u> form of the verb. See p.153.

   Quisiera que <u>me reembolse</u>, por favor.   *__I'd like you (form., sing.) to give me a refund__*, please.

Me encanta esta rebeca pero me queda grande. ¿Hay otra talla?

I love this cardigan, but it's too big for me. Is there another size?

Estoy buscando un bolso de cuero que no sea muy caro.

I'm looking for a leather bag which is not too expensive.

Quisiera un collar pero no quiero gastar demasiado.

I'd like a necklace, but I don't want to spend too much.

Use 'quedar' with 'grande' or 'pequeño' to say that something is too big or small for you.

When you're imagining something that may or may not exist, you need the present subjunctive. 'Sea' is the present subjunctive form of 'ser'. See p.154.

some earrings — unos pendientes
a tie — una corbata
a dress — un vestido

Quiero quejarme porque la falda tiene un agujero. Quisiera un reembolso, por favor.

I want to complain because the skirt has a hole. I'd like a refund, please.

Hoy hay muchas rebajas. Compré este chándal a mitad de precio.

There are a lot of sales today. I bought this tracksuit half-price.

has a stain — tiene una mancha
is ripped — está rasgada
is broken — está rota
I had to queue for ages. — Tuve que hacer cola durante mucho tiempo.
'Tener' is irregular in the preterite tense. See p.141.

Shopping

It's not just clothes shopping you need to get your head around — you need to know about buying food too.

En la tienda de comestibles — In the grocery shop

la cantidad	*quantity*	una ración	*a portion*
una caja	*a box*	una bolsa	*a bag*
un cartón	*a carton*	lleno/a	*full*
una lata	*a tin*	vacío/a	*empty*
un pedazo	*a piece*	pesar	*to weigh*
un trozo	*a slice, piece*	un kilo	*a kilogram*
un tarro	*a jar*	un gramo	*a gram*
un paquete	*a packet*	varios/as	*several*

Grammar — agreement with weights

When you're talking in <u>hundreds</u> in Spanish, the <u>number</u> has to <u>agree</u> with the <u>weight</u>.

Doscien<u>tos</u> gra<u>mos</u> de uvas, por favor.
Two hundred grams of grapes, please.

In Spanish, when you say '<u>half a kilo</u>', you <u>don't need</u> the '<u>a</u>' like in English.

Medio kilo de fresas, por favor.
Half <u>a</u> kilo of strawberries, please.

Quisiera un trozo de tarta, por favor. ¿Cuánto cuesta?

I would like a slice of cake, please. How much does it cost?

Deme dos kilos de naranjas, por favor.

Give me two kilos of oranges, please.

¿Puede usted pesar estas peras, por favor?

Could you weigh these pears, please?

Necesitamos unos tomates.

We need some tomatoes.

a portion of Manchego cheese — una ración de queso manchego

Although this sounds a bit rude, it's normal to use the imperative 'give me' in Spanish when you're at a market. See p.155 for more imperatives.

We need — Nos hacen falta
Use 'hace' instead of 'hacen' to say you need a singular item.

Hacer las compras en la red — Shopping online

Question

¿Te gusta hacer las compras en la red?
Do you like shopping online?

Simple Answer

Sí, me gusta hacer las compras en la red porque es fácil.
Yes, I like shopping online because it's easy.

Grammar — before / after doing something

To say '<u>before doing something</u>', use '<u>antes de</u>' and the <u>infinitive</u>. To say '<u>after doing something</u>', use '<u>después de</u>' followed by the <u>infinitive</u>.

<u>Después de hacer</u> las compras, tomo un café.
<u>After doing</u> the shopping, I have a coffee.

Extended Answer

Sí, me gusta hacer las compras en la red porque resulta más barato. Además, no tienes que salir de casa porque hay un servicio de reparto a domicilio.
Yes, I like shopping online because it turns out cheaper. Besides, you don't have to leave the house because there's a home delivery service.

Prefiero ir de compras en un centro comercial porque para mí, es mejor ver las cosas antes de comprarlas.
I prefer to go shopping in a shopping centre because, for me, it's better to see things before buying them.

Being able to ask for things is useful in loads of situations...

Montse is in a grocery shop. Listen to the dialogue and answer the questions in **English**.

e.g. What is Montse making a tortilla for? *a birthday party*

1. What quantity of onions does she need? [1]
2. Which ingredient doesn't she need to buy? [1]
3. Why doesn't the shopkeeper have any olive oil? [1]
4. How much does the shopping cost in total? [1]

Giving and Asking for Directions

Don't just wander around aimlessly — learn how to ask for the directions to GCSE Spanish success.

¿Dónde está? — Where is it?

cruzar	*to cross*
tomar	*to take (a road)*
seguir	*to continue*
a la izquierda	*on the left*
a la derecha	*on the right*
al lado de	*next to*
detrás de	*behind*
delante de	*in front of*
entre	*between*
enfrente de	*opposite*
en la esquina	*on the corner*
al final de	*at the end of*

For more prepositions, see p.133.

Question

¿Dónde está la peluquería?
Where's the hairdresser's?

Simple Answer

La peluquería está al final de la calle.
The hairdresser's is at the end of the street.

Extended Answer

La peluquería está justo al lado de la piscina, enfrente del cine. Es muy fácil encontrarla.

The hairdresser's is right next to the swimming pool, opposite the cinema. It's very easy to find it.

Grammar — 'estar' for locations

In Spanish, there are <u>two verbs</u> for '<u>to be</u>' — '<u>ser</u>' and '<u>estar</u>'. To describe <u>where things are</u>, you need to use '<u>estar</u>' — see p.139. You can also use '<u>estar situado</u>' to say <u>where something is situated</u>.

La estación está enfrente de Correos, en el norte de la ciudad.

The station is opposite the post office, in the north of the city.

El banco está situado detrás de la iglesia.

The bank is situated behind the church.

Los servicios están en la esquina.

The toilets are on the corner.

See p.16 for the other compass points.

is on the right of — está a la derecha de

on the left — a la izquierda

¿Cómo se llega a...? — How do you get to...?

Siga todo recto y el museo está entre la catedral y la biblioteca.

Continue straight on and the museum is between the cathedral and the library.

behind — detrás de

El parque está detrás del colegio. Tome esa calle y verá un semáforo. Luego gire a la izquierda.

The park is behind the school. Take that road and you'll see some traffic lights. Then turn left.

the police station — la comisaría

Grammar — giving instructions

To give <u>instructions</u>, use the <u>imperative</u>. See how to form it on p.155.
You probably <u>won't know</u> the person who's asked for directions, so you should use the '<u>usted</u>' form.

<u>Siga</u> todo recto y <u>cruce</u> la calle.
<u>Continue</u> straight on and <u>cross</u> the street.

<u>Tome</u> la segunda calle a la derecha.
<u>Take</u> the second street on the right.

Make sure you know your 'entre' from your 'enfrente de'...

Escucha a Iker describir su barrio y escribe verdadero (V) o falso (F) para cada frase.

e.g. Es un barrio muy viejo. **V**

1. El teatro está al lado del supermercado. *[1]*
2. Hay tres supermercados. *[1]*
3. Hay un supermercado enfrente de la comisaría. *[1]*
4. Para llegar a la iglesia, hay que seguir la calle San Felipe y tomar una calle a la izquierda. *[1]*

Weather

Knowing which verbs to use with which types of weather in Spanish is tricky — but help is at hand...

Hace buen / mal tiempo — It's good / bad weather

Está...	It's...	caluroso	hot
despejado	*clear*	fresco	*fresh*
nublado	*cloudy*	húmedo	*humid*
lloviendo	*raining*	tormentoso	*stormy*
nevando	*snowing*	seco	*dry*

Hace...	It's...
sol	*sunny*
viento	*windy*
calor	*hot*
frío	*cold*

Hay...	There is / there are...
niebla	*fog*
hielo	*ice*
tormenta	*a storm*
chubascos	*showers*

el clima	*climate*	el pronóstico	*weather forecast*	el cielo	*sky*

Question

¿Qué tiempo hace?
What's the weather like?

Simple Answer

Hace buen tiempo hoy.
It's good weather today.

Extended Answer

Hoy hace mucho sol en el sur, pero mañana cambiará: habrá truenos y relámpagos.

Today it's really sunny in the south, but tomorrow it will change: there will be thunder and lightning.

Grammar — weather verbs

To describe the weather in English, you often use '<u>to be</u>', e.g. '<u>it's</u> rainy'. You can do this in Spanish with some types of weather:

<u>Está</u> despejado / nublado / nevando / lloviendo.
***It's** clear / cloudy / snowing / raining.*

But sometimes, you have to use the verb '<u>hacer</u>' instead:

<u>Hace</u> sol / viento / frío. ***It's** sunny / windy / cold.*

And sometimes, you need the verb '<u>haber</u>':

<u>Hay</u> niebla / hielo. ***There's** fog / ice.*

It sounds complicated, but just learn which types of weather go with which verb. Remember you can put the verbs into <u>different tenses</u> too.

¿Qué tiempo habrá? — What will the weather be like?

Estará tormentoso por todas partes.	*It will be stormy everywhere.*
Nevará en Inglaterra este invierno.	*It will snow in England this winter.*
Hará mucho calor en el sur de Europa este verano. Sería mejor si no hiciera tanto calor porque prefiero las temperaturas más bajas.	*It will be very hot in the south of Europe this summer. It would be better if it weren't so hot because I prefer lower temperatures.*

dry — seco

It will rain — Lloverá

See p.3 for the seasons.

It would be perfect if it were just as hot all the time. — Sería perfecto si hiciera tanto calor todo el tiempo.

Don't let revision rain on your parade...

Read this weather forecast, and then answer the questions in **English**.

Hoy en el norte de España, habrá niebla, mientras que en el sur, estará despejado. En el oeste, cerca de Portugal, hará frío, con la posibilidad de lluvia. Para el fin de semana, hará buen tiempo por toda España, pero para la semana que viene, podemos esperar que las temperaturas bajen, con un riesgo de tormentas.

e.g. What will the weather be like in the north of Spain today? **It will be foggy.**

1. Which part of Spain will have clear weather? [1]
2. Where will it be cold? [1]
3. What will it be like at the weekend? [1]
4. What'll happen to the temperatures next week? [1]
5. What else might happen next week? [1]

Listening Questions

Phew, that was a long section. Now, if only you could test yourself with some practice questions...

1   Listen to the following conversation between Emilia and Santiago. Decide which **three** statements are true for each person and write the letters in the boxes.

TRACK LISTENING 19

1 a   Choose the three statements that are true for **Emilia**:

A	She lives with her parents.	D	She'd like a smaller house.
B	She lives in a flat.	E	She lives in a safe area.
C	She lives in the city centre.	F	It's modern inside.

☐ ☐ ☐

[3 marks]

1 b   Choose the three statements that are true for **Santiago**:

A	He owns his flat.	D	He lives on the fifth floor.
B	He lives with his cousin.	E	The flat has a washing machine.
C	He shares a bathroom.	F	He likes living there.

☐ ☐ ☐

[3 marks]

2   Escucha las opiniones de Manuela y Juana y contesta a las preguntas en **español**.

TRACK LISTENING 20

2 a   ¿Qué hace Juana para ayudar en casa?

.... *[1 mark]*

2 b   Manuela tiene que hacer mucho en casa. ¿Por qué?

.... *[1 mark]*

2 c   ¿Qué hace Manuela para ayudar en casa durante la semana? Da **dos** detalles.

.... *[2 marks]*

2 d   ¿Qué hace Manuela los fines de semana?

.... *[1 mark]*

Speaking Question

- Spend a couple of minutes looking at the photo and the questions below it.

- You can make notes on a separate piece of paper.

You will be asked the following **three** questions, and **two** questions you haven't prepared:

- ¿Qué hay en la foto?

- ¿Te gusta ir de compras? ¿Por qué (no)?

- ¿Qué compraste la última vez que fuiste de compras?

- Allow the student to develop his / her answers as much as possible.

- You need to ask the student the following questions **in order**:

> - ¿Qué hay en la foto?
>
> - ¿Te gusta ir de compras? ¿Por qué (no)?
>
> - ¿Qué compraste la última vez que fuiste de compras?
>
> - ¿Crees que los jóvenes gastan demasiado dinero en la ropa?
>
> - Si tuvieras mucho dinero, ¿qué comprarías? ¿Por qué?

Reading Questions

1 Read this small advert from a Spanish newspaper, then complete the text
   using the words from the list. Write the correct letter in each box.

Yo ☐ buscando una compañera porque ☐ decidido ☐ mi piso.

Hay ☐ central y el ☐ de un patio. Está en el ☐ de la ciudad,

cerca del ☐ . El ☐ cuesta €250 por mes.

A	he	F	uso	K	centro
B	calefacción	G	hay	L	compartir
C	ático	H	césped	M	vendo
D	alquiler	I	estabas	N	comisaría
E	habéis	J	ayuntamiento	O	estoy

[8 marks]

2 Translate the following text into **English**.

Hoy tengo una lista larguísima de cosas que hacer. Primero, tengo que ir a los grandes
almacenes para devolver unos calcetines negros. Mi abuela necesita un abrigo nuevo, pero lo
voy a comprar en el Internet y aprovechar el servicio de reparto a domicilio. Finalmente, tengo
que llevar una docena de pasteles a la casa de mis tíos. ¡Debería empezar ahora mismo!

....

....

....

....

....

....

....

[9 marks]

Writing Questions

1 Vas a escribir un artículo sobre el lugar donde vives para un concurso organizado por el ayuntamiento.

Menciona:

- cómo es el lugar

- cómo ha cambiado el lugar en los últimos diez años

- si hay suficientes instalaciones para los jóvenes

- cómo sería tu pueblo o tu ciudad ideal.

Escribe aproximadamente **90** palabras en **español**.
Responde a todos los aspectos de la pregunta.

[16 marks]

2 Translate the following into **Spanish**.

> Today the weather is good. Last week, there was a storm and it rained for three days. The worst thing was that I couldn't go out with my friends. I saw the weather forecast last night and they said that tomorrow it will be sunny and windy here in the north.

....

....

....

....

....

....

[12 marks]

Revision Summary for Section Six

Section Six has it all, from describing your town to asking for a refund. It's a long section, so don't worry if you can't tick all these questions off straight away. You know what to do next by now — check over anything that tripped you up, give it a tick once you've got it and then continue on your merry way.

Talking About Where You Live (p.60) ☑

1) What's the Spanish for...?
   a) town hall   b) factory   c) mosque   d) hairdresser's   e) port ☑

2) Ruth says: 'Vivo en las afueras de una ciudad bastante grande. Aunque hay un parque, sería mejor si tuviera un parque más grande.' What would make Ruth's city better? ☑

3) Describe tu barrio. ¿Qué hay? ¿Te gusta? ☑

4) ¿Es mejor vivir en el campo o en la ciudad? Contesta en español, con frases completas. ☑

The Home (p.61-62) ☑

5) ¿Qué hay en tu dormitorio? ☑

6) You read this description in the window of an estate agent's office: 'Esta casa tiene una cocina grande pero no muy moderna. Hay una ventana encima del fregadero.'
   What's the kitchen like? ☑

7) Para ti, ¿es importante que tu casa tenga jardín? Escribe dos frases en español. ☑

8) ¿A qué hora te acuestas los fines de semana? ☑

9) ¿Qué haces para ayudar en casa? ☑

Shopping (p.63-64) ☑

10) How do you say...?
    a) department store   b) clothes size   c) the sales   d) receipt ☑

11) How would you ask politely for a discount in Spanish? ☑

12) You see a sign by the till saying 'Solo se puede pagar en efectivo'. What does this mean? ☑

13) You are at a grocery shop and need a tin of tuna, a bag of carrots and a carton of milk.
    How would you ask for these items in Spanish? ☑

Giving and Asking for Directions (p.65) ☑

14) 'Para llegar a la playa, tome la tercera calle a la izquierda.' How do you get to the beach? ☑

15) You're on holiday and you want to go to the museum. Ask a Spanish person how to get there. ☑

16) How would you say in Spanish that the Post Office is at the end of the street, next to the library? ☑

Weather (p.66) ☑

17) What's the English for...?   a) chubascos   b) caluroso   c) despejado   d) niebla ☑

18) While in Barcelona, you hear this weather forecast: 'Mañana hará calor. A lo mejor las temperaturas máximas alcanzarán los 32 grados.' What will the weather be like? ☑

19) ¿Qué tiempo hace hoy? Contesta en español, con frases completas. ☑

Environmental Problems

Time to think green and start talking about the things that affect the environment.

El medio ambiente — The environment

el cambio climático	*climate change*	el combustible	*fuel*	agotar	*to use up*
el calentamiento global	*global warming*	la lluvia ácida	*acid rain*	la escasez	*shortage*
el efecto invernadero	*greenhouse effect*	nocivo	*harmful*	la inundación	*flood*
la capa de ozono	*ozone layer*	la marea negra	*oil spill*	la sequía	*drought*
los productos químicos	*chemicals*	el vertedero	*rubbish tip*	echar la culpa	*to blame*
los gases de escape	*exhaust fumes*	dañar	*to damage*	preocuparse	*to worry*

Question	**Simple Answer**	**Extended Answer**
¿El medio ambiente es importante para ti?	Sí, creo que es muy importante proteger el medio ambiente.	Es importantísimo proteger el medio ambiente. Si no actuamos ahora, las selvas y los bosques desaparecerán.
Is the environment important to you?	*Yes, I think it's very important to protect the environment.*	*It's really important to protect the environment. If we don't act now, the jungles and forests will disappear.*

El cambio climático — Climate change

El cambio climático es un problema que me preocupa bastante. El uso de ciertos combustibles contamina el aire y causa el calentamiento global.

Debido al efecto invernadero, las temperaturas suben, lo que amenaza la supervivencia de unos animales, por ejemplo los pingüinos.

Climate change is a problem that worries me quite a lot. The use of certain fuels pollutes the air and causes global warming.

Due to the greenhouse effect, temperatures rise, which threatens the survival of some animals, for example penguins.

Exhaust fumes can be harmful and they damage the ozone layer. — Los gases de escape pueden ser nocivos y dañan la capa de ozono.

causes a shortage of water in some regions of the world — causa una escasez de agua en algunas regiones del mundo

El desperdicio de agua — Water wastage

El agua es necesaria para todo el mundo. Sin agua, los cultivos no pueden sobrevivir.

Debemos usar menos agua en nuestra vida diaria.

Water is necessary for everyone. Without water, crops can't survive.

We should use less water in our daily lives.

It's an important resource that we shouldn't use up. — Es un recurso importante que no deberíamos agotar.

use — utilizar

waste — malgastar

La deforestación — Deforestation

Los bosques son importantes porque reducen la cantidad de dióxido de carbono en la atmósfera.

Hoy en día cortamos muchos árboles para producir combustibles. Esto contribuye a la destrucción de los bosques, y al cambio climático.

Forests are important because they reduce the amount of carbon dioxide in the atmosphere.

Nowadays we cut down lots of trees to produce fuel. This contributes to the destruction of forests, and to climate change.

Environmental Problems

Raise your nature-loving credentials and impress the examiners by spicing up your opinions.

La contaminación — Pollution

Las mareas negras ensucian el mar y las playas. Luego, los peces y los pájaros sufren mucho y muchas veces mueren.

Oil spills make the sea and the beaches dirty. Then, the fish and birds suffer a lot and often they die.

Oil is harmful for the creatures that live in the sea. — El petróleo es nocivo para las criaturas que viven en el mar.

Aquí, tenemos un problema con la cantidad de basura. Es muy fácil olvidarse de la basura cuando está en un vertedero y no en la calle, pero sí existe.

Here, we have a problem with the amount of rubbish. It's very easy to forget about rubbish when it's in a tip and not in the street, but it does exist.

I don't understand it, because it's very easy to recycle cardboard and plastic packaging. — No lo entiendo, porque es muy fácil reciclar cartón y envases de plástico.

Algunos problemas graves — Some serious problems

Grammar — using the subjunctive

Use the subjunctive to give your opinion and say what you want to happen. Check how to form it on p.153-154.

- You need it after '<u>no pienso que...</u>' (*I don't think that...*).

  No pienso que <u>sea</u> justo echar la culpa a las fábricas. *I don't think that <u>it's</u> fair to put the blame on factories.*

- It can also be used to express an <u>emotion</u> about something.

  Es terrible que <u>haya</u> tanta basura en la calle. *It's terrible that <u>there is</u> so much rubbish in the street.*

- And when you're saying what you want <u>someone else</u> to do, use '<u>quiero que</u>' followed by the subjunctive.

  Quiero que el gobierno <u>haga</u> más por la naturaleza. *I want the government to <u>do</u> more for nature.*

Grammar — the future

To talk about what things might be like in the <u>future</u>, you can use the <u>immediate future</u> tense (<u>ir</u> + <u>a</u> + <u>infinitive</u>) or the <u>proper future tense</u> (<u>iré</u> — *I will go*, <u>tendré</u> — *I will have*, etc.). See p.145.

Es esencial que protejamos la naturaleza porque sin ella, no podremos vivir.

It's essential that we protect nature because we won't be able to live without it.

we combat the effects of climate change, because if not, we're going to suffer — combatamos los efectos del cambio climático porque si no, vamos a sufrir

Quiero que todos hagan más para reducir la cantidad de basura que producimos. Si no, los vertederos estarán llenos pronto.

I want everyone to do more to reduce the amount of rubbish that we produce. If not, the rubbish tips will be full soon.

think more about the environment and not waste so many things — piensen más en el medio ambiente y no gasten tantas cosas

Es terrible que no pensemos más en el futuro de la Tierra.

It's terrible that we don't think more about the Earth's future.

future generations — las generaciones del futuro

Give opinions using the subjunctive for top marks...

Translate this text into **Spanish**. *[12 marks]*

Climate change worries me a lot. Factories and cars contribute to the greenhouse effect. For me, the worst thing is that people in some poor countries suffer due to floods and droughts. It isn't fair. I think we should work together to reduce the effects of climate change, but it will be very difficult.

Problems in Society

Time to move on to social problems and — yep, you guessed it — you'll have to give opinions on them.

Los problemas sociales — Social problems

el gobierno	*government*	la desigualdad	*inequality*
la libertad	*freedom*	el prejuicio	*prejudice*
el peligro	*danger*	la guerra	*war*
la pobreza	*poverty*	los "sin techo"	*homeless people*
la violencia	*violence*	el desempleo	*unemployment*
la igualdad	*equality*	estar en paro	*to be unemployed*

Los efectos de la guerra — The effects of war

Grammar — 'me parece'

Use '<u>me parece</u>' to say how something '<u>seems</u>' to you. You can use it to <u>vary</u> the way you give <u>opinions</u>.

Me parece inquietante que...
It seems worrying to me that...

Me parece interesante que...
It seems interesting to me that...

Debido a la guerra, muchas personas tienen que emigrar a otro país y empezar la vida de nuevo.

Due to war, many people have to emigrate to another country and start their lives all over again.

No me parece justo que la libertad que tienes dependa tanto del país en que naciste.

It seems unfair to me that the freedom you have depends so much on the country in which you were born.

La igualdad social — Social equality

Sería agradable creer que todos somos iguales en nuestro país, pero no es así.

It would be nice to believe that we're all equal in our country, but that's not the case.
→ inequality doesn't exist — la desigualdad no existe

A veces, la desigualdad provoca violencia entre los ricos y los pobres.

Sometimes, inequality causes violence between the rich and the poor.
→ discrimination against immigrants — discriminación contra los inmigrantes

Me encantaría vivir en un mundo más justo.

I would love to live in a fairer world.
→ Here we are lucky because our country is quite fair. — Aquí tenemos suerte porque nuestro país es bastante justo.

La violencia juvenil — Youth violence

Question	**Simple Answer**	**Extended Answer**
¿Crees que la violencia es un problema grave hoy en día?	Sí, en mi barrio, hay un grupo de jóvenes violentos que nos dan miedo.	Sí, hay grupos de gamberros que salen por la noche. Son muy violentos e intimidan a la gente mayor, lo que me enfada mucho.
Do you think that violence is a serious problem nowadays?	*Yes, in my neighbourhood, there's a group of violent youths who scare us.*	*Yes, there are groups of troublemakers who go out at night. They are very violent and they intimidate the older people, which makes me really angry.*

Problems in Society

And the social problems don't end there — you still have poverty and unemployment to get through.

La pobreza — Poverty

Question

¿Crees que hay mucha pobreza en este país?

Do you believe there is a lot of poverty in this country?

Simple Answer

Creo que hay más pobreza que hace diez años. El gobierno debería apoyar a los "sin techo".

I think there's more poverty than ten years ago. The government should support homeless people.

Grammar — 'deber'

To say what someone should do, use 'deber' followed by the infinitive.

Deberíamos luchar contra la pobreza.
We should fight against poverty.

Extended Answer

Creo que hay demasiada pobreza en nuestra sociedad. Vivo en un país rico, pero todavía hay mucha gente sin comida y sin hogar. Deberíamos ayudar a los más necesitados porque es fácil acabar en la pobreza si pierdes tu trabajo. La pobreza puede afectar a cualquier persona.

I think there's too much poverty in our society. I live in a rich country, but there are still lots of people without food and without a home. We should help the most needy people because it's easy to end up in poverty if you lose your job. Poverty can affect anyone.

El desempleo — Unemployment

This could be the examiner's favourite topic in the speaking exam, so learn how to talk about it.

Hay mucha gente en paro en mi ciudad.

There are lots of unemployed people in my city.

Nobody has a problem finding work — Nadie tiene problemas para encontrar trabajo

Casi todos los estudiantes por aquí se preocupan por el desempleo. Si pudiera cambiar algo, crearía más trabajos.

Nearly all the students around here worry about unemployment. If I could change anything, I'd create more jobs.

It is a big problem that we must solve. — Es un gran problema que debemos solucionar.

El desempleo es un problema muy grave porque los que están en paro se encuentran en un círculo vicioso. Los expertos dicen que si estás en paro, es más difícil encontrar otro trabajo.

Unemployment is a very serious problem because those who are unemployed find themselves in a vicious circle. Experts say that if you're unemployed, it's harder to find another job.

the worst affected are young people — los más afectados son los jóvenes

Try to vary the structure of your sentences...

A charity for the homeless is talking about the situation in Spain. Listen, and then fill the gaps.

e.g. ‎Thousands‎ of people are homeless in Spain.

1) Many people have lost their jobs and homes due to .... [1]
2) Homeless people often have a .... life. [1]
3) Homeless people are often the victims of .... [1]
4) According to the report, many people think homeless people are .... [1]
5) To change the situation for homeless people, we should .... [1]

Contributing to Society

So now you've battled through all the problems, it's time to get creative and find some solutions.

¿Qué podemos hacer? — What can we do?

la basura	*rubbish*	renovable	*renewable*
los desechos / los residuos	*rubbish*	salvar el planeta	*to save the planet*
el reciclaje	*recycling*	la organización benéfica	*charitable organisation*
reciclar	*to recycle*	la tienda solidaria	*charity shop*

Question	**Simple Answer**	**Extended Answer**
¿Qué haces para proteger el medio ambiente?	Apago las luces para ahorrar energía.	Cuando voy de compras, siempre reutilizo las bolsas en vez de comprar nuevas.
What do you do to protect the environment?	*I turn the lights off to save energy.*	*When I go shopping, I always reuse the bags instead of buying new ones.*
¿Qué haces para ayudar a otras personas?	Los domingos trabajo en una tienda solidaria.	Ayudo con el club de jóvenes en mi pueblo. Es esencial que hagamos algo para los demás.
What do you do to help other people?	*On Sundays I work in a charity shop.*	*I help with the youth club in my town. It's essential that we do something for others.*

¿Cómo podemos ayudar? — How can we help?

Me gustaría ayudar a los refugiados que vienen a vivir en nuestro país.

I would like to help the refugees who come to live in our country.

> the victims of natural disasters like hurricanes and fires — las víctimas de desastres naturales como huracanes e incendios

Es importante que apoyemos a las organizaciones benéficas.

It's important that we support charitable organisations.

> 'Acabar de' + infinitive means 'to have just done something'. See p.150.

Acabo de participar en una protesta en contra del uso de los combustibles fósiles.

I have just participated in a protest against the use of fossil fuels.

> a campaign — una campaña

SPEAKING

Use lots of different tenses to impress the examiner...

Look at the answers to these questions — then it's time for a photo question.
¿Recicláis mucho en casa?
¿Qué haremos en el futuro para proteger el medio ambiente?

Tick list:
✓ tenses: present, future present subjunctive
✓ topical vocab, e.g. cartón, vertedero

Sí, intentamos reciclar muchas cosas. Reciclamos envases de plástico, botellas y cartón. Si no podemos reciclar algo, intentamos reutilizarlo **para que no acabe**[1] en un vertedero.

Grade 8-9

Creo que tendremos coches eléctricos. También reduciremos la cantidad de basura que producimos y reutilizaremos las cosas más antes de tirarlas.

[1] so that it doesn't end up

To improve:
+ explain opinions more
+ more complex connectives e.g. sin embargo

*Answer these questions in **Spanish**. Talk for **2** minutes.*

- ¿Qué hay en la foto?
- ¿Podríamos hacer más para salvar el planeta?
- ¿Crees que es importante reciclar? [10 marks]

Global Events

Covering everything from music festivals to hard-hitting campaigns, global events is a pretty wide topic. Use this page to make sure you're well prepared for anything that might come up in the exam.

Los eventos internacionales — International events

asistir a	*to attend*
el evento	*event*
la campaña	*campaign*
recaudar dinero	*to raise money*
a beneficio de	*in aid of*
la organización caritativa	*charitable organisation*
el festival (de música)	*(music) festival*
los Juegos Olímpicos	*Olympic Games*
el Mundial	*World Cup (football)*

> **Grammar** — capital letters
>
> Just as in English, there are some nouns which have <u>capital letters</u> in Spanish, <u>wherever in the sentence</u> they come, like the <u>Olympic Games</u> and the <u>World Cup</u> — 'los <u>J</u>uegos Olímpicos' and 'el <u>M</u>undial'.
>
> Sometimes you might see '<u>m</u>undial' with a lower case '<u>m</u>' — in this case, it's an adjective meaning '<u>worldwide</u>' or '<u>global</u>'.

Question	**Simple Answer**	**Extended Answer**
¿Has asistido a algún evento internacional?	No, pero me gustaría asistir a los Juegos Olímpicos.	El año pasado fui a Benicàssim para un festival internacional de música. Atrae a gente de muchos países.
Have you attended any international events?	*No, but I would like to attend the Olympic Games.*	*Last year I went to Benicàssim for an international music festival. It attracts people from all around the world.*
	Sí, fui a un festival de música rock en Escocia.	No, pero planeamos ir al próximo Mundial. Habrá un ambiente fenomenal.
	Yes, I went to a rock music festival in Scotland.	*No, but we're planning to go to the next World Cup. There will be a great atmosphere.*

Las campañas mundiales — Global campaigns

Las campañas mundiales nos enseñan sobre los problemas del mundo.

Global campaigns teach us about the world's problems. ← *the importance of working together* — la importancia de trabajar juntos

Lo malo de las campañas es que cuando terminan, mucha gente se olvide de ellas rápidamente. Es difícil cambiar el mundo para siempre.

The bad thing about campaigns is that when they finish, many people forget about them quickly. It's difficult to change the world permanently. ← *people's behaviour* — el comportamiento de la gente

Dedicar días especiales a las campañas mundiales es una buena manera de recaudar dinero y cambiar el mundo.

Dedicating special days to global campaigns is a good way of raising money and changing the world. ← *attracting people's attention* — llamar la atención de la gente

You'll need opinions on events even if you haven't been to one...

Traduce el texto siguiente al **español**. *[12 marks]*

> This year, we have worked with a charity which helps disadvantaged children in Asia. We organised a concert and we wrote to some singers to ask them if they would support us. Three of them came and everyone had a good time. In the future, I would love to go to the World Cup. I think it would be really fun.

Listening Questions

You know the drill now — four pages of exam-style questions are ready and waiting for you.
They say practice makes perfect and all that... so what are you waiting for?

---

1   A radio show is interviewing people about environmental issues.
For each person, decide which problem they are most worried about.
Then write the correct letter on the dotted line.

TRACK LISTENING 22

1 a   Briana   ....

1 b   Alberto   ....

1 c   Raquel   ....

A	Rubbish
B	Deforestation
C	Flooding
D	Climate change
E	Drought

[3 marks]

2   A local politician hoping to be elected soon is giving a television interview.
Listen to what she says and answer the questions in **English**.

TRACK LISTENING 23

2 a   What is the first problem that the politician mentions?

....   *[1 mark]*

2 b   What can't some people living in poverty earn enough to do? Give **two** details.

....   *[2 marks]*

2 c   According to the politician, what does social inequality cause?

....   *[1 mark]*

2 d   What is the last problem that the politician mentions?

....   *[1 mark]*

Speaking Question

Candidate's Material

- Spend a couple of minutes looking at the photo and the questions below it.

- You can make notes on a separate piece of paper.

You will be asked the following **three** questions, and **two** questions you haven't prepared:

- ¿Qué hay en la foto?

- ¿Te preocupa la contaminación? ¿Por qué (no)?

- ¿Qué has hecho recientemente para proteger el medio ambiente?

Teacher's Material

- Allow the student to develop his / her answers as much as possible.

- You need to ask the student the following questions **in order**:

  - ¿Qué hay en la foto?

  - ¿Te preocupa la contaminación? ¿Por qué (no)?

  - ¿Qué has hecho recientemente para proteger el medio ambiente?

  - ¿Hay algo más que podrías hacer para proteger el medio ambiente?

  - ¿Qué piensas de la destrucción de los bosques? ¿Por qué?

Reading Questions

1 Translate the following passage into **English**.

> — ¡Espero que no vayas a salir con esos chicos! Creo que son muy maleducados, Pedro.
> — No te preocupes, no voy a salir con ellos. Ahora sé que son violentos. El otro día, intimidaron a una mujer en la calle. Fueron muy agresivos y ella creyó que le iban a hacer daño. Eso no me gustó para nada y ahora no somos amigos.

....

....

....

....

....

....

....

[9 marks]

2 Lee el blog de Pavel.

> Recientemente participé en los Juegos Paralímpicos. Fue una experiencia inolvidable, sobre todo gracias a los espectadores que aplaudían cuando entramos en el estadio. Lo que más me encanta de los eventos así es la idea de influenciar a los jóvenes. Es decepcionante ver a tantos jóvenes que no hacen deporte nunca y quiero cambiar esta situación. Sé que los eventos así cuestan mucho, sobre todo para el país que acoge los Juegos, pero creo que vale la pena apoyar eventos que facilitan la cooperación internacional.

Completa cada frase con una palabra o expresión del recuadro de abajo.
No necesitas todas las palabras.

> inactiva   aburrida   una pérdida de tiempo   acoger
>
> bienvenidos   buenas oportunidades   participar

2 a Pavel cree que mucha gente joven es ....   *[1 mark]*

2 b Según Pavel, una desventaja de .... un evento es el coste.   *[1 mark]*

2 c Pavel piensa que eventos internacionales son ....   *[1 mark]*

Writing Questions

1   Quieres hacer una práctica con una organización benéfica. Escribes al jefe / a la jefa para contarle sobre tu experiencia.

Menciona:

- el problema social que más te preocupa

- por qué quieres hacer una práctica en una organización benéfica

- algo que has hecho para contribuir a la sociedad

- qué más podríamos hacer para apoyar a otra gente.

Escribe aproximadamente **90** palabras en **español**.
Responde a todos los aspectos de la pregunta.
[16 marks]

2   Translate the following passage into **Spanish**.

> In my opinion, there are many problems with the environment. Due to the greenhouse effect, temperatures have increased a lot. My grandmother told me that when she was younger, it used to snow every winter, but it doesn't snow much now. In the future, I think there will be more droughts.

....

....

....

....

....

....

[12 marks]

Revision Summary for Section Seven

Section Seven might be the trickiest in the whole book — it's full of vocab and contains some pretty complex grammatical structures. That's why you shouldn't worry if there are a fair few questions you can't do straight away. Just keep coming back to tick things off once you've got the hang of them.

Environmental Problems (p.72-73) ☑

1) What's the Spanish for...?
   a) global warming   b) greenhouse effect   c) fuel   d) rubbish tip   e) drought ☑

2) Translate into English: 'Los productos químicos pueden ser nocivos.' ☑

3) Naomi says: 'Acid rain can damage the forests.' How could she say this in Spanish? ☑

4) ¿Cuál es el problema medioambiental que más te preocupa?
   Contesta en español, con frases completas. ☑

5) ¿Hay demasiada contaminación en tu país? Escribe dos frases en español. ☑

Problems in Society (p.74-75) ☑

6) How do you say these words in Spanish?
   a) war   b) government   c) poverty   d) equality ☑

7) 'Tenemos mucha suerte porque vivimos en un país en el que la gente tiene libertad.'
   Translate this into English. ☑

8) You read a newspaper headline: 'El número de personas "sin techo" ha bajado en los
   últimos meses.' What does the newspaper claim has happened recently? ☑

9) Aitor says: 'Estuve en paro durante seis meses.' Translate this into English. ☑

10) ¿Crees que hay suficiente igualdad en nuestra sociedad? ☑

11) ¿El desempleo es un problema muy serio en tu región? Explica tu opinión. ☑

Contributing to Society (p.76) ☑

12) Give three ways of saying 'rubbish' in Spanish. ☑

13) You read a leaflet about the environment which says: 'Antes de tirar algo a la basura,
    debemos preguntarnos si podríamos reciclarlo, reutilizarlo o si otra persona podría usarlo'.
    What is the leaflet advising? ☑

14) ¿Qué haces para proteger el planeta? ☑

15) How do you say...?   a) charitable organisation   b) youth club ☑

16) Para ti, ¿es importante ayudar a otra gente? ☑

17) Resul says: 'Hay dos tiendas solidarias en mi pueblo. Me gusta comprar libros allí porque
    es una manera de ayudar a los "sin techo".' How does he help homeless people? ☑

Global Events (p.77) ☑

18) How do you say...?   a) event   b) campaign   c) festival ☑

19) ¿Te gustaría asistir a algún evento internacional? Contesta en español, con frases completas. ☑

20) Shara says: 'Hace unos años fui a los Juegos Olímpicos. Había una atmósfera increíble.'
    Translate this into English. ☑

21) Lucas has just participated in a campaign. How could he say this in Spanish? ☑

22) Write down two advantages of global campaigns in Spanish. ☑

Healthy Living

Time for a whole page about healthy living, complete with some reflexive verbs. Pass the biscuits, then.

¿Te mantienes en forma? — Do you keep fit?

mantenerse en forma	*to keep fit / in shape*	entrenar(se)	*to train*	activo/a	*active*
el ejercicio (físico)	*(physical) exercise*	equilibrado/a	*balanced*	la salud	*health*
el entrenamiento	*training*	estar en forma	*to be fit*	saludable	*healthy*

Question

¿Es importante mantenerse en forma?

Is it important to keep fit?

Simple Answer

Sí, creo que es importante entrenarse y comer bien.

Yes, I think it's important to train and to eat well.

Grammar — reflexive verbs

'Mantenerse' and 'entrenarse' are reflexive verbs. Check p.149 for a reminder of how to form them.

Extended Answer

Diría que es importante entrenarse, pero no tengo tiempo para hacerlo todos los días. Voy al gimnasio dos veces a la semana para mantenerme en forma. Para mí, es importante elegir comida saludable también.

I would say that it's important to train, but I don't have time to do it every day. I go to the gym twice a week to keep myself in shape. For me, it's important to choose healthy food too.

Una vida sana — A healthy life

Intento comer una dieta equilibrada todos los días.

I try to eat a balanced diet every day.

to avoid junk food — evitar la comida basura

Para mantenerme en forma, juego al tenis dos veces a la semana.

To keep fit, I play tennis twice a week.

I do exercise almost every day — hago ejercicio casi todos los días

Vale la pena comer menos comida rápida y más verduras.

It's worth eating less fast food and more vegetables.

drinking two litres of water every day — beber dos litros de agua todos los días

Para mí, es importante dormir al menos ocho horas.

For me, it's important to sleep for at least eight hours.

to relax a bit after school — relajarme un poco después del colegio

Time to give your Spanish a workout...

Selina has written an article about healthy living.

La salud es muy importante para mí. Voy al colegio a pie todos los días, y hago deporte tres veces a la semana. Normalmente como bien — tengo una dieta equilibrada. Recientemente he aprendido a cocinar y me encanta la comida saludable. Además es **un buen consejo**[1] beber agua en vez de **bebidas gaseosas**[2] porque contienen mucho azúcar, lo que puede llevar a problemas con los dientes. Para evitar **el estrés**[3], se debe hacer algo que te relaje todos los días. Se puede hacer ejercicio físico o escuchar música o **sencillamente**[4] hablar con tu familia. Por último, es una buena idea acostarte temprano.

Grade 8-9

[1] a good piece of advice

[2] fizzy drinks

[3] stress

[4] simply

Tick list:
✓ tenses: present, perfect, subjunctive
✓ use of impersonal verbs
✓ good topical vocab and time phrases

To improve:
+ give reasons for opinions

Escribe aproximadamente **90 palabras** en **español** para una revista. Menciona:

- lo que haces para mantenerte en forma;
- si tienes una dieta equilibrada;
- si tienes una vida más o menos sana que hace cinco años;
- dos cosas que podrías hacer para llevar una vida más sana   [16 marks]

Unhealthy Living

Time to tackle drinking, smoking and drugs — you might be asked about these in your exams.

Una vida malsana — An unhealthy life

el cigarrillo	*cigarette*	el fumador (pasivo)	*(passive) smoker*
fumar	*to smoke*	el tabaquismo	*addiction to tobacco*
el humo	*smoke*	el síndrome de abstinencia	*withdrawal symptoms*
oler	*to smell*	la droga blanda / dura	*soft / hard drug*
los pulmones	*lungs*	el sobrepeso	*obesity*
respirar	*to breathe*	borracho/a	*drunk*
hacer daño	*to harm*	emborracharse	*to get drunk*
cansarse	*to get tired*	el botellón	*drinking party in the street*

Question

¿Qué piensas de
los cigarrillos?

*What do you think
of cigarettes?*

Simple Answer

Los cigarrillos son peligrosos
porque es difícil dejar de fumar.

*Cigarettes are dangerous because
it's difficult to stop smoking.*

Grammar — to stop ...ing

To say 'to stop ...ing', use 'dejar de'
followed by the infinitive.

Quiero dejar de fumar.
I want to stop smoking.

Extended Answer

Estoy convencido/a de que los cigarrillos perjudican la salud. Incluso cuando una persona ha dejado
de fumar, los cigarrillos causan una variedad de problemas debido al síndrome de abstinencia.

*I am convinced that cigarettes damage your health. Even when a person has stopped
smoking, cigarettes cause a variety of problems due to withdrawal symptoms.*

No quiero probar las drogas
porque son peligrosas.

*I don't want to try drugs
because they are dangerous.*

Una vez, me emborraché,
pero no me gustó.

*Once, I got drunk,
but I didn't like it.*

No se puede fumar en
espacios públicos.

*You can't smoke in public
spaces.*

to smoke because it smells really horrible
— fumar porque huele fatal

'Oler' (*to smell*) is an irregular verb.

I went to a drinking party in the street
— fui a un botellón

buy cigarettes if you're under 18 — comprar
cigarrillos si tienes menos de 18 años

Some of this vocab's pretty tricky — so keep testing yourself...

Have a look at Karima's answer to this question.

¿Piensas que el alcohol es peligroso?

Desde mi punto de vista, no hay ningún problema si
alguien quiere beber una cerveza o un poco de vino.
A mis padres les gusta probar vinos de varios países y no
se emborrachan. Sin embargo, creo que hay problemas con
el alcohol cuando los jóvenes se emborrachan sin pensar en
las consecuencias. Es peligroso porque no saben ni dónde
están ni cuánto han bebido. Hace unos meses, mi amigo
bebió demasiado y tuvo que ir al hospital. Es muy
irresponsable beber tanto alcohol.

Grade
8-9

Tick list:
✓ tenses: present, preterite
✓ good use of quantifiers
✓ lots of opinions

To improve:
+ include another tense
  e.g. future
+ use more topical vocab

*Now answer the following questions.
Try to speak for about 2 minutes. [10 marks]*

- *¿Qué piensas de las drogas?*
- *¿Piensas que el alcohol es más peligroso
  que las drogas? ¿Por qué?*
- *¿Qué le dirías a un joven que toma drogas?*

Illnesses

They might not be the cheeriest of topics, but you do need to know about illness and general health issues.

Las enfermedades — Illnesses

encontrarse / sentirse mal	*to feel ill*	doler	*to hurt*	el cerebro	*brain*
encontrarse / estar enfermo/a	*to be ill*	el dolor	*pain*	el ataque cardíaco	*heart attack*
mejorarse	*to get better*	el cuerpo	*body*	el estrés	*stress*
los primeros auxilios	*first aid*	el corazón	*heart*	el sida	*AIDS*
tener dolor (de)...	*to have a pain (in)...*	el hígado	*liver*	seropositivo/a	*HIV-positive*

Question

¿Cómo te sientes?
How do you feel?

Simple Answer

Me duele la garganta.
My throat hurts.

Extended Answer

Me duelen el pie y el brazo, y tengo dolor de espalda.
My foot and arm hurt, and I have backache.

Grammar — 'doler' — to hurt

'Doler' works in a similar way to 'gustar' — to say what's <u>hurting you</u>, you need to use an <u>indirect object pronoun</u> (see p.130) <u>before</u> the verb.
You also need to add an '<u>n</u>' in the <u>plural</u>.

<u>Me duele</u> la pierna. *<u>My</u> leg <u>hurts</u>.* ← Literally, 'the leg
<u>Me duelen</u> los pies. *<u>My</u> feet <u>hurt</u>.*   hurts me'.

<u>Le duelen</u> el brazo *<u>His</u> / <u>her</u> arm
y la mano. *and hand <u>hurt</u>.*

You also need to remember that '<u>doler</u>' is a <u>radical-changing verb</u>. See p.138.

Necesito ir al médico — I need to go to the doctor

Hace un mes, me encontré enfermo y tuve que ir al médico.

A month ago, I felt ill and I had to go to the doctor.

the doctor gave me a prescription — el médico me dio una receta

De niño, tenía muchos problemas respiratorios.

As a child, I had a lot of respiratory problems.

problems with my liver — problemas con el hígado

Creo que todos deberían hacer un curso de primeros auxilios.

I think everyone should do a first aid course.

learn about what you should do if someone has a heart attack — aprender lo que se debe hacer si alguien tiene un ataque cardíaco

El sida es un problema muy grave en algunos países.

AIDS is a very serious problem in some countries.

The lack of doctors — La falta de médicos

Muchos jóvenes se preocupan por su peso y su apariencia.

Many young people worry about their weight and their appearance.

their exams, which causes a lot of stress — sus exámenes, lo que causa mucho estrés

'Doler' works in a similar way to 'gustar'...

Translate this text into **English**. *[9 marks]*

Me siento muy mal. La semana pasada, fui al campo, pero desafortunadamente estaba lloviendo y no había traído mi paraguas. Me duele muchísimo la garganta y apenas puedo hablar. He tenido que beber muchos líquidos durante unos días y no tengo ganas de comer. Tendré que ir al médico si no me mejoro pronto. Lo peor es que si todavía estoy enfermo el sábado, no podré ir a la fiesta de mi amigo.

Listening Questions

Section Eight's only short, but that doesn't mean you can just leave it out. Use these questions to make sure you can talk about lifestyle — they're just like the ones you'll get in the real exam.

1 Escuchas esta entrevista con Julia en un programa sobre comida saludable. Escribe la letra correcta en cada casilla.

TRACK LISTENING 24

1 a ¿Qué animó a Julia a interesarse por el desayuno?

A	Ella había dejado de desayunar.
B	Su hija mayor tenía miedo de engordarse.
C	Su hija menor no quería consumir tanta comida.

[1 mark]

1 b Según los expertos, hay una relación entre...

A	la gente que come mucho y la gente que hace deporte.
B	los que desayunan y los que disfrutan de buena salud.
C	la gente que desayuna y la gente que pesa más.

[1 mark]

1 c ¿Cuál es la desventaja de desayunar cereales? Contesta en **español**.

.... *[1 mark]*

2 Listen to a reporter interviewing Tom about his attitude to alcohol and smoking, and then complete the sentences that follow. You will not need all the answers.

TRACK LISTENING 25

2 a	Tom would like his friends to...	
2 b	To reduce alcohol consumption, he thinks the government should...	
2 c	Tom hates...	
2 d	It really worries him...	

A	give up alcohol.	E	the smell of smoke.
B	drink less.	F	that you can't smoke in bars.
C	ban the advertising of alcohol.	G	that smoking could affect his girlfriend's health.
D	increase taxes on alcohol.	H	that he might get ill because of passive smoking.

[4 marks]

Speaking Question

Candidate's Role

- Your teacher will play the role of the doctor. They will speak first.

- You should use *usted* to address the doctor.

- – ! – means you will have to respond to something you have not prepared.

- – ? – means you will have to ask the doctor a question.

> Usted está hablando con el médico/la médica porque ha tenido un accidente.
>
> - El accidente — cuándo.
>
> - Los síntomas que tienes (**dos** detalles).
>
> - !
>
> - Otros problemas de salud (**dos** detalles).
>
> - **?** Consejos.

Teacher's Role

- You begin the role-play using the introductory text below.

- You should address the candidate as *usted*.

- You may alter the wording of the questions in response to the candidate's previous answers.

- Do not supply the candidate with key vocabulary.

> Introductory text: *Usted está hablando con el médico/la médica porque ha tenido un accidente. Yo soy el médico/la médica.*
>
> - Veo que usted ha tenido un accidente. ¿Cuándo fue?
>
> - ¿Cómo se siente ahora?
>
> - ! ¿Cuántas horas durmió anoche?
>
> - ¿Tiene usted otros problemas de salud?
>
> - **?** Allow the candidate to ask you a question.

Reading Questions

1   Translate this text into **English**.

> — ¿Conoce usted a alguna persona que tome drogas?
>
> — No, pero mi madre es médica y ha trabajado mucho con la gente drogadicta.
>
> — Entonces, ¿qué les dijo su madre sobre las drogas?
>
> — Les dijo que no vale la pena tomar drogas porque te hacen sentir fatal.
>   Además, cuestan muchísimo dinero e incluso te pueden matar.
>
> — Es verdad. No tomaría drogas nunca.

....

....

....

....

....

[9 marks]

2   Translate the following conversation into **English**.

> — Hola, señora. ¿En qué puedo ayudarle hoy?
>
> — Me encuentro mal. Me duele mucho la garganta y tengo dolor de estómago.
>
> — Vamos a ver... Recomiendo que intente descansar y tome esta medicina. Voy a darle una
>   receta. Aparte de esto, no puedo hacer nada más. Si quiere mejorarse, hay que relajarse.
>
> — Bueno, gracias por su ayuda, doctora. Adiós.

....

....

....

....

....

[9 marks]

Writing Questions

1 Quieres hacer una campaña sobre el peligro de llevar una vida malsana y decides empezar con un artículo en tu revista escolar.

Menciona:

- las desventajas de beber demasiado alcohol y fumar

- tus consejos para las personas que llevan una vida malsana.

Escribe aproximadamente **150** palabras en **español**.
Responde a los dos aspectos de la pregunta.

[32 marks]

2 Translate the following text into **Spanish**.

> I think that it is important to keep fit. When I was young, I used to be very lazy. I never did exercise and I ate junk food. Now I run or swim at least three times a week and I feel better. However, I still need to eat a more balanced diet. I will try to eat five pieces of fruit a day and I will drink more water.

....

....

....

....

....

....

....

....

[12 marks]

Revision Summary for Section Eight

As always, we've put together a set of questions so you can test yourself on what you've learned in this section. Tick away and be sure to go back over the tougher bits. You'll soon have a long line of ticks and a clean bill of health...

Healthy Living (p.83) ☑

1) What does 'estoy en forma' mean in English?

2) ¿Crees que haces suficiente ejercicio para mantenerte en forma?

3) Rashid says: 'Recientemente he intentado comer una dieta más equilibrada.' What's Rashid been trying to do?

4) Belén wants to be healthier. Which one of the following options would help her?
    a) comer menos verduras
    c) comer más comida basura
    b) dejar de hacer ejercicio
    d) beber más agua

5) ¿Cuál sería tu mejor consejo para alguien que quiere llevar una vida sana?

Unhealthy Living (p.84) ☑

6) What's the Spanish for...?
    a) to breathe   b) to get tired   c) drug   d) obesity

7) ¿Piensas que los jóvenes beben demasiado alcohol? ¿Por qué (no)?

8) Your Spanish friend explains: 'Un botellón es una actividad en la que los jóvenes se juntan en la calle o en una plaza para beber alcohol.' What is a 'botellón'?

9) ¿Cuáles son los peligros de fumar? Contesta en español.

10) Isabel says: 'Me molesta cuando la gente fuma cerca de mí. El humo huele mal y no quiero ser fumadora pasiva.' Why does Isabel dislike smoking?

11) What is 'el tabaquismo' in English?

12) How would you say: 'I think it's more dangerous to take drugs than to smoke cigarettes.'

Illnesses (p.85) ☑

13) You've hurt yourself while playing rugby. How would you tell a doctor your leg and arm hurt?

14) Eva says: 'Me duele casi todo el cuerpo. Pienso que es a causa del estrés. El médico me dijo que tengo que relajarme un poco.' Why does Eva feel so ill?

15) On a job advertisement, you read the following: 'Buscamos a alguien que haya hecho un curso de primeros auxilios.' What is the company looking for?

16) How would you say: 'As a child, my brother had a lot of problems with his heart.'

17) 'El año pasado, el abuelo de Juan tuvo un ataque cardíaco.' What happened last year?

18) ¿Cómo se dice 'seropositivo' en inglés?

Where to Go

Grab some sun cream and pack your suitcase because you're off on holiday...

Los países y las nacionalidades — Countries and nationalities

España	*Spain*	español	*Spanish*	los Estados Unidos	*United States*
Inglaterra	*England*	inglés	*English*	Canadá	*Canada*
Escocia	*Scotland*	escocés	*Scottish*	la India	*India*
Gales	*Wales*	galés	*Welsh*	Australia	*Australia*
Irlanda	*Ireland*	irlandés	*Irish*	Rusia	*Russia*
Irlanda del Norte	*Northern Ireland*	norirlandés	*Northern Irish*	Brasil	*Brazil*
Gran Bretaña	*Great Britain*	británico	*British*	México	*Mexico*
Francia	*France*	francés	*French*	Argentina	*Argentina*
Alemania	*Germany*	alemán	*German*	Perú	*Peru*
Portugal	*Portugal*	portugués	*Portuguese*	Chile	*Chile*
Italia	*Italy*	italiano	*Italian*	Colombia	*Colombia*
Grecia	*Greece*	griego	*Greek*	Cuba	*Cuba*
Europa	*Europe*	europeo	*European*		

Mi padre es medio irlandés, así que vamos de vacaciones a Irlanda a menudo.

My father is half Irish, so we often go on holiday to Ireland.

Mi padre es griego y solía ir a Grecia para quedarme con mi familia.

My father is Greek and I used to go to Greece to stay with my family.

Luisa fue a Londres el año pasado y le gustó mucho la comida británica.

Luisa went to London last year and she really liked British food.

Grammar — nationalities

Nationalities are <u>adjectives</u> — some have an <u>accent</u> when they're used in the <u>masculine singular</u> form, but drop the accent and add '<u>a</u>' in the <u>feminine</u> form.

inglés (m., sing.) — **inglesa** (f., sing.)
ingleses (m., pl.) — **inglesas** (f., pl.)
Las chicas <u>son inglesas</u>.
The girls <u>are English</u>.

Remember — always use the verb '<u>ser</u>' with nationalities (p.139).

Question	**Simple Answer**	**Extended Answer**
¿Adónde quisiera ir de vacaciones?	Quisiera ir al norte de España.	Me gustaría ir al norte de España porque mi tía nació en Asturias. Quisiera visitar el pueblo donde vivía.
Where would you like to go on holiday?	*I would like to go to the north of Spain.*	*I would like to go to the north of Spain because my aunt was born in Asturias. I would like to visit the town where she used to live.*

Don't just name places — give opinions about them too...

Arturo has written a leaflet to help promote his region.

¡Ven a visitar la región bellísima de Galicia! Está situada en la costa del Océano Atlántico en el norte de España. Aquí se puede conocer las ciudades famosas de Vigo, Pontevedra, Ourense, o Santiago de Compostela, que es más conocida por su catedral y sus **peregrinaciones**[1] todos los años. ¡Hay tantas cosas que hacer! Por ejemplo, se puede **alquilar**[2] un barco en Pontevedra, explorar las calles antiguas de Vigo, o nadar en uno de los **ríos**[3] en Ourense!

*Lee este texto, y luego contesta a las preguntas en **español**.*

e.g. ¿Qué región se menciona? *Galicia.*

1. ¿Dónde está Galicia? Da dos detalles. *[2]*

2. ¿Por qué es la ciudad de Santiago de Compostela famosa? Da dos razones. *[2]*

3. ¿Qué se puede hacer en Ourense? *[1]*

[1]pilgrimages [2]to rent, hire [3]rivers

Accommodation

So you've chosen which country you're going to visit — now all you need is somewhere to stay...

Busco alojamiento... — I'm looking for accommodation...

alojarse / quedarse	to stay	las instalaciones	facilities
el albergue juvenil	youth hostel	media pensión	half board
la pensión	boarding house (B&B)	pensión completa	full board
el parador	state-owned hotel	la habitación doble	double room
(irse de) camping	(to go) camping	la habitación individual	single room
la tienda	tent	la cama de matrimonio	double bed
el crucero	cruise	el aire acondicionado	air-conditioning

Quisiera quedarme aquí cuatro noches. *I would like to stay here for four nights.*

a room with a balcony — una habitación con balcón

Siempre nos quedamos en una pensión. *We always stay in a boarding house.*

a luxury hotel — un hotel de lujo

Es esencial encontrar una habitación que tenga aire acondicionado. *It's essential to find a room that has air-conditioning.*

that has a bathroom — que tenga cuarto de baño

Question	**Simple Answer**	**Extended Answer**
¿Qué tipo de habitación quisiera usted?	Quisiera una habitación con vista al mar.	Somos una familia de tres, así que quisiéramos dos habitaciones — una individual y una doble.
What type of room would you like?	*I would like a room with a sea view.*	*We are a family of three, so we would like two rooms — a single and a double.*

Quisiera alojarme en... — I would like to stay in...

Mi amigo/a quisiera encontrar alojamiento de media pensión. *My friend would like to find half-board accommodation.*

full-board — pensión completa

Preferiríamos alojarnos en un parador porque tienen buenas instalaciones. *We would prefer to stay in a state-owned hotel because they have good facilities.*

on a campsite because we have a caravan and like nature — en un camping porque tenemos una caravana y nos gusta la naturaleza

Nos gustaría quedarnos en un albergue juvenil para conocer a gente nueva. *We would like to stay in a youth hostel in order to meet new people.*

to save money — ahorrar dinero

TRACK LISTENING 26

Use plenty of adjectives to describe your accommodation...

Listen to this extract about hotels in Rio de Janeiro from a book by Gorgonio Petano y Mazariegos.

1. How are the hotels in general described?

   A) average   B) fantastic   [1]

2. How many hotels are mentioned when discussing the best hotels in the city?   [1]

3. How is the *Hotel de los Extranjeros* described? Choose the two correct adjectives from the list below.

small	old-fashioned
modern	strange
elegant	ugly [2]

4. What do the people of the *Cuerpo Diplomático extranjero* do at the hotel?

   A) eat dinner

   B) live

   C) have meetings   [1]

Getting Ready to Go

That holiday won't book itself. Thankfully, there's plenty of vocab here to help you get something sorted.

Reservando unas vacaciones — Booking a holiday

la agencia de viajes	*travel agent's*	el folleto	*leaflet*
libre / disponible	*available*	el regreso	*return*
el pasaporte	*passport*	el guía	*guide*
el carnet de conducir	*driving licence*	la guía	*guidebook*
la maleta	*suitcase*	buscar	*to look for*
el equipaje	*luggage*	informarse	*to find out*
la ficha / el formulario	*registration form*	el lugar / sitio	*place*

Grammar — I need...

When talking about the features of something you <u>require</u>, use the <u>subjunctive</u> (p.153-154).

Busco un hotel grande que <u>tenga</u> una piscina.

I'm looking for a big hotel that <u>has</u> a pool.

Question

¿Estás listo/a para tus vacaciones?

Are you ready for your holidays?

Simple Answer

Sí, he hecho mi maleta.

Yes, I have packed my suitcase.

Extended Answer

Sí, he hecho mi maleta, pero todavía no he comprado una guía. Necesito una guía que incluya información sobre España e Italia.

Yes, I've packed my suitcase, but I haven't bought a guidebook yet. I need a guidebook that includes information about Spain and Italy.

¿En qué puedo servirle? — How can I help you?

Por favor, ¿puedo reservar la mejor habitación disponible?

Please can I reserve the best room available?

Quisiera ir a un lugar donde pueda nadar.

I would like to go to a place where I can swim.

¿Puede usted darnos unos folletos? Queremos informarnos sobre lo que hay en esta región.

Can you give us some leaflets? We want to find out about what there is in this region.

a room on the ground floor — una habitación en la planta baja

canoe — hacer piragüismo

tell us if there are rooms available — decirnos si hay habitaciones libres

to know what time the museum opens — saber cuándo abre el museo

---

This is another possible role-play scenario...

Read the following scene from a Spanish TV show script. A travel agent is speaking to Bea.

Agente de Viajes (AV): Dígame, Señora.

Bea: Buenos días. Quisiera reservar unas vacaciones en España pero no sé el mejor lugar para quedarnos. Quiero ir con cuatro amigos.

AV: Bueno. Pues, ¿cuándo quisiera usted venir?

Bea: Preferiríamos ir durante las vacaciones de verano, desde el 3 de agosto hasta el 11 de agosto. Nos gustan las montañas.

AV: Hace buen tiempo durante agosto. Le recomendaría ir a Gijón, en el norte de España, porque se puede visitar la costa y los Picos de Europa, que son estupendos.

Grade 6-7

Tick list:
✓ tenses: present, imperfect subjunctive, conditional
✓ superlative

To improve:
+ use subjunctive to say what you require
+ include more adjectives
+ use more conjunctions

Escribe un diálogo con un agente de viajes y menciona:

- *el tipo de lugar donde te gustaría ir;*
- *cuándo quieres ir;*
- *qué actividad quieres poder hacer;*
- *que te gustaría alquilar un coche.*

Escribe aproximadamente **90** *palabras en* **español**. *[16 marks]*

How to Get There

Cars, trains, planes — they'll get you to your destination and knowing about them will help you collect marks.

Cómo llegar a tu destino — How to get to your destination

el avión	aeroplane	el pasajero / viajero	passenger / traveller
el aeropuerto	airport	hacer transbordo	to change, transfer
el vuelo	flight	el billete (de ida / de ida y vuelta)	(single / return) ticket
el barco	boat	la estación (de autobuses / de trenes)	(bus / train) station
conducir	to drive	el andén	platform
la autopista	motorway	la red de ferrocarril	railway network
el tranvía	tram	la estación de servicio	service station
el viaje	journey	la gasolina (sin plomo)	(unleaded) petrol

Preferiría ir a España en avión porque me encuentro mal cuando voy en barco.

I would prefer to go to Spain by plane because I feel ill when I go by boat.

by car because it's cheaper — en coche porque es más barato

Fuimos a la playa a pie ya que está cerca de nuestro hotel.

We went to the beach on foot since it's near our hotel.

by taxi because our feet were hurting — en taxi porque nos dolían los pies

Viajaremos en autobús porque siempre nos perdemos cuando vamos en coche.

We will travel by bus because we always get lost when we go by car.

the airport workers are on strike — los empleados del aeropuerto están en huelga

El tren está retrasado — The train is delayed

¿A qué hora sale el tranvía?

At what time does the tram leave?

does the train arrive — llega el tren

Necesito reservar un coche. ¿Tengo que rellenar una ficha?

I need to reserve a car. Do I have to fill in a registration form?

have my driving licence with me — tener mi carnet de conducir conmigo

Coge el metro porque hay un atasco en la autopista.

Take the underground because there's a traffic jam on the motorway.

the train has been cancelled — el tren ha sido cancelado

No me importa viajar en autocar, pero prefiero ir en tren porque es más cómodo.

I don't mind travelling by coach, but I prefer to go by train because it's more comfortable.

by plane because it's faster — en avión porque es más rápido

You can use this transport vocab in other situations too...

Translate this text into **English**. *[9 marks]*

Mi ciudad tiene varios tipos de transporte. El metro, que abrió en 1924, es muy limpio y rápido. Además, existe una red de tranvías en la que se puede visitar la mayoría de los barrios de la ciudad. Desde el aeropuerto, es posible volar a todas las ciudades importantes de Europa y no está muy lejos del centro. Pronto, van a mejorar la red de autobuses, lo que será fenomenal.

What to Do

This is a good chance to practise using different tenses to talk about what you did, like doing, or will do.

Hay varias actividades... — There are various activities...

la excursión	*trip, excursion*	caminar	*to walk*
el mar	*the sea*	esquiar	*to ski*
bañarse	*to swim*	sacar / hacer fotos	*to take photos*
tomar el sol	*to sunbathe*	el parque de atracciones	*fairground*
broncearse	*to get a tan*	el parque temático	*theme park*
los deportes acuáticos	*water sports*	el recuerdo	*souvenir*

Question	**Simple Answer**	**Extended Answer**
¿Qué actividades hiciste durante tus vacaciones?	Fuimos a la playa — fue muy relajante.	Pasamos mucho tiempo en la playa porque hacía sol. Me bañé e tomé el sol con mis primos.
What activities did you do during your holiday?	*We went to the beach — it was very relaxing.*	*We spent a lot of time on the beach because it was sunny. I swam and sunbathed with my cousins.*

Grammar — la foto

<u>Watch out</u> for nouns that don't fit the masculine / feminine rule of ending with an '-o' or '-a' (p.116):

<u>la</u> fot<u>o</u>   *the photo*
<u>el</u> agua   *the water*

('Water' is actually a feminine noun, but it takes 'el' as its article because 'la agua' is too awkward to pronounce.)

Estamos de vacaciones — We're on holiday

Para mí, lo importante es encontrar un parque de atracciones.

For me, the important thing is to find a fairground. ← to buy souvenirs — comprar recuerdos
to go to a museum — visitar un museo

Nos gusta nada más que dar un paseo por las calles.

We like nothing more than to go for a stroll around the streets. ← *to try the region's typical food* — probar la comida típica de la región

Cuando estoy de vacaciones, suelo sacar muchas fotos.

When I'm on holiday, I usually take lots of photos. ← *go on various excursions* — hacer varias excursiones

Think about the sorts of activities you might want to say...

Tom and his teacher are discussing holiday activities. Look at Tom's response to this question:
¿Te gusta ir de vacaciones a lugares donde se puede practicar deportes acuáticos?

Depende del lugar. Cuando voy a un país donde hace calor, como España, tengo ganas de hacer deportes acuáticos. Voy a ir a **Noruega**[1] el año que viene. Practicaremos el piragüismo, pero pienso que el agua estará muy fría.

Grade 6~7

[1]Norway

Tick list:
✓ tenses: present, immediate future, proper future

To improve:
+ be more descriptive
+ more tenses
+ more topic vocab

*Now answer these questions in **Spanish**. Try to talk for **2** minutes. [10 marks]*

- *¿Qué hay en la foto?*
- *¿Cómo fueron tus últimas vacaciones?*
- *¿Cuáles serían tus vacaciones ideales?*

Practical Stuff

You might need to speak or write about practical stuff in your exam — and it'll be useful in real life too.

¡He perdido mi billete! — I've lost my ticket!

la comisaría	*police station*
el monedero	*purse*
la cartera	*wallet*
robar	*to steal / rob*
el garaje	*garage*
la gasolina	*petrol*
la avería	*breakdown*
el desvío	*diversion*
el cajero automático	*ATM / cashpoint*
confirmar	*to validate (ticket)*

Question

¿Usted ha perdido su billete?
Have you lost your ticket?

Simple Answer

Sí, lo perdí en el andén.
Yes, I lost it on the platform.

Extended Answer

No sé dónde está. Lo he buscado por todas partes pero no lo he encontrado.

I don't know where it is. I've looked for it everywhere but I haven't found it.

> When you use public transport in Spain, you often have to validate your ticket in a machine before you travel.

Grammar — the perfect tense

Say what you 'have done' using the perfect tense. To make the perfect tense, you need the right form of the verb 'haber' in the present tense for the 'have' bit and the past participle of the verb for the 'done' bit.

He confirmado mi billete.   ***I have validated** my ticket.*

El coche ha chocado contra un árbol.   *The car **has crashed** into a tree.*

For more information, have a look at p.144.

Tengo un problema — I have a problem

El coche de mi madre tiene una avería. ¿Hay un garaje por aquí?

My mother's car has broken down. Is there a garage around here?

→ *a service station* — una estación de servicio

Tengo que ir a la comisaría porque alguien me ha robado la cartera.

I have to go to the police station because someone has stolen my wallet.

← *I left my keys on the bus* — dejé mis llaves en el autobús

Cuando estaba de vacaciones en Francia tuve un accidente y me llevaron al hospital.

When I was on holiday in France I had an accident and they took me to hospital.

→ *I broke my arm* — me rompí el brazo

WRITING

Time to validate your one-way ticket to exam success...

Gael has written about a problem that occurred last weekend.

El fin de semana pasado estaba viajando a Liverpool en tren cuando **me di cuenta de que**[1] había dejado mi cartera en el andén. Cuando vino **el revisor**[2], le expliqué que no tenía mi billete porque lo había perdido. Yo estaba muy preocupado porque pensé que él no me creería, pero **sonrió**[3] y me dio mi cartera. Alguien lo había encontrado en la estación y **se lo había entregado**[4] al revisor. ¡Qué suerte!

(Grade 8-9)

[1] I noticed that   [3] he smiled
[2] the ticket inspector [4] he/she had handed it in

Tick list:
- ✓ tenses: preterite, imperfect, pluperfect, conditional
- ✓ good subject-specific vocab
- ✓ good use of pronouns

To improve:
+ use more varied conjunctions e.g. ya que, por eso

Escriba usted un artículo sobre los problemas que tuvo cuando estaba de vacaciones el año pasado:

Debe incluir los puntos siguientes:
- *dónde estaba usted y con quién*
- *qué le pasó*
- *cómo usted solucionó el problema*
- *sus planes de vacaciones para el año que viene.*

*Escriba aproximadamente **150** palabras en **español**.* [32 marks]

Listening Questions

To keep the holiday fun going a little while longer, we've got some questions for you to try. Don't worry if you get stuck on something — just flick back through the section and give them another crack.

1 Escucha a unos clientes que están llamando al Hotel Cristal. ¿De qué se tratan las llamadas? Elige **tres** frases de la tabla que resumen las llamadas de los dos clientes.

TRACK LISTENING 27

1 a

A	Reservar una habitación doble
B	Una vista
C	La dirección
D	La piscina
E	El restaurante

☐ ☐ ☐

1 b

F	Media pensión
G	Pensión completa
H	La seguridad
I	El aparcamiento
J	Reservar una habitación individual

☐ ☐ ☐

[6 marks]

2 Listen to this conversation between a travel agent and a customer, then answer the questions below in **English**.

TRACK LISTENING 28

2 a When do they want to go on holiday? .... *[1 mark]*

2 b Why does she choose a nearby country? ....

.... *[1 mark]*

2 c What does her husband like to do on holiday? .... *[1 mark]*

2 d Where does the travel agent recommend they go? .... *[1 mark]*

2 e How much would the holiday cost per person? .... *[1 mark]*

Speaking Question

Topic: Holidays

- Spend a couple of minutes looking at the photo and the prompts below it.

- You can make notes on a separate piece of paper.

Mira la foto y prepara las respuestas a los puntos siguientes:

- la descripción de la foto

- la importancia de sacar fotos cuando estás de vacaciones

- tus últimas vacaciones

- si te gustaría ir de vacaciones con tus amigos

- !

- Allow the student to develop his / her answers as much as possible.

- You need to ask the student the following questions **in order**:

  - Describe esta foto. ... ¿Algo más?

  - Para ti, ¿es importante sacar fotos cuando vas de vacaciones? ... ¿Por qué (no)?

  - ¿Qué hiciste la última vez que fuiste de vacaciones? ... ¿Algo más?

  - ¿Te gustaría ir de vacaciones con tus amigos? ... ¿Por qué (no)? / ¿Algo más?

  - ¿Prefieres visitar ciudades o ir a la playa cuando estás de vacaciones? ... ¿Por qué?

Reading Questions

1 Translate the following text into **English**.

> El viaje más estresante de mi vida fue el año pasado. Tuvimos que ir al aeropuerto en autobús, pero desafortunadamente, había un atasco en la autopista, así que llegamos bastante tarde. Luego nos dijeron que el vuelo había sido cancelado debido a la nieve y que tendríamos que esperar unas siete u ocho horas. ¡Qué horroroso!

....

....

....

....

....

....

[9 marks]

2 Read Andrea's review of her recent school trip and answer the questions in **English**.

> Mis compañeros de clase y yo acabamos de visitar el centro Campos Verdes y puedo decir que ha sido una experiencia inolvidable. Hemos hecho una multitud de actividades que no habríamos podido hacer de otro modo. Un día hicimos un paseo a caballo y casi me morí de risa porque mi caballo no quiso salir de la granja y se quedó inmóvil en medio del camino. Para mí, lo mejor de este tipo de vacaciones es que hay una gran variedad de activitidades y puedes elegir lo que quieres hacer. Cuando vas de vacaciones con tus amigos, suele haber por lo menos una pelea que tiene que ver con la ducha o con el ruido que una persona hace cuando los otros quieren dormirse. Esta vez, sorprendentemente, no hubo ni una disputa, los profesores no tuvieron que salir de su sala privada para atendernos, y todos siguen siendo amigos. ¡Ha sido un verdadero éxito!

2 a How did Andrea feel about her horse-riding experience?

.... *[1 mark]*

2 b What does Andrea think is the main advantage of an activity holiday?

.... *[1 mark]*

2 c Why might the teachers have been pleased with the students? Give **two** details.

.... *[2 marks]*

Writing Questions

1   Usted acaba de volver de vacaciones.
    Escriba usted un informe para otros turistas que quieren visitar el mismo lugar.

Debe incluir los puntos siguientes:

• una descripción del lugar

• lo que hizo durante sus vacaciones

• el transporte público en el lugar que visitó

• si recomendaría el lugar y por qué.

Justifique sus ideas y sus opiniones.
Escriba aproximadamente 150 palabras en **español**.

[32 marks]

2   Translate the following text into **Spanish**.

> My favourite country is Wales because there are lots of mountains and Welsh people are very nice. Another advantage is that you can visit some towns by train. I would love to go to Conwy in the future. However, the last time we went to Wales, it rained for the entire week!

....

....

....

....

....

....

[12 marks]

Revision Summary for Section Nine

Hopefully Section Nine's got you in a holiday mood. To help you have even more fun, here are some more questions. You know the score by now — have a look at the questions, tick off the ones you can do, and then sort out any problems by going back over the section.

Where to Go (p.91) ☑

1) How do you say...?
   a) Blake is from Scotland.
   b) Kevin is Welsh.
   c) They live in Germany.
   d) Marie and Élise are French. ☑

2) Translate into English: 'El año pasado fui a los Estados Unidos.' ☑

3) ¿Te gustaría viajar a la India? ☑

Accommodation (p.92) ☑

4) Jamila says: 'El verano que viene vamos a hacer un crucero por el mediterráneo. No sé si me va a gustar o no. Por un lado, habrá muchas instalaciones, como por ejemplo un bar y una discoteca. Sin embargo, tendremos poco tiempo para explorar los lugares que vamos a visitar.'
   What's the advantage of the cruise for Jamila? What's the disadvantage? ☑

5) How do you say 'I am going to go camping at the weekend'? ☑

6) Da dos ventajas de quedarse en un albergue juvenil. ☑

Getting Ready to Go (p.93) ☑

7) How do you say...?
   a) suitcase   b) leaflet   c) passport   d) guide ☑

8) Where could you go to book a holiday? Answer in Spanish. ☑

9) How would you say that you're looking for a hotel that has rooms available? ☑

How to Get There (p.94) ☑

10) Georgia says: 'Fuimos al sur de Francia en avión.' How did she get to the south of France? ☑

11) How would you ask for a return ticket to San Sebastián? ☑

12) On the aeroplane, someone says: 'Si estás de vacaciones y quieres alquilar un coche, necesitarás rellenar un formulario.' What are they telling you? ☑

What to Do (p.95) ☑

13) ¿Qué te gusta hacer cuando estás de vacaciones? Contesta con frases completas. ☑

14) Ivy likes to take photos and buy souvenirs for her friends. How would she say this in Spanish? ☑

15) 'Lo mejor de las vacaciones es broncearse en la playa.' Translate this into English. ☑

16) What's the Spanish for 'theme park'? ☑

17) ¿Cómo serían tus vacaciones ideales? ¿Adónde irías, y qué harías allí? ☑

Practical Stuff (p.96) ☑

18) You're on a Spanish road and you see a sign saying 'desvío'. What does it mean? ☑

19) How would you tell someone you've lost your keys in Spanish? ☑

20) Someone tells you: 'Usted tiene que confirmar su billete antes de viajar.' What must you do? ☑

School Subjects

School subjects — as if you don't get enough of that at school. However, it's important to learn them and to be able to say what you think about them.

Las asignaturas — School subjects

el español	*Spanish*	el dibujo	*art*
el alemán	*German*	el arte dramático	*drama*
el francés	*French*	la música	*music*
el inglés	*English*	las matemáticas	*maths*
las ciencias	*science*	las ciencias económicas	*economics*
la biología	*biology*	el comercio	*business studies*
la química	*chemistry*	la informática	*IT*
la física	*physics*	la cocina	*food technology*
la geografía	*geography*	los trabajos manuales	*handicrafts*
la historia	*history*	la gimnasia	*gymnastics*
la religión	*RE*	la educación física	*PE*

Mi asignatura preferida es... — My favourite subject is...

Question	**Simple Answer**	**Extended Answer**
¿Cuál es tu asignatura preferida?	Mi asignatura preferida es la música. Me encanta tocar la guitarra.	El español es mi asignatura preferida ya que es muy interesante. Es útil también porque espero ir a España el verano que viene.
What's your favourite subject?	*My favourite subject is music. I love to play the guitar.*	*Spanish is my favourite subject as it's very interesting. It's useful too because I hope to go to Spain next summer.*

Me encanta la historia. Es interesante aprender sobre el pasado.

I love history. It's interesting to learn about the past.

Nos gustan mucho las matemáticas. Es fascinante trabajar con números.

We really like maths. It's fascinating to work with numbers.

Miguel odia la química porque es tan difícil.

Miguel hates chemistry because it's so difficult.

I hate — Odio

boring — aburrido

useful — útil

José finds art awful — José encuentra el dibujo horrible

Subject yourself to learning all the asignaturas...

Gabriela has written about her school subjects in a chat room.

Generalmente, me gustan mis asignaturas. Me encantan las lenguas porque son divertidas, así que **opté por estudiar**[1] el francés y el inglés este **curso**[2]. Sin embargo, lo malo es que son difíciles. Por otro lado, me fastidia la profesora de ciencias porque es demasiado estricta. Pero a decir verdad, mi asignatura preferida es la educación física porque me gusta jugar al baloncesto.

Grade 6-7

Tick list:
✓ adjectives agree
✓ range of vocabulary and conjunctions

To improve:
+ use different tenses
+ more complex adjectives
+ extend opinions

Escribe tu propio comentario. Menciona:
- *qué asignaturas (no) te gustan, y por qué;*
- *qué asignaturas quieres estudiar el curso que viene, y por qué.*

*Escribe aproximadamente **150** palabras en **español**.*
Responde a los dos aspectos de la pregunta. [32 marks]

[1] I chose to study [2] school year

School Routine

Same old routine, day in, day out. At least routines are quite easy to talk about in the exam...

Mi rutina escolar — My school routine

el trimestre	*(school) term*
la agenda	*diary*
el horario	*timetable*
la clase	*lesson*
el recreo	*break*

> **Grammar** — telling the time
>
> If you're saying what time something is at, remember to put '<u>a</u>' first.
> **La hora de comer es <u>a la una</u>.** *Lunchtime is <u>at one o'clock</u>.*
> For more about time, see p.2.

Mi colegio empieza a las nueve, y a las nueve y cinco, el profesor pasa la lista.

My school starts at nine o'clock, and at five past nine, the teacher calls the register.

at twenty to nine — a las nueve menos veinte

we go to the assembly room — vamos al salón de actos

Tengo cinco clases por día, y cada clase dura cuarenta minutos. El día escolar termina a las tres y media.

I have five lessons a day, and each lesson lasts forty minutes. The school day finishes at half past three.

I return home at quarter past three. — Vuelvo a casa a las tres y cuarto.

¿Qué haces durante el recreo? — What do you do during break?

Durante el recreo, juego al fútbol con mis amigos, y a la hora de comer, vamos a la cantina para almorzar.

During break, I play football with my friends, and at lunchtime, we go to the canteen to eat lunch.

I chat — charlo

we sit outside and eat lunch — nos sentamos afuera y almorzamos

Prefiero pasar el recreo en la biblioteca porque mis amigos van al club de tenis, que a mí no me gusta.

I prefer to spend my break in the library because my friends go to tennis club, which I don't like.

go to gymnastics club — van al club de gimnasia

En mi mochila, pongo... — In my rucksack, I put...

el bolígrafo	*pen*	la regla	*ruler*	el cuaderno	*exercise book*
el lápiz	*pencil*	las tijeras	*scissors*	el libro	*book*

En mi mochila, hay un estuche.

In my rucksack, there's a pencil case.

Se me ha olvidado mi lápiz.

I have forgotten my pencil.

¿Me puedes prestar un boli por favor?

Can you lend me a pen please?

In Spanish, 'bolígrafo' (*pen*) is often shortened to 'boli'.

Make sure you can say what time you do things...

Juan y Marta hablan de su horario. Completa la tabla con las asignaturas en **español**. *[3 marks]*

día / hora	08.30 — 09.20	09.20 — 10.10	10.10 — 10.30	10.30 — 11.20
lunes	las matemáticas	1)	RECREO	el inglés
martes	las ciencias	el francés	RECREO	2)
miércoles	los trabajos manuales	el español	RECREO	3)

School Life

Now's your chance to talk about what your school's like and what it has and hasn't got.

¿A qué tipo de colegio asistes? — What type of school do you go to?

el instituto	*secondary school*	mixto	*mixed*	privado	*private*
la escuela primaria	*primary school*	religioso	*religious*	público	*state*

Mi instituto es un colegio mixto. Está a unos cinco kilómetros de mi casa.

My school is a mixed school. It's about five kilometres from my house.

→ *modern state* — público y moderno

→ *about 400* — unos cuatrocientos
950 — novecientos cincuenta

Hay quinientos alumnos en mi instituto y llevamos uniforme.

There are 500 students at my school and we wear a uniform.

we don't have to wear a uniform — no tenemos que llevar uniforme

Soy alumno/a aquí desde hace tres años. Me gusta este colegio y me llevo bien con los profesores.

I've been a student here for 3 years. I like this school and I get on well with the teachers.

the teachers are very nice — los profesores son muy simpáticos

¿Cómo es tu instituto? — What's your school like?

Grammar — el aula

'Aula' is <u>feminine</u>, but it uses '<u>el</u>' when it's <u>singular</u>. Any <u>adjectives</u> must be in the <u>feminine</u> form.

El aula es <u>estupenda</u>.
<u>The</u> classroom is <u>fantastic</u>.

las instalaciones	*facilities*	el taller	*workshop*
el aula (f)	*classroom*	el campo de deportes	*sports field*
la pizarra interactiva	*smart board*	el gimnasio	*gymnasium*
la sala de profesores	*staffroom*	los vestuarios	*changing rooms*

Mi colegio tiene un campo de deportes grande donde podemos jugar al hockey.

My school has a big sports field where we can play hockey.

a small gym where we can keep fit — un gimnasio pequeño donde podemos mantenernos en forma

En general, mi instituto es muy moderno. Encuentro las aulas maravillosas porque tienen pizarras interactivas.

In general, my school is very modern. I find the classrooms marvellous because they have smart boards.

quite old — bastante antiguo

horrible because the heating doesn't work well — horribles porque la calefacción no funciona bien

---

Use adjectives to make your answers interesting...

Read what Sofía has written about her school below. Then in the table, indicate the three sentences that are true by ticking the correct boxes. *[3 marks]*

¡Hola! Soy Sofía. Te escribo para hablarte de mi colegio. Está situado en Madrid a unos siete kilómetros de mi casa y hay ochocientos alumnos. Normalmente, mi padre me lleva en coche al colegio. Tengo suerte porque puedo coger el metro también — es muy eficaz si hay atascos en las carreteras. El día empieza a las ocho menos diez. Las clases duran unos cuarenta minutos y tengo un recreo de quince minutos. El descanso para comer empieza a la una y media y dura una hora y media. Generalmente las instalaciones en mi colegio son modernas, pero lo malo es el gimnasio. Es muy sucio. ¡Qué horror! ¿Cómo es tu colegio? ¡Adiós!

1.	Sofía usually takes the underground to school.	
2.	Sofía is positive about the underground.	
3.	Sofía is negative about the underground.	
4.	The facilities are old.	
5.	The facilities are modern.	
6.	Sofía dislikes the gym.	

School Pressures

A chance to vent your frustrations now — should be refreshing after all this stressful revision...

Las reglas — The rules

(no) hay que...	*you (don't) have to...*
(no) tienes que...	*you (don't) have to...*
(no) se debe...	*you must (not)...*
(no) es obligatorio...	*it's (not) compulsory...*
(no) deberías...	*you shouldn't...*

No deberías comer chicle ni beber bebidas gaseosas.	*You shouldn't eat chewing gum nor drink fizzy drinks.*
Hay que levantar la mano antes de hablar.	*You have to raise your hand before speaking.*

Estoy muy estresado/a por... — I'm really stressed about...

estresante	*stressful*	el éxito	*success*	suspender	*to fail*	el apoyo	*support*
la presión	*pressure*	aprobar	*to pass*	repasar	*to revise*	apoyar	*to support*

La vida escolar es estresante. Hay mucha presión y tengo muchos deberes. Afortunadamente, los profesores apoyan a los alumnos estresados.

School life is stressful. There's a lot of pressure and I have a lot of homework. Luckily, the teachers support stressed students.

I'm afraid of failing my exams — tengo miedo de suspender mis exámenes

Si no saco sobresalientes, no podré ir a la universidad.

If I don't get outstanding marks, I won't be able to go to university.

get good marks — saco buenas notas

pass this exam — apruebo este examen

El acoso (escolar) — (School) bullying

El acoso es un problema muy grave en mi colegio.

Bullying is a serious problem in my school.

Bullying doesn't happen much — La intimidación no ocurre mucho

El mal comportamiento arruina las clases.

Bad behaviour ruins lessons.

is a distraction — es una distracción

Practise using as much subject-specific vocab as possible...

Have a look at this photo question. Use the example to give you some inspiration.

¿Hay mucha violencia en los institutos hoy en día?

En mi instituto, la violencia no es un problema. Si la conducta de un alumno es peligrosa, el director **castigará**[1] a ese alumno. Pero a mi modo de ver, muchos institutos tienen problemas con peleas y **falta de respeto**[2]. Sería difícil estudiar en esos colegios.

Grade 6-7

*Now answer these questions — talk for about **3** minutes.*

- *¿Qué hay en la foto?*
- *¿Cómo era la vida escolar en tu escuela primaria?*
- *¿Hay mucha violencia en los institutos hoy en día?*
  [15 marks]

[1]will punish [2]lack of respect

Tick list:
✓ tenses: present, future, conditional
✓ varied vocab

To improve:
+ more opinion phrases with explanations
+ use past tenses, e.g. preterite and imperfect

After you've answered the three questions you've prepared, your teacher will ask you two more questions that you haven't seen. See p.159 for more tips for doing well in the speaking exam.

School Events

Every year, schools up and down the country hold exciting events, like trips and... err... parents' evenings.

¿Qué pasa en tu colegio? — What's happening at your school?

participar en	to participate in	la vuelta al colegio	first day back at school
la excursión (del colegio)	(school) trip	el autobús escolar	school bus
el intercambio	exchange	el grupo escolar	school group
(al) extranjero	abroad	la reunión de padres	parents' evening

Question

¿Qué pasa en tu colegio esta semana?

What's happening at your school this week?

Simple Answer

Esta semana hay una excursión del colegio al campo.

This week there's a school trip to the countryside.

Extended Answer

Esta semana hay reunión de padres. Mis padres hablarán con mis profesores sobre mi rendimiento escolar.

This week it's parents' evening. My parents will talk to my teachers about my academic achievement.

Grammar — saying what's happening

In Spanish, you can use the normal present tense to say things like 'I am doing' as well as 'I do'.

You only have to use the present continuous form (see p.150) when you really want to emphasise that something's happening right now.

Participo en un intercambio.
I'm participating in an exchange (soon).

Estoy participando en un intercambio.
I'm participating in an exchange (right now).

El año pasado hice un intercambio al extranjero. Me quedé con Miguel durante una semana y ahora somos amigos por correspondencia.

Last year I did an exchange trip abroad. I stayed with Miguel for a week and now we're penfriends.

I participated in — participé en

Pronto haremos una excursión a un museo. Ya que somos un grupo escolar, nos darán una visita guiada.

Soon we will go on a trip to a museum. As we're a school group, they'll give us a guided tour.

a discount — un descuento

A veces hay ventas de pasteles durante el recreo. Damos todo el dinero a organizaciones caritativas.

Sometimes there are cake sales during break time. We give all the money to charities.

there is a fancy dress day — hay un día de disfraces

Todos los años el instituto realiza una entrega de premios. Los profesores dan premios a los alumnos que han sacado las mejores notas.

Every year the school holds a prize-giving ceremony. The teachers give prizes to the students who have got the best marks.

who have tried the hardest — que se han esforzado más

Prepare for any event-uality with this question...

Yann ha escrito una carta sobre un evento en su colegio.

El 3 de septiembre, mi instituto **cumplirá setenta años**[1] y habrá una gran fiesta para toda la comunidad. Cualquier persona que asistía al instituto podrá venir para celebrar con nosotros. Mis amigos van a hacer un pastel, y yo voy a ayudar con las visitas guiadas. Lo mejor es que han cancelado las clases ese día. ¡Qué suerte!

Grade 6-7

[1] will be seventy years old

Tick list:
✓ tenses: present, imperfect, perfect and future
✓ 'lo' + adjective
✓ good use of exclamation

To improve:
+ use more varied conjunctions
+ add more opinions

Ahora escribe una carta sobre una excursión del colegio reciente. Debes incluir los puntos siguientes:

• lo que hiciste
• lo bueno de las excursiones
• alguna desventaja de las excursiones
• una excursión del colegio que te gustaría hacer

Escribe aproximadamente **90** palabras en **español**. [16 marks]

Education Post-16

It might not be something you've thought a lot about, but your future plans could come up in the exam. Learn this page and it might even give you some ideas...

Cuando tenga 16 años... — When I'm 16...

el/la aprendiz/a	*apprentice*	la academia	*academy, school post-16*
la experiencia laboral	*work experience*		*(for certain careers)*
la práctica	*work placement*	las perspectivas	*employment*
hacer el bachillerato	*to do A-levels*	laborales	*prospects*

Quiero seguir mis estudios y hacer el bachillerato porque espero estudiar Derecho en la universidad.

I want to continue my studies and do my A-levels because I hope to study law at university.

to do a work placement — hacer una práctica

Para mejorar nuestras perspectivas laborales, el profesor recomienda que busquemos experiencia laboral.

In order to improve our employment prospects, the teacher recommends that we look for work experience.

to become a plumber's apprentice — hacerme aprendiz/a de fontanero

to get a degree — conseguir un título

You often need to use the subjunctive when someone wants someone else to do something. See p.153-154

Después del bachillerato... — After A-levels...

el año libre / sabático	*gap year*	la carrera	*career, profession*
la formación (profesional)	*vocational training*	calificado	*competent, skilled*

Question	Simple Answer	Extended Answer
¿Qué quieres hacer después de terminar el bachillerato? *What do you want to do after you finish your A-levels?*	Después de terminar el bachillerato, quiero empezar a trabajar. *After finishing my A-levels, I want to start working.*	Voy a dedicarme a mis estudios porque quiero ser traductor/a. Si quiero ser traductor/a calificado/a, tendré que estudiar mucho. *I'm going to focus on my studies because I want to be a translator. If I want to be a competent translator, I'll have to study a lot.*

Quisiera tomarme un año sabático, luego me gustaría ir a la universidad porque quiero hacer carrera en medicina.

I would like to take a gap year, then I would like to go to university because I want to have a career in medicine.

Me gustaría ser electricista, pero primero, necesito formación profesional.

I would like to be an electrician, but first, I need vocational training.

Grammar — conditional

To talk about something that could, should or would happen, use the conditional tense (p.146).

Me gustaría estudiar música.
I would like to study music.

Remember that 'quisiera' can be used to say 'I would like' too (p.146).

Show that you can use the future and conditional tenses...

Translate this text into **Spanish**. *[12 marks]*

When I was young, I thought I would like to be a teacher. My parents are teachers and although they find the work interesting, my father says that it is quite stressful. Now I have decided that I'm going to go to an academy to study photography. I would love to take photos of weddings!

Career Choices and Ambitions

All this revising is hard work and now you've got another job to do — learn about careers.

Los empleos — Jobs

el/la empleado/a	*employee*	el/la fontanero/a	*plumber*	
el/la abogado/a	*lawyer*	el/la ingeniero/a	*engineer*	
el/la arquitecto/a	*architect*	el/la mecánico/a	*mechanic*	
el/la bombero/a	*firefighter*	el/la médico/a	*doctor*	
el/la cocinero/a	*chef*	el/la oficial de policía	*police officer*	
el/la constructor/a	*builder*	el/la periodista	*journalist*	
el/la contable	*accountant*	el/la veterinario/a	*vet*	
el/la enfermero/a	*nurse*	estar en paro	*to be unemployed*	

Grammar — I'm a...

When talking about jobs, <u>usually</u> you <u>don't</u> need the article '<u>un(a)</u>' (p.117).

Quiero ser funcionario/a
***I want to be a** civil servant*.

You <u>do</u> though if you use an <u>adjective</u>.

Soy <u>un(a)</u> buen(a) técnico/a.
I'm <u>a good</u> technician.

a tiempo completo	*full-time*	ganar	*to earn*
a tiempo parcial	*part-time*	el sueldo	*salary*

For more jobs, have a look at the vocab list starting on p.208.

Mi empleo ideal sería periodista. Trabajaría en una oficina y escribiría artículos interesantes.	*My ideal job would be a journalist. I would work in an office and I would write interesting articles.*
Para mí, es importante tener un empleo desafiante.	*For me, it's important to have a challenging job.*
Mi madre es enfermera. Es un trabajo difícil porque tiene mucha responsabilidad, pero a ella le encanta ayudar a la gente.	*My mother is a nurse. It's a difficult job because she has a lot of responsibility, but she loves helping people.*

full time — a tiempo completo

stimulating — estimulante
rewarding — gratificante
varied — variado

there's a lot of pressure — hay mucha presión

Tengo un empleo a tiempo parcial — I have a part-time job

Soy dependiente en una tienda de ropa. Lo mejor es charlar con los clientes.	*I'm a shop assistant in a clothes shop. The best thing is chatting with customers.*
No tengo empleo a tiempo parcial, pero a veces cuido a mi hermana y recibo paga.	*I don't have a part-time job, but sometimes I look after my sister and I receive pocket money.*
Trabajo en una peluquería los sábados. Me gusta el empleo pero no gano mucho.	*I work in a hairdresser's on Saturdays. I like the job, but I don't earn a lot.*

waiter/waitress in a restaurant — camarero/a en un restaurante

that there are discounts for employees — que hay descuentos para los empleados

I hope to find another job and earn more money — espero conseguir otro empleo y ganar más dinero

Think about the positives and negatives of jobs...

Translate this text into **English**. *[9 marks]*

— Cuando yo tenía quince años, era difícil conseguir un trabajo — dijo mi madre.

— Sí, pero mucho ha cambiado en los últimos años — le respondí. — Quiero ser abogada. Ganan un buen sueldo y me gustaría ayudar a la gente. ¡El trabajo sería tan variado!

Languages for the Future

There's life beyond GCSE — your Spanish might help you make friends, or even land you a job.

¿Hablas otro idioma? — Do you speak another language?

la lengua / el idioma	language
conocer a alguien	to get to know someone
viajar por el mundo	to travel the world
expresarse	to express yourself
comunicarse	to communicate
traducir	to translate
pronunciar	to pronounce
el/la auxiliar de lengua	foreign language assistant
el laboratorio de idiomas	language lab

Grammar — articles + languages

When a language is the subject of the sentence, you need to use the definite article with it.

El español es fácil. *Spanish is easy.*

However, when you use a language as the object of the verbs 'saber', 'aprender' or 'hablar', you don't need to use the article.

Aprendo árabe. *I'm learning Arabic.*

Have a look at p.129-130 for a reminder about subjects and objects.

Quiero trabajar por una empresa internacional, así que los idiomas son importantes para mí.

I want to work for an international company, so languages are important to me.

En mi instituto tenemos auxiliares de lenguas. Me parece un trabajo muy divertido. Me gustaría hacer algo parecido en el futuro.

In my school we have foreign language assistants. It seems like a very fun job. I'd like to do something similar in the future.

Voy a viajar por Asia después del bachillerato, así que he aprendido algunas frases útiles para poder comprar cosas y pedir comida.

I'm going to travel around Asia after my A-Levels, so I have learnt some useful phrases so I can buy things and order food.

Aprender una lengua extranjera — To learn a foreign language

Question

¿Es importante aprender otro idioma?
Is it important to learn another language?

Simple Answer

Sí, porque no todo el mundo habla inglés.
Yes, because not everyone speaks English.

Extended Answer

Sí, es importante que aprendamos idiomas extranjeros porque vivimos en una sociedad multicultural.
Yes, it's important that we learn foreign languages because we live in a multicultural society.

En mi opinión es una pérdida de tiempo aprender una lengua extranjera. Si necesitas comunicarte en el extranjero, hay aplicaciones que te pueden ayudar.
In my opinion it's a waste of time to learn a foreign language. If you need to communicate abroad, there are apps that can help you.

Articles may be small, but it's important to get them right...

Read what David says about the languages he speaks and then answer the questions in **English**.

Me llamo David y soy **azafato**[1]. Para nosotros es esencial saber por lo menos tres lenguas para poder comunicarnos con los clientes. Aprendí inglés y francés en el instituto, y pronto asistiré a **clases nocturnas**[2] de alemán en una escuela donde hay laboratorios de idiomas. Creo que la parte más difícil para mí será la pronunciación.

[1]flight attendant [2]evening classes

1. Give one requirement of David's job. [1]
2. What will he do in the near future? [1]
3. What will the venue be like? [1]
4. What does he think will be challenging? [1]

Applying for Jobs

Trawling through job adverts isn't exactly entertaining — but actually getting a job's a pretty good reward.

Solicitar un puesto de trabajo — To apply for a job

el anuncio de trabajo	*job advertisement*	las condiciones de empleo	*terms of employment*
la vacante	*vacancy*	las posibilidades de promoción	*promotion prospects*
la carta de solicitud	*application letter*	el sueldo	*salary*
la solicitud	*application form*	bien pagado	*well-paid*
adjuntar	*to attach*	por hora	*per hour*
la entrevista	*interview*	el/la jefe	*boss*

Question

¿Por qué decidió usted solicitar este puesto de trabajo?

Why did you decide to apply for this job?

Simple Answer

Cuando leí el anuncio de trabajo, me interesó mucho.

When I read the job advertisement, it really interested me.

Extended Answer

Es un trabajo bien pagado y las condiciones de empleo me parecen justas. Además, hay buenas posibilidades de promoción.

It's a well-paid job and the terms of employment seem fair to me. Moreover, there are good promotion prospects.

Mi amigo me dijo que había vacantes en su empresa, así que decidí rellenar el formulario y mandarles mi currículum.

My friend told me that there were vacancies in his company, so I decided to fill in the form and send them my CV.

La semana que viene tengo una entrevista de trabajo. Tendré que prepararme bien, porque conoceré al director.

Next week I have a job interview. I'll have to prepare myself well because I'll meet the manager.

Cuando buscas un trabajo, es una buena idea pensar en las condiciones de empleo y el sueldo.

When you're looking for a job, it's a good idea to think about the terms of employment and the salary.

to write an application letter — escribir una carta de solicitud

it's a very well-paid job — es un trabajo muy bien pagado

the skills you have — las habilidades que tienes

Learn this page and get promoted to high-flying student...

Read this role-play. Blanca is having an interview with Carlos, a careers adviser.

Carlos:	¿Qué tipo de trabajo le gustaría hacer?
Blanca:	No sé exactamente. Ese es el problema que tengo.
Carlos:	¿Qué habilidades tiene usted?
Blanca:	Aprendo rápidamente y me gusta trabajar con los ordenadores.
Carlos:	¿Tiene usted alguna experiencia laboral?
Blanca:	Sí, hice una práctica en una oficina hace un año.
Carlos:	¿Ha visto este anuncio? Lo acabamos de recibir. Buscan individuos que tengan buenas **habilidades informáticas**[1] y que sepan trabajar en grupo. ¿Le interesa?
Blanca:	Sí. A lo mejor les mandaré un correo. Gracias.

Grade 8-9

[1]computer skills

Tick list:
✓ good variety of tenses
✓ correct use of 'usted'

To improve:
+ try to use more subject-specific vocab

Usted está hablando con el director de su instituto.
- trabajo ideal — opinión
- experiencia laboral
- !
- ? ser profesor — opinión
- ? consejos para encontrar un trabajo

*Now prepare the role-play on the right. You must address the head teacher as 'usted', and try to speak for about **two** minutes. [15 marks]*

Listening Questions

You'll soon be ready to deal with whatever the examiners throw at you. Don't forget there's a practice exam at the back of the book, so you can try questions on different topics under time pressure.

---

1 Nuria, Syed and Lucía are on the school council and are discussing the biggest problems in their school.

(TRACK LISTENING 30)

Listen to their points of view and answer the questions in **English**.

1 a What does Nuria suggest to help the victims of bullying?

.... *[1 mark]*

1 b Give an example of a rule that Syed finds unfair.

.... *[1 mark]*

1 c How much homework does Lucía think is reasonable?

.... *[1 mark]*

1 d Give **two** things that Lucía says would happen if students had less homework.

1. ....

2. .... *[2 marks]*

---

2 Kyra, Rafael and Laura are exchanging ideas about possible careers. For each person, write down a positive and a negative aspect of the job they talk about.

(TRACK LISTENING 31)

		Positive	Negative
2 a	Kyra		
2 b	Rafael		
2 c	Laura		

[6 marks]

Speaking Question

Candidate's Role

Topic: What school is like

- Your teacher will play the role of your Colombian friend. They will speak first.

- You should use *tú* to address your friend.

- – ! – means you will have to respond to something you have not prepared.

- – ? – means you will have to ask your friend a question.

> Estás en la cantina de tu colegio. Hablas con tu amigo/a colombiano/a.
>
> - Colegio — descripción
>
> - Uniforme — opinión
>
> - !
>
> - ? Reglas — opinión
>
> - ? Planes para el año que viene

Teacher's Role

Topic: What school is like

- You begin the role play using the introductory text below.

- You should address the candidate as *tú*.

- You must ask the questions below exactly as they are written.

- You may repeat the questions, but no more than twice.

> Introductory text: *Estás en la cantina de tu colegio. Hablas con tu amigo/a colombiano/a.*
>
> - ¿Cómo es tu colegio?
>
> - ¿Te gusta llevar uniforme?
>
> - ! Háblame de lo que hiciste durante el recreo ayer.
>
> - ? Allow the candidate to ask you about your opinion of school rules.
>
> - ? Allow the candidate to ask you about your plans for next year.

Reading Questions

1 Translate the following passage into **English**.

> Yo no tuve la oportunidad de aprender ningún idioma en el instituto. Cuando empecé a trabajar en un restaurante de comida italiana, el cocinero me enseñó un poco de su idioma. Voy a buscar un curso de italiano porque sería muy interesante. Creo que es esencial que todos aprendan por lo menos un idioma extranjero.

....

....

....

....

....

....

[9 marks]

2 Lee este anuncio y contesta a las preguntas en **español**.

> **¿Eres trabajador/a? ¿Quieres trabajar desde casa?**
> **¿Quieres trabajar a tiempo parcial cuando quieras?**
>
> Buscamos a una persona para ayudarnos este verano. Somos una agencia de viajes bastante nueva y necesitamos ayuda con nuestro sitio web.
>
> ¡Puedes hacer el trabajo con tu ordenador en casa mientras te pagamos!
>
> Si tienes un ordenador, tiempo y experiencia en cuanto a la creación de sitios web, ponte en contacto ahora. Llámanos al 96 578 0989 o mándanos un email a servicio@gmail.es.

2 a ¿Qué tipo de empresa es?

.... *[1 mark]*

2 b ¿Dónde trabajará el/la empleado/a?

.... *[1 mark]*

2 c ¿Qué necesitas para hacer el trabajo? Menciona **dos** detalles.

1. ....

2. .... *[2 marks]*

Writing Questions

1   Jorge es un chico español que va a asistir a tu instituto el año que viene.
Escribe un correo electrónico a Jorge para contarle sobre tu instituto.

Debes incluir los puntos siguientes:

* una descripción de tu instituto

* tus opiniones del instituto cuando empezaste

* si crees que es importante aprender lenguas extranjeras

* el tipo de trabajo que te gustaría hacer en el futuro.

Escribe aproximadamente **90** palabras **en español**.   *[16 marks]*

2   Translate the following passage into **Spanish**.

> After my exams, I would like to be an apprentice. Last summer, I had two weeks of work experience in a small company. It was really interesting and I learned a lot. I don't want to do A-levels because exams are very stressful for me and I don't like doing homework.

....

....

....

....

....

....

[12 marks]

Revision Summary for Section Ten

This is your chance to go back over school and education and see what's what. Take your time when you're going through this checklist and be honest with yourself about what you found easy and what you could do with working on a bit more.

School Subjects (p.102) ☑

1) Write down the names of these subjects in Spanish: a) chemistry   b) RE   c) maths   ☑
2) ¿Cuál es la asignatura que más te gusta? ¿Por qué?   ☑

School Routine (p.103) ☑

3) Escribe tres frases sobre tu rutina escolar.   ☑
4) ¿Qué haces normalmente durante el recreo?   ☑

School Life (p.104) ☑

5) What are these types of school in English?
   a) una escuela primaria   b) un colegio religioso   c) un colegio público   ☑
6) ¿Qué hay en tu instituto? Contesta en español, con frases completas.   ☑

School Pressures (p.105) ☑

7) Escribe tres reglas que hay en tu colegio.   ☑
8) ¿Te preocupas mucho por los exámenes?   ☑

School Events (p.106) ☑

9) How do you say these events in English?   a) la vuelta al colegio   b) la reunión de padres   ☑
10) ¿Adónde te gustaría ir con tu clase?   ☑

Education Post-16 (p.107) ☑

11) ¿Qué quieres hacer después de los exámenes?   ☑
12) How do you say 'a gap year' in Spanish?   ☑

Career Choices and Ambitions (p.108) ☑

13) While in Peru, someone asks: '¿Tienes un trabajo a tiempo parcial?' What do they want to know?   ☑
14) ¿Qué tipo de trabajo te gustaría hacer en el futuro? ¿Por qué?   ☑

Languages for the Future (p.109) ☑

15) You meet someone who says: 'Soy auxiliar de lengua.' What do they do?   ☑
16) ¿Es importante aprender una lengua extranjera? Contesta en español, con frases completas.   ☑

Applying for Jobs (p.110) ☑

17) Eduardo says: 'He solicitado un puesto en una compañía. Tuve que escribir una carta
    de solicitud al jefe. Mañana tengo que ir a una entrevista.' Translate this into English.   ☑
18) You're in Spain and you see a job advert. It mentions 'el sueldo'. What is this in English?   ☑

Nouns	**Words for People and Objects**

Nouns are like the building blocks of a language — it's really important to know how to use them.

Every Spanish noun is masculine or feminine

When you learn a new noun, learn its gender too.

1) Whether a word is masculine, feminine or plural affects lots of things.

2) All 'the' and 'a' words change depending on the word's gender, and so do any <u>adjectives</u> which describe the noun.

> el árbol alto (m.)   *the tall tree*
> la casa alta (f.)   *the tall house*

These rules help you guess what gender a word is

1) If you see a word with '<u>el</u>' or '<u>un</u>' before it, it's usually <u>masculine</u>.

2) '<u>La</u>' or '<u>una</u>' in front of a word means it's <u>feminine</u>.

3) If you don't have these clues, there are <u>other tricks</u> you can use to help you guess.

MASCULINE	Most nouns that end in: -o -l -n -r -s -ta -aje	AND	Male people, days, months, languages, seas, rivers, oceans and mountains.
FEMININE	Most nouns that end in: -a -ción -sión -tad -tud -dad -umbre	AND	Female people, letters of the alphabet.

4) You <u>can't tell</u> whether a noun ending in '<u>e</u>' or '<u>ista</u>' is masculine or feminine — you have to learn them.

el coche *the car*	la gente *the people*	el turista *the tourist (male)*	la turista *the tourist (female)*

These are some of the exceptions to the rules. You'll just need to learn these ones off by heart.

el día	*day*	la foto	*photo*
el problema	*problem*	la moto	*motorbike*
el mapa	*map*	la mano	*hand*

Making nouns plural

1) Some nouns in Spanish end in a <u>vowel</u>. To make them <u>plural</u>, just add '<u>s</u>' — '<u>una cama</u>' (*one bed*) becomes '<u>dos camas</u>' (*two beds*).

2) There are some <u>exceptions</u> to these rules though:

Type of noun	To make it plural...	Example
ends in a consonant except 'z'	add 'es'	una flor *one flower* ⟹ dos flores *two flowers*
ends in 'z'	drop the 'z' and add 'ces'	un lápiz *one pencil* ⟹ dos lápices *two pencils*
days ending in 's'	make the article plural but keep the noun the same	el viernes *Friday* ⟹ los viernes *Fridays*
family surnames		Los Simpson *The Simpsons*

Sometimes you need to add or remove an accent in the plural to avoid changing the pronunciation of the word. Here are a couple of common examples.

> un inglés *one English person* ⟹ dos ingleses *two English people*
> un joven *one young man* ⟹ dos jóvenes *two young men*

Ignore genders at your peril...

Write 'el' or 'la' for each of these words. Then write each one in the plural form with 'los' or 'las'.

1. sombrero	**3.** tradición	**5.** porcentaje	**7.** tensión	**9.** ciudad
2. problema	**4.** viernes	**6.** francés	**8.** dificultad	**10.** mapa

'The', 'A', 'Some' and Other Little Words

In Spanish, 'the' and 'a' change depending on the gender of the noun and whether it's singular or plural.

El, la, los, las — the

'El', 'la', 'los' and 'las' are definite articles.

	Masculine	Feminine
singular	el	la
plural	los	las

1) The word for 'the' changes depending on the gender of the noun, and whether it's singular or plural.

2) Use 'el' before feminine nouns which start with a stressed 'a'.

> El agua está fría.   *The water is cold.*

3) Sometimes you need a definite article in Spanish where you wouldn't use one in English...

> a) with nouns used in a general sense: No me gusta el café. *I don't like coffee.*
> b) in front of the days of the week and times: los lunes a las seis *Mondays at six o'clock*
> c) in front of weights and measurements: dos euros el kilo *two euros a kilo*
> d) when you use a person's title: ¿Cómo está el señor Gómez? *How is Mr Gómez?*

4) There's a neuter article 'lo' for things that aren't masculine or feminine.

When you use 'lo' in front of an adjective, the adjective has to be in the masculine form — see p.118.

> lo mejor / peor / aburrido es que...   *the best / worst / boring thing is that...*

Un, una, unos, unas — a and some

'Un', 'una', 'unos' and 'unas' are indefinite articles.

1) 'Un' and 'una' mean 'a'.

2) 'Un' is used for masculine words and 'una' is used for feminine words.

> un gato   *a cat*
> una casa   *a house*

3) When you make 'un' or 'una' plural, they become 'unos' and 'unas' — they mean 'some' or 'a few'.

> unos gatos   *some cats*
> unas casas   *some houses*

4) Watch out, though — 'a' is left out...

> a) ...after the verb 'ser' when talking about someone's occupation or nationality: Soy estudiante. *I'm a student.*
> b) ...after a negative verb: No tengo perro. *I haven't got a dog.*

Any, another, each, all

These are known as indefinite adjectives. See p.118-120 for more adjectives.

1) There's no special word for 'any' in Spanish.

> ¿Tienes manzanas?   *Have you got any apples?*

2) Use 'otro' or 'otra' for 'another'.

> Lo haré otro día.   *I'll do it another day.*

You don't need to write 'un' or 'una' before 'otro/a'.

3) 'Cada' means 'each'. It's the same for masculine and feminine nouns.

> Cada otoño voy a Gales.   *Each autumn I go to Wales.*

4) 'Todo/a/os/as' means 'all'.

> Compré todos los libros en la tienda.   *I bought all the books in the shop.*

Check you know when to use each of the articles on this page...

Translate these sentences into **Spanish**.

1. I like chocolate.
2. I don't have any water.
3. She is a teacher.
4. He wants some potatoes.
5. I want to speak to Mrs López.
6. Each person has two dogs.

| Adjectives | # Words to Describe Things |

Jazz up your work with some flashy describing words — and collect more marks while you're at it.

Adjectives describe things — learn these common ones

grande	*big*	viejo/a	*old*	interesante	*interesting*
pequeño/a	*small*	joven	*young*	simpático	*kind*
alto/a	*tall / high*	guapo/a	*good-looking*	aburrido	*boring*
bajo/a	*short / low*	feliz	*happy*	malo/a	*bad*
largo/a	*long*	triste	*sad*	nuevo/a	*new*
gordo/a	*fat*	fácil	*easy*	rápido/a	*fast*
delgado/a	*slim*	difícil	*difficult*	lento/a	*slow*

When you look up an adjective in the dictionary, it'll be in the masculine singular form.

Adjectives need to agree with the noun

1) Adjectives have to <u>agree</u> with the <u>noun</u> they refer to, <u>even if they aren't right next to it</u>.

2) This means the <u>adjective changes</u> depending on the <u>gender</u> of the <u>noun</u> and whether it's <u>singular</u> or <u>plural</u>.

3) Adjectives that end in '<u>o</u>' in the <u>masculine singular</u> form change the '<u>o</u>' to '<u>a</u>' in the <u>feminine</u> form. When <u>plural</u>, the adjective ends in '<u>os</u>' (masculine) or '<u>as</u>' (feminine).

Masculine singular	Feminine singular	Masculine plural	Feminine plural
el chico pequeño	la chica pequeña	los chicos pequeños	las chicas pequeñas
the small boy	*the small girl*	*the small boys*	*the small girls*

4) Adjectives which <u>don't</u> end in '<u>o</u>' or '<u>a</u>' <u>don't change</u> in the singular. If the noun is <u>plural</u>, add '<u>s</u>' if it ends in a vowel, or '<u>es</u>' if it ends in a consonant.

Masculine singular	Feminine singular	Masculine plural	Feminine plural
el hombre triste	la mujer triste	los hombres tristes	las mujeres tristes
the sad man	*the sad woman*	*the sad men*	*the sad women*

If the adjective ends in 'z', remove the 'z' and add 'ces'. See p.116 for nouns that work in a similar way.

Some adjectives don't change to agree

Some adjectives <u>don't change at all</u>.

Most adjectives that don't change are colours.

beis	*beige*	rosa	*pink*
lila	*lilac*	turquesa	*turquoise*
naranja	*orange*	violeta	*violet*

tres coches naranja	*three orange cars*
siete trenes rosa	*seven pink trains*

You'll lose marks if your adjectives don't agree...

Translate these phrases, making sure the adjectives agree with the nouns (where they need to).

1. the happy dog
2. seven red skirts
3. the blue cars
4. two short women
5. five small cats
6. nine violet chairs
7. four beige books
8. one sad person

Words to Describe Things

Once you know loads of adjectives, you need to know where to put them.

Most adjectives go after the word they describe

1) In Spanish, <u>most adjectives go after the noun</u> (the word they describe).

2) But that's not always the case — some adjectives always go <u>in front of the noun</u> they're describing, like these ones:

> Es un vestido horrible.
> *It's a horrible dress.*

mucho/a	*a lot of*	tanto/a	*so much*	primero/a, segundo/a...	*first, second...*
muchos/as	*lots of*	tantos/as	*so many*	próximo/a	*next*
otro/a	*another*	poco/a	*little*	último/a	*last*
otros/as	*other*	pocos/as	*few*		
alguno/a	*some*	cada	*each*		

'Otro', 'cada' and 'alguno/a' are all indefinite adjectives.
For more on indefinite adjectives, see p.117.

Some adjectives change before masculine nouns...

Some adjectives <u>lose</u> the final 'o' when they go in front of a <u>masculine noun</u>.

bueno/a	*good*	tercero/a	*third*	ninguno/a	*none*
primero/a	*first*	alguno/a	*some*	malo/a	*bad*

un buen día	*a good day*	el tercer libro	*the third book*	algún día	*some day*

① 'Alguno' and 'ninguno' <u>drop</u> the final 'o' and <u>add</u> an accent.	No hay ningún taxi libre.	*There's no taxi free.*
② 'Grande' is the only adjective that <u>drops</u> 'de' in front of both <u>masculine and feminine</u> words.	una gran señora	*a great lady*

...and some change their meaning depending on their position

Adjective	Before the noun...	After the noun...
grande	un gran hombre *a great man*	un hombre grande *a big man*
mismo	el mismo día *the same day*	yo mismo *I myself*
nuevo	un nuevo coche *a new (to owner) car*	un coche nuevo *a brand new car*
viejo	un viejo amigo *a long-standing friend*	un amigo viejo *an old (elderly) friend*

Don't let those adjectives trip you up — learn where they go...

Translate these phrases and sentences into **Spanish**, making sure the adjectives go in the right place.

1. There are lots of cats.
2. the first day
3. the same dog
4. the other pupils
5. Some people think that...
6. He's a great teacher.

Words to Describe Things

Adjectives are also really useful for saying what's yours and for pointing things out.

Mi, tu, nuestro — my, your, our

'Mi', 'tu', 'nuestro' etc. are possessive adjectives.

Words like '<u>my</u>' and '<u>your</u>' in Spanish have to <u>agree</u> with the <u>noun</u> they're describing — <u>not the owner</u>.

Possessive	Masculine singular	Feminine singular	Masculine plural	Feminine plural
my	mi (mío)	mi (mía)	mis (míos)	mis (mías)
your (inf., sing.)	tu (tuyo)	tu (tuya)	tus (tuyos)	tus (tuyas)
his/her/its/your (form., sing.)	su (suyo)	su (suya)	sus (suyos)	sus (suyas)
our	nuestro	nuestra	nuestros	nuestras
your (inf., pl.)	vuestro	vuestra	vuestros	vuestras
their/your (form., pl.)	su (suyo)	su (suya)	sus (suyos)	sus (suyas)

'Su(s)' can mean 'his', 'her', 'its', 'their' and 'your' (formal). Use the rest of the information in the sentence to work out which of these it is.

mi libro	su perro
my book	*his dog*

The forms <u>in burgundy</u> (in brackets) are the <u>special long forms</u> — put them <u>after the noun</u>:

las casas tuyas	*your houses*		el gato nuestro	*our cat*

The 'our' and 'your (inf., pl.)' forms are the same in the short and long forms.

Este, ese, aquel — this, that, that over there

'Este', 'ese' and 'aquel' are demonstrative adjectives.

1) Use '<u>este</u>' to say '<u>this</u>'. It's an adjective, so it <u>changes to agree</u> with the noun. When the noun is <u>feminine</u>, use '<u>esta</u>', and when it's <u>plural</u>, use '<u>estos</u>' (masculine) or '<u>estas</u>' (feminine).

este tigre	*this tiger*	esta leche	*this milk*	estos huevos	*these eggs*	estas caras	*these faces*

2) In Spanish, there are <u>two words</u> for '<u>that</u>', but their meanings are slightly different. '<u>Ese</u>' is used when you'd normally say '<u>that</u>' in English. Use '<u>esa</u>' for feminine nouns, and '<u>esos</u>' or '<u>esas</u>' for plural nouns.

ese tigre	*that tiger*	esa leche	*that milk*	esos huevos	*those eggs*	esas caras	*those faces*

3) '<u>Aquel</u>' is used for things that are <u>even further away</u> — in English, you might say '<u>that over there</u>'. 'Aquel' changes to '<u>aquella</u>' in the <u>feminine</u> form and '<u>aquellos</u>' and '<u>aquellas</u>' for the <u>plural</u> forms.

| aquel tigre | *that tiger over there* | aquellos huevos | *those eggs over there* |
| aquella leche | *that milk over there* | aquellas caras | *those faces over there* |

Cuyo — whose

'Cuyo' is a relative adjective.

To say '<u>whose</u>' in Spanish, use '<u>cuyo/a/os/as</u>'. The <u>ending</u> agrees with the <u>noun following</u>, <u>not with its owner</u>.

	Masculine singular	Feminine singular	Masculine plural	Feminine plural
whose	cuyo	cuya	cuyos	cuyas

Eva es la chica cuyo gato está allí.
Eva is the girl whose cat is there.

It's your turn now — help yourself to these quick questions...

Translate these sentences into **Spanish**.

1. Their books are new.
2. I want that apple.
3. That lion over there is eating.
4. These pears are good.
5. That man, whose wife is Spanish, is tall.
6. Lucas is the boy whose parents are nice.

Words to Compare Things

To make your Spanish even more brilliant, learn how to compare things.

Más, el más — more, the most

'More' is a comparative and 'the most' is a superlative.

1) In Spanish you can't say 'cheaper' or 'cheapest' — you have to say 'more cheap' or 'the most cheap'.

Este piso es barato.	Este piso es más barato.	Este piso es el más barato.
This flat is cheap. →	*This flat is cheaper.* →	*This flat is the cheapest.*
	i.e. 'more cheap'	i.e. 'the most cheap'

2) To say 'less cheap' or 'the least cheap', use 'menos'.

Este piso es barato.	Este piso es menos barato.	Este piso es el menos barato.
This flat is cheap. →	*This flat is less cheap.* →	*This flat is the least cheap.*

3) To say 'the most / least' if the word you're describing is <u>feminine</u>, use 'la más / menos'. For <u>plural</u> words, use 'los/las más / menos'.

Laura es la más baja.   *Laura is the shortest.*
Jo y Ed son los menos altos.   *Jo and Ed are the least tall.*

Más / menos ... que — more / less ... than

1) Use 'más ... que' *(more ... than)* and 'menos ... que' *(less ... than)* to <u>compare</u> two things <u>directly</u>.

Catalina es más inteligente que Jorge.   *Catalina is more intelligent than Jorge.*
Jorge es menos inteligente que Catalina.   *Jorge is less intelligent than Catalina.*

2) Or to say two things are <u>as</u> young or old or brilliant <u>as</u> each other, use 'tan ... como' *(as ... as)*.

Catalina es tan feliz como Jorge.   *Catalina is as happy as Jorge.*

There are some exceptions...

If the noun is feminine or plural, you'll need to change the 'el' to 'la', 'los' or 'las'.

As usual, there are a few trickier ones — learn these exceptions.

bueno	*good*	→	mejor	*better*	→	el mejor	*the best*
malo	*bad*	→	peor	*worse*	→	el peor	*the worst*
viejo	*old (for people only)*	→	mayor	*older*	→	el mayor	*the oldest*
joven	*young (for people only)*	→	menor	*younger*	→	el menor	*the youngest*

Manuela es la mayor de mis hermanas.   *Manuela is the oldest of my sisters.*

All the comparatives and superlatives stay the same for the masculine and feminine forms, but they add 'es' for the plural forms.

Blanca y Renata son las menores.   *Blanca and Renata are the youngest.*

El gorro azul es el mejor.   *The blue cap is the best.*

Making comparisons is the best thing ever...

Translate these sentences into **Spanish** — watch out for the irregular adjectives though.

1. My cat is the fattest.
2. I am as tall as my father.
3. The dog is older than the child.
4. It was the worst day of the week.
5. The film is better than the book.
6. Our novel is the most interesting.

Quick Questions

Knowing your Spanish grammar inside out and back to front is absolutely crucial — you just won't be able to get high marks in your GCSE without it. Check you're up to speed with these quick questions.

Quick Questions

1) Write either 'm' or 'f' after each noun to show whether it's masculine or feminine.

   a) queso   e) azúcar   i) espejo   m) taza

   b) árbol   f) virtud   j) pájaro   n) papel

   c) playa   g) canción   k) prisión   o) falda

   d) drama   h) autobús   l) maldad   p) clase

2) Make each of these nouns plural — don't forget to include 'los' or 'las'.

   a) fresa   f) jardín   k) luz

   b) sábado   g) edad   l) limón

   c) conejo   h) nariz   m) jueves

   d) pez   i) mujer   n) examen

   e) mes   j) reloj   o) camisa

3) Circle the correct definite articles (el, la, los or las) to complete the sentences below.

   a) A **los** / **las** chicas les gusta jugar en el parque.

   b) **El** / **La** agua está muy limpia.

   c) Dame **el** / **los** lápiz, por favor.

   d) Me gustan **la** / **las** fresas.

   e) **El** / **Los** lunes siempre voy al polideportivo.

4) Fill in the gaps in these sentences using the correct indefinite article (un, una, unos or unas).

   a) He comprado .... estuche, ... goma y .... tijeras.

   b) Tengo .... hermano y .... hermana.

   c) En mi ciudad, hay .... mercado enorme y .... edificios feos.

5) Translate these phrases into Spanish using the correct articles.

   a) We like ham and cheese.   e) Mrs García is my teacher.

   b) On Saturdays, I get up late.   f) I don't have a computer.

   c) In the future, I want to be a waiter.   g) The boring thing is that we can't go out.

   d) I would like some tomatoes, please.

6) Underline all of the adjectives in the following sentences.

   a) Las ciencias son muy fáciles.   e) Leí una novela muy emocionante.

   b) Vi a una mujer muy vieja.   f) A mucha gente le gusta ir a la playa.

   c) Tantas personas vinieron a la fiesta.   g) Es una idea fenomenal.

   d) Tiene el pelo castaño, largo y liso.   h) Según mi padre, la película es estupenda.

7) Circle the correct adjective to complete each of these phrases.

   a) un conejo **grande** / **grandes**   f) dos dentistas **feliz** / **felices**

   b) el gato **gordo** / **gorda** / **gordas**   g) el examen **difícil** / **difíciles**

   c) tres chicas **delgada** / **delgadas**   h) las flores **bonito** / **bonitos** / **bonitas**

   d) dos asignaturas **fácil** / **fáciles**   i) el león **peligroso** / **peligrosa** / **peligrosos**

   e) un camarero **alto** / **alta** / **altos**   j) una cara **hermosa** / **hermosos** / **hermosas**

Quick Questions

Quick Questions

8) Fill in the correct form of the adjective in each of these sentences.
   a) Vi tres casas .... *(big)*
   b) Compró tres blusas .... *(orange)*
   c) Quisiera un abrigo .... *(lilac)*
   d) Las paredes son .... *(blue)*
   e) Conocí a cuatro personas .... *(sad)*

9) Translate these sentences into Spanish.
   a) I live in a small flat.
   b) Maria is a happy girl.
   c) My teachers are nice.
   d) Football is easy.
   e) She buys three interesting books.
   f) Ben and Adam are young.

10) Complete the sentences below by circling the correct form of each adjective.
    a) Hace **bueno** / **buen** tiempo.
    b) No había **ninguno** / **ningún** coche.
    c) Es un **mal** / **malo** profesor.
    d) Probé un **buen** / **bueno** zumo.
    e) **Algún** / **Alguna** gente cree que es una **mal** / **mala** idea.

11) Fill in the gaps in the Spanish sentences with the correct possessive adjectives in brackets.
    a) .... hermanos son traviesos. *(My)*
    b) Vi a .... amigo en la calle. *(your — inf., pl.)*
    c) .... primos se llaman Rita y Pau. *(Our)*
    d) ¿Dónde están .... zapatos? *(your — inf., sing.)*
    e) .... bicicletas son rojas. *(Their)*
    f) ¿Ha visto .... cara? *(your — form., sing.)*

12) Sometimes you need the longer possessive adjectives.
    Complete these sentences using the bit in brackets to help you.
    a) Las manzanas son .... *(mine)*
    b) La televisión es .... *(yours — inf., pl.)*
    c) Los guantes son .... *(yours — inf., sing.)*
    d) Este piso es .... *(ours)*

13) Translate these phrases into Spanish using the correct demonstrative adjectives.
    Demonstrative adjectives are words like 'this' (este).
    a) I live in this street.
    b) They live in that street over there.
    c) I would like those potatoes.
    d) Would you *(inf., pl.)* like this book?

14) Translate these sentences into Spanish.
    a) Strawberries are more delicious than grapes.
    b) Barcelona is as interesting as Madrid.
    c) Badminton is less boring than hockey.
    d) My father is as strict as my mother.

Adverbs	# Words to Describe Actions

Adverbs describe verbs by adding more information about how an action is done. Using them makes your Spanish much more interesting and complex, which can only be a good thing...

Adverbs help you describe how actions are done

1) If you wanted to <u>describe how you run</u>, you could say 'I run <u>slowly</u>' — '<u>slowly</u>' is an <u>adverb</u>.

2) In English, you add '-<u>ly</u>' to the adjective '<u>slow</u>' to make '<u>slowly</u>'.

3) It's similar in Spanish — to form an adverb, you add '-<u>mente</u>' to the end of the <u>adjective</u>. <u>But</u>, you need to make sure the adjective is in the <u>feminine form</u> first.

> lento (*slow*) ⟹ lenta (*feminine form of 'slow'*) **+** -mente ⟹ lentamente (*slowly*)

4) With adjectives that <u>don't end</u> in '<u>o</u>', you can just add '-<u>mente</u>'.

> fácil (*easy*) **+** -mente ⟹ fácilmente (*easily*)

5) Unlike with adjectives (see p.118), adverbs don't need to <u>agree</u>. This is because they're <u>describing</u> an <u>action</u>, not the <u>person</u> doing the action.

> Hablamos sinceramente.   *We speak sincerely.*
> Habla alegremente.   *She speaks happily.*

6) Adverbs come <u>after</u> the <u>verb</u>.

> Estudio tranquilamente.   *I study quietly.*

Some adverbs are formed differently

1) Just like in English, there are a couple of <u>exceptions</u>.

2) You don't say 'I sing <u>goodly</u>' in English, and you can't say '<u>buenamente</u>' in Spanish either.

> bueno/a *good* ⟹ bien *well*
> malo/a *bad* ⟹ mal *badly*

> Canto bien. ⟹ *I sing well.*
> Canto mal. ⟹ *I sing badly.*

3) Even though you can use '<u>rápidamente</u>' and '<u>lentamente</u>' for '<u>quickly</u>' and '<u>slowly</u>', you can also use the <u>irregular</u> forms — '<u>deprisa</u>' (*quickly*) and '<u>despacio</u>' (*slowly*). They <u>don't</u> add '-<u>mente</u>' or <u>change their ending</u>.

> Escribes deprisa.   *You write quickly.*

> Escribes despacio.   *You write slowly.*

> Just like regular adverbs, these ones come after the verb.

Use adverbs to make your Spanish stand out...

Try translating these sentences into **Spanish**.

1. They cry noisily.   **3.** She speaks clearly.   **5.** The baby sleeps well.   **7.** You dance badly.

2. He lives healthily.   **4.** We speak intelligently.   **6.** I run quickly.   **8.** I read slowly.

Words to Describe Actions

And here's another page on adverbs. This time, it's how to form adverbs using 'con', and some handy lists of adverbs that help you say where or when something is happening.

You can also form adverbs using 'con' + noun

1) In English, you can say someone did something '<u>with ease</u>' instead of saying '<u>easily</u>'.

2) You can do the same in Spanish by putting '<u>con</u>' with a <u>noun</u>.

Lo hago con facilidad. *I do it with ease / easily.*	Hablaste con arrogancia. *You spoke with arrogance / arrogantly.*	¡Con cuidado! *With care! / Carefully!*

Adverbs can tell you where something is done...

You can put these handy words into sentences to say <u>where</u> things happen.

aquí	*here*
ahí	*just there*
allá / allí	*over there*
cerca	*near*
lejos	*far away*
en / por todas partes	*everywhere*

Mi tía trabaja aquí.	*My aunt works here.*
Hay gatos por todas partes.	*There are cats everywhere.*
Está muy cerca.	*It's very near.*

there — ahí

far away — lejos

To say where something is, you need the verb 'estar' (p.139).

...or when it's happening

1) Use these adverbs to help you say <u>when</u> something is being done.

ahora	*now / nowadays*	antes (de)	*before*
ya	*already*	después (de)	*after(wards)*
al mismo tiempo	*at the same time*	en seguida	*straightaway*
de momento	*at the moment*	mientras tanto	*meanwhile*
de repente	*suddenly*	pronto	*soon*
de nuevo	*again*	todavía	*still, yet*

Ya tengo un reloj.
 I already have a watch.

Estaré allí pronto.
 I'll be there soon.

2) These ones are really useful for saying <u>how often</u> something is done.

a diario	*daily*
a menudo	*often*
a veces	*sometimes*
de vez en cuando	*from time to time*
pocas veces	*rarely, a few times*
siempre	*always*

Siempre juego al fútbol en el parque con mis amigos.
 I always play football in the park with my friends.

A veces voy a la tienda.
 I sometimes go to the shop.

Use loads of adverbs and start raking in the marks with ease...

Translate these sentences into **Spanish** using all your adverb knowledge.

1. My shoes are here. **3.** I did it patiently. (Use 'con'.) **5.** She did it straightaway.

2. I want to do it again. **4.** We live far away. **6.** He danced enthusiastically. (Use 'con'.)

Words to Compare Actions

Now you've got to grips with adverbs, you can use some of the same techniques you learned on p.121 to compare how people do things.

Using adverbs to say 'more ...ly' and 'less ...ly'

Adverbial phrases like this are called comparatives.

1) To say that something is done 'more ...ly', use 'más ... que'.

> Eva trabaja más alegremente que Inés.   *Eva works more happily than Inés.*

2) If you want to say that something is done 'less ...ly', use 'menos ... que'.

> Inés trabaja menos alegremente que Eva.   *Inés works less happily than Eva.*

3) To say that someone does something 'as ... as' someone else, use 'tan ... como'.

> Eva trabaja tan alegremente como Inés.   *Eva works as happily as Inés.*

Using adverbs to say the 'most ...ly'

This kind of construction is called a 'superlative'.

To say someone does something 'the most ...ly', follow this pattern.

(Make sure you remember to change 'el' to 'la' if the subject is feminine, 'los' if it's a masculine plural subject, and 'las' for a feminine plural subject.)

> Daniela es la que trabaja más alegremente.   *Daniela works the most happily.*
> Juan es el que baila menos rápidamente.   *Juan dances the least quickly.*

Watch out for irregular comparatives and superlatives

Yes, you guessed it — there are some more lovely irregular forms.

bien (*well*) ⟹	mejor (*better*) ⟹	el que mejor ... (*the one who ... the best*)
mal (*badly*) ⟹	peor (*worse*) ⟹	el que peor ... (*the one who ... the worst*)

> Cocino mejor que mis amigos.   *I cook better than my friends.*
> Escribes peor que un niño.   *You write worse than a child.*
> Él es el que peor juega.   *He's the one who plays the worst.*
> Ellas son las que mejor bailan.   *They are the ones who dance the best.*

That's it for adverbs — use them well...

Have a go at using what you know about adverbs to translate these sentences.

1. Carmen eats more quickly.
2. Luis sings as well as Adela.
3. Selina drives the best.
4. I study better than my friends.
5. We walk more slowly than Rob.
6. Ed is the one who runs the worst.

Words to Say How Much

You can use quantifiers and intensifiers with other words to give more detailed descriptions.

Use quantifiers to say how many or how much

1) Just saying 'I have apples' is boring. Use quantifiers to say you only have a few apples — or loads.

2) Quantifiers go before the noun, and most change their endings to agree with it, just like adjectives do.

mucho	a lot/lots of
poco	only a little/only a few
un poco de	a bit of
demasiado	too much/too many
tanto	so much/so many
bastante	enough

'Un poco de' doesn't change its ending.

Tengo muchos deberes.	I have a lot of homework.
Tengo pocas cartas.	I only have a few letters.
Haces demasiado ruido.	You make too much noise.
Hay tanta gente.	There are so many people.
Tienes bastantes zapatos.	You have enough shoes.
Comí un poco de chocolate.	I ate a bit of chocolate.

3) You don't just have to use these quantifiers with nouns — you can also use them with verbs. When you use them with verbs, they work like adverbs, so they go after the verb and don't change their endings.

Hablas demasiado.	You talk too much.
Come mucho.	She eats a lot.

Use intensifiers to strengthen what you're saying

1) You can use intensifiers like 'very' and 'quite' to add detail to what you're saying.

2) Intensifiers go before the word they're modifying, but their endings don't change at all.

muy	very
poco	not very
demasiado	too
bastante	quite

Simón está muy feliz.	Simón is very happy.
Es poco cortés.	He's not very polite.
Habla demasiado tranquilamente.	She speaks too quietly.
Comes bastante bien.	You eat quite well.

Add '-ito' or '-ísimo' to make adjectives smaller or stronger

1) You can add 'ito/a/os/as' to the end of most adjectives to make something seem smaller or cuter.

El bebé está enfermito.	The baby is poorly.

2) Add 'ísimo/a/os/as' to make the meaning of what you're saying stronger. It's as if you're adding 'really' to the adjective — so if 'bueno' is 'good', then 'buenísimo' would mean 'really good' or 'wonderful'.

La bruja es malísima.	The witch is evil.

That's enough of quantifiers and intensifiers for now...

Translate these sentences into **Spanish**.

1. There are too many cats here.
2. It's quite interesting.
3. I have lots of friends.
4. They speak too slowly.
5. There are so many beaches in Spain.
6. The book is really good.

Quick Questions

You're really blasting through the grammar section now — but don't be tempted to sail on into pronouns without stopping to check you've understood all the stuff you've just learned.

Quick Questions

1) Turn each of these adjectives into adverbs.
   a) lento
   b) normal
   c) ruidoso
   d) claro
   e) simple
   f) obvio
   g) completo
   h) honesto

2) Translate these sentences into Spanish.
   a) They speak very sadly. *(triste)*
   b) We have to listen carefully. *(cuidadoso)*
   c) He drives dangerously. *(peligroso)*
   d) She sings sweetly. *(dulce)*

3) Fill in the gaps by choosing the most appropriate adverb from each list.
   a) Voy a hacer mis deberes .... **en seguida** / **de repente**
   b) Me despierto y .... me levanto. **ahora** / **de nuevo** / **después**
   c) Mi primo .... ha comido así. **pronto** / **siempre**
   d) .... es difícil saber la respuesta. **antes** / **a veces** / **ya**
   e) Haz las compras, y ...., iré allí. **mientras tanto** / **siempre**
   f) .... estoy listo. **después de** / **a menudo** / **ahora**

4) Adverbs can be used to form comparatives and superlatives.
   Make these sentences make sense by circling one of the words in bold.
   a) Claudia habla más rápidamente **que** / **como** Irene.
   b) A Ian le encanta trabajar. Trabaja **más** / **menos** alegremente que sus colegas.
   c) Mi hijo menor no duerme tan **tranquilamente** / **tranquila** como su hermano.
   d) Corro más **deprisa** / **despacio** que mis amigas. ¡No voy a ganar nunca!
   e) Yo canto bien, pero ella canta **mejor** / **mayor**.
   f) Él baila **peor** / **el peor** que sus hermanos.

5) Translate these sentences into English.
   a) Elisa es la que estudia más diligentemente.
   b) Julia es la que canta más alegremente.
   c) José y Luna son los que hablan más claramente.
   d) Ellos son los que celebran más frecuentemente.

6) Translate these sentences into Spanish.
   a) For me, English is quite difficult.
   b) I think rugby is very boring.
   c) Normally he's too honest.
   d) Jodie was very ill on Monday.

7) Complete the sentences by translating the bit in brackets into Spanish. You should use a suffix (either -ísimo or -ito) in each one. Make sure the suffix agrees with the noun.
   a) El campo es .... *(really beautiful)*
   b) Mi casa es .... *(tiny)*
   c) Creo que los patos son .... *(really ugly)*

I, You, We

Pronouns are really handy little words that save you from needing to repeat nouns all the time.

Subject and object

Before you get started on pronouns, you need to know how to find the <u>subject</u> and the <u>object</u> of a sentence.

The subject of a sentence is the noun doing the action. → **Pau come la pera.** *Pau eats the pear.* ← The object of a sentence is the noun having the action done to it.

Yo, tú, él, ella — I, you, he, she

1) <u>Pronouns</u> are words that <u>replace nouns</u> — like 'you' or 'them'. You use them to <u>avoid repeating nouns</u>.

Jessica went to the beach and she sat on the sand. ← In English, the pronoun 'she' replaces Jessica's name. 'She' is a 'subject pronoun' because it replaces the subject of the sentence — Jessica.

2) You <u>don't normally</u> include <u>subject pronouns</u> in Spanish sentences — but you <u>still</u> need to know them.

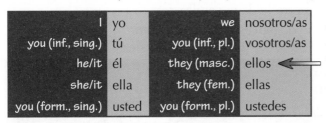

I	yo	we	nosotros/as
you (inf., sing.)	tú	you (inf., pl.)	vosotros/as
he/it	él	they (masc.)	ellos
she/it	ella	they (fem.)	ellas
you (form., sing.)	usted	you (form., pl.)	ustedes

The masculine 'they' form is also used for groups made up of masculine and feminine nouns.

There's also 'se' which means 'one'. It's used in phrases like 'se puede' (one can / you can). It uses the third person singular form of the verb. See p.152 for more impersonal verbs.

Here, you don't need the pronoun 'yo' because you can see from the first person verb forms 'fui' and 'comí' that the person speaking ('I') is doing the action.

Remember there are four ways to say 'you' in Spanish — see p.7 for more.

Fui a la playa y comí un helado. *I went to the beach and I ate an ice cream.*

You can use subject pronouns for emphasis

Although you <u>don't usually</u> need <u>subject pronouns</u> in Spanish, they help <u>emphasise</u> exactly <u>who</u> does what:

¿Qué queréis hacer el fin de semana que viene? *What would you (inf., pl.) like to do next weekend?*

Pues, yo quiero ir de compras, pero él quiere ir al cine. ← You include the pronouns here to emphasise who wants what. They're used in Spanish in cases when extra stress is put on pronouns in English.
*Well, **I** want to go shopping, but **he** wants to go to the cinema.*

¿Quieren visitar el museo? *Do they / you (form., sing.) want to visit the museum?* ← Remember that if you're using 'ustedes', you need the 'they' form of the verb.

Pues, yo sí, pero ella no. *Well, **I** do but **she** doesn't.*

Pronouns make your writing sound smoother — use them...

Write down the Spanish subject pronoun you'd use to replace each of these subjects.

1. Juan y Jorge
2. Anabel
3. Pedro y yo
4. Alberto y tú
5. Ramón
6. el señor Pérez y usted
7. Miranda, Alicia y Lina
8. Alberto y Tania

Object Pronouns	Me, You, Them

Now you've got to grips with subject pronouns, it's time for object pronouns...

Me, te, lo — me, you, him

'Me', 'you', 'him' and 'her' are direct object pronouns. They replace the object of a sentence — the thing having an action done to it.

Use <u>direct object pronouns</u> when you're talking about <u>who</u> or <u>what</u> an action is <u>done to</u>.

me	me	us	nos
you (inf., sing.)	te	you (inf., pl.)	os
him/it	lo	them (masc.)	los
her/it	la	them (fem.)	las
you (form., sing.)	lo/la	you (form., pl.)	los/las

The pronoun usually goes before the verb.

Ricardo lava el perro. → Ricardo lo lava.
Ricardo washes the dog. *Ricardo washes it.*

The action is done to the dog ('el perro' — masculine), so the pronoun 'it' needs to be in the masculine singular form.

Me, te, les — to me, to you, to them

1) If you want to talk about doing something '<u>to</u>' or '<u>for</u>' <u>someone</u>, you need an <u>indirect object pronoun</u>.

El perro da el cepillo a Ricardo. → El perro le da el cepillo.
The dog gives the brush to Ricardo. *The dog gives the brush to him.*

2) These pronouns are the same ones you use with the verb '<u>gustar</u>' when you say you <u>like something</u>. This is because 'me gusta el chocolate' literally means 'chocolate is pleasing <u>to me</u>'.

to me	me	to us	nos
to you (inf., sing.)	te	to you (inf., pl.)	os
to him / her / it / you (form., sing.)	le	to them / you (form., pl.)	les

3) If the thing you like is <u>singular</u>, you need '<u>gusta</u>'. If it's <u>plural</u>, you need '<u>gustan</u>'.

¿Te gusta el español? *Do you like Spanish?*
Le gustan los parques. *He likes the parks.*

Getting the order right

1) Object pronouns <u>normally</u> come <u>before the verb</u>, but they can go <u>before</u> or <u>after</u> the verb if it's an <u>infinitive</u> (p.137) or a <u>present participle</u> (p.150).

Often you need to add an accent to keep the pronunciation right.

Lo quiero ver. **OR** Quiero verlo.
I want to see it.

Le estamos hablando. **OR** Estamos hablándole.
We're talking to him.

2) With <u>commands</u>, the pronoun is <u>tacked on to the end</u>. | Escríbeme, por favor. *Write to me, please.*

3) When <u>two object pronouns</u> come together, the <u>indirect</u> one comes <u>first</u>.

4) And if the <u>indirect object pronoun</u> is '<u>le</u>' or '<u>les</u>', it becomes '<u>se</u>' when it's in front of '<u>lo</u>', '<u>la</u>', '<u>los</u>' or '<u>las</u>'.

direct object pronoun

Te la envío. *I send it to you.*

indirect object pronoun

direct object pronoun

Debo dárselo. *I must give it to him/her/them/you (form.).*

indirect object pronoun

Pronouns are tricky — but if you can use them, you'll be flying...

Translate these sentences into **Spanish** — try to use the correct pronouns and get the order right.
1. She breaks it (the window).
2. I drink it (the milk).
3. He bought a skirt for her.
4. I send him an email.
5. I want to do it.
6. He said it to us.

More Pronouns

Pronouns can be a bit confusing — but they're really useful for adding extra detail and asking questions.

Some pronouns change after certain prepositions

Watch out — 'mí' needs an accent, but 'ti' doesn't.

1) The words for '<u>me</u>' and '<u>you</u>' (inf., sing.) become '<u>mí</u>' and '<u>ti</u>' after <u>prepositions</u> like '<u>a</u>' (*to*), '<u>para</u>' (*for*), and '<u>sobre</u>' / '<u>de</u>' (*about*).

> Lo compré para él. *I bought it for him.*

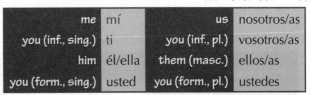

me	mí	us	nosotros/as
you (inf., sing.)	ti	you (inf., pl.)	vosotros/as
him	él/ella	them (masc.)	ellos/as
you (form., sing.)	usted	you (form., pl.)	ustedes

2) '<u>With me</u>' becomes '<u>conmigo</u>' and '<u>with you</u>' becomes '<u>contigo</u>':   Está conmigo. *He's with me.*

Que — that, which, who

1) '<u>Que</u>' can mean '<u>that</u>', '<u>which</u>' or '<u>who</u>' — it's a <u>relative pronoun</u>.

2) You can use it to start a <u>relative clause</u>, which is a way of <u>adding detail</u> to a sentence.

> Fui a Menorca, que es una isla preciosa. *I went to Menorca, which is a beautiful island.*
>
> ¿Dónde está el pan que compraste ayer? *Where's the bread that you bought yesterday?*
>
> Allí está el hombre que vive en nuestra calle. *There's the man who lives on our road.*

3) If you're talking about an <u>idea</u> instead of an object, you need '<u>lo que</u>'.

> Van a venir, lo que es maravilloso. *They're going to come, which is wonderful.*

4) <u>After prepositions</u>, like '<u>con</u>', '<u>a</u>' and '<u>de</u>', use '<u>quien</u>' for 'who' or '<u>el / la que</u>' or '<u>el / la cual</u>' for 'that / which.'

If you were talking about a plural noun, you'd need to use 'con quienes' or 'de los / las cuales' instead.

> el hombre con quien estoy hablando
> *the man with whom I'm talking*

> el mercado del cual compro flores
> *the market from which I buy flowers*

Using pronouns to ask questions

Pronouns for asking questions are called 'interrogative pronouns'.

1) Normally, you can use '<u>¿Qué...</u>' to ask a question that starts with '<u>What...</u>' in English.

> ¿Qué te gustaría hacer? *What would you like to do?*

2) Use '<u>¿Cuál...</u>' when you'd use '<u>Which...</u>' or '<u>Which one...</u>' in English. But remember — sometimes you need '<u>¿Cuál...</u>' when you'd actually use 'What...' in English — see p.4.

If 'cuál' is being used before a noun, it needs to agree with it. Use 'cuál' for all singular nouns and 'cuáles' for all plural nouns.

> ¿Cuál es mejor? *Which (one) is better?*

> ¿Cuál es tu apellido? *What is your surname?*

3) '<u>¿Quién...</u>' means '<u>Who...</u>'. You often use '<u>¿Quién...</u>' with <u>prepositions</u>.

> ¿Quién es? *Who is it?*

> ¿Con quién? *With whom?*

> ¿De quién son? *Whose are they?*

This page, which is very useful, will help you greatly...

Pronouns are tricky — so practise tackling them. Translate these sentences into **Spanish**.

1. My sister, who is seven, is short.
2. I went to Madrid, which is the capital of Spain.
3. What's your address?
4. Who do you live with?
5. Whose is this dog?
6. Which do you prefer?

More Pronouns

It's well worth being able to use these pronouns, so make sure you get your head around them.

El mío, el tuyo... — mine, yours...

'el mío', 'el tuyo', 'el nuestro' etc. are possessive pronouns.

1) Use possessive pronouns to say '<u>mine</u>' or '<u>yours</u>'.

2) Possessive pronouns <u>agree</u> in <u>gender</u> and <u>number</u> with the <u>noun</u> they're replacing.

Possessive pronoun	Masculine singular	Feminine singular	Masculine plural	Feminine plural
mine	el mío	la mía	los míos	las mías
yours (inf., sing.)	el tuyo	la tuya	los tuyos	las tuyas
his/hers/its/yours (form.)	el suyo	la suya	los suyos	las suyas
ours	el nuestro	la nuestra	los nuestros	las nuestras
yours (inf., pl.)	el vuestro	la vuestra	los vuestros	las vuestras
theirs/yours (form., pl.)	el suyo	la suya	los suyos	las suyas

¿Es tu casa?   *Is it your house?*
No, la mía es más alta. *No, mine is taller.*

¿Es vuestro hotel?   *Is it your (inf., pl.) hotel?*
No, el nuestro está allí. *No, ours is there.*

Algo, alguien — something, someone

'Algo' and 'alguien' are indefinite pronouns.

'<u>Algo</u>' means '<u>something</u>':   ¿Queréis algo?   *Do you (inf., pl.) want something?*

'<u>Alguien</u>' means '<u>someone</u>':   Vi a alguien. *I saw someone.*

When you 'see someone' in Spanish, you have to add the personal 'a'. See p.134.

Este, ese, aquel — this one, that one, that one over there

1) <u>Demonstrative pronouns</u> are <u>the same as</u> the <u>demonstrative adjectives</u> on p.120.

2) Remember to <u>change the ending</u> to <u>agree</u> with the noun it refers back to.

Sometimes you might see these pronouns written with an accent on the first 'e' — e.g. 'éste'.

Demonstrative pronoun	Masculine singular	Feminine singular	Masculine plural	Feminine plural
this/these one(s)	este	esta	estos	estas
that/those one(s)	ese	esa	esos	esas
that/those one(s) over there	aquel	aquella	aquellos	aquellas

Me gustaría este.
I'd like this one.

Prefiere esas.
She prefers those.

3) Use the <u>neuter forms</u> '<u>esto</u>', '<u>eso</u>' and '<u>aquello</u>' if you <u>don't</u> know the <u>gender</u> of the noun.

¿Qué es eso? *What's that?*

Using pronouns correctly helps you get good marks...

Translate these sentences into **Spanish**, using the correct pronouns.

1. They're mine. *(cats)*
2. What's that over there?
3. This bed is bigger than that one over there.
4. This book is more interesting than that one.
5. Is it yours (inf., pl.)? *(hat)*
6. Someone's talking quietly.

Prepositions

Prepositions are sneaky little words — but you've got to learn them if you want the highest marks.

Use these words to say where something is...

Don't forget to use 'estar' (see p.139) to say where something is.

al lado de	*next to*	bajo / debajo de	*below / under*	enfrente de	*opposite*
detrás de	*behind*	en / sobre	*on / upon*	en / dentro de	*in / into / inside*
delante de	*in front of*	encima de	*above / on top of*	al fondo de	*at the back of*
entre	*between*	contra	*against*	hacia	*towards*

A, hasta — to

To say '<u>to</u>' in Spanish, you <u>normally</u> say '<u>a</u>'. But when '<u>to</u>' means '<u>as far as</u>', use '<u>hasta</u>'.

Va a Liverpool.	*She's going to Liverpool.*	Solo va hasta Manchester.	*He's only going to Manchester.*

En, dentro de — in, inside

'<u>In</u>' is just '<u>en</u>' and '<u>inside</u>' is '<u>dentro de</u>'. The verb '<u>entrar</u>' (*to go in / enter*) is normally followed by '<u>en</u>'.

En Leeds...	*In Leeds...*	dentro de la caja	*inside the box*	Entro en la tienda.	*I enter the shop.*

De — of

'<u>De</u>' is usually '<u>of</u>'. You can also use '<u>de</u>' to say what something's <u>made of</u>.

Es de oro.	*It's made of gold.*	al final del pasillo	*at the end of the corridor*

You can't say 'de el' or 'a el' in Spanish. Instead, you combine 'a' or 'de' with the definite article (p.117).

	el	la
a	al	a la
de	del	de la

En, a — at

You can <u>normally</u> use '<u>en</u>' when you want to say '<u>at</u>'. Sometimes you need '<u>a</u>' instead...

Está en el colegio.	*He's at school.*	en casa	*at home*	a las seis	*at six o'clock*

Sobre, en — on

You don't need 'on' for days of the week.

For '<u>on (top of)</u>', use '<u>sobre</u>' or '<u>en</u>'. When you mean '<u>on</u>' but not '<u>on top of</u>', use '<u>en</u>'.

Está sobre la mesa.	*It's on the table.*	Lo vi en la tele.	*I saw it on TV.*	El lunes...	*On Monday...*

De, desde, a partir de — from

'<u>From</u>' is normally '<u>de</u>'. Use '<u>desde</u>' when there's a <u>starting</u> and <u>ending</u> point and '<u>a partir de</u>' for dates.

Es de Kent.	*He's from Kent.*	desde Fife hasta Ayr	*from Fife to Ayr*	a partir de julio	*from July*

Learn when to use each of these prepositions...

Use what you know about prepositions to translate these sentences into **Spanish**.

1. The house is opposite the bank.
2. The train goes as far as Italy.
3. I heard it on the radio.
4. I enter the supermarket.
5. I'm from Hull, but I live in Crewe.
6. From September, I will have a job.

'Por', 'Para' and the Personal 'a'

'Por', 'para' and the personal 'a' are also prepositions, but they don't always translate easily into English.

Use 'para' to...

1) ...say who something is for. | Este dinero es para ti.   *This money is for you.*

2) ...talk about destinations. | el tren para Bilbao   *the train to Bilbao*

3) ...say 'to' or 'in order to'. | Veo la tele para descansar.   *I watch TV to relax.*

4) ...say 'by' in time phrases. | para mañana   *by tomorrow*

5) ...say 'for' in phrases like 'for X days' when you're talking about the future. | Quiero el coche para un día.   *I want the car for one day.*

6) ...say 'in my / your opinion'. | Para mí, es muy bonito.   *In my opinion, it's very pretty.*

7) ...say 'about to'. | Según él, está para llover.   *According to him, it's about to rain.*

'Según' is another preposition. It means 'according to'.

Use 'por' to...

1) ...say 'for' in phrases like 'for X years / months' in the past. | Vivió allí por un año.   *He lived there for a year.*

In certain cases, for the future you need to use 'por': Estaré en Galicia por dos años.

2) ...talk about parts of the day when you want to say 'in'. | por la mañana   *in the morning*

3) ...say 'through'. | Entré por la puerta sin hablar.   *I came through the door without speaking.*

'Sin' is a preposition which means 'without'.

4) ...say 'per' or 'a' in number phrases. | tres veces por día   *three times a day*

5) ...talk about exchanges. | Pagó dos euros por el té.   *He paid 2 euros for the tea.*

6) ...say 'on behalf of'. | Lo hice por ti.   *I did it for you.*

7) ...say 'thank you'. | Gracias por el pastel.   *Thanks for the cake.*

The personal 'a'

You don't usually use the personal 'a' after 'tener' or 'ser'.

You need an extra 'a' before the word for any human being or pet after every single verb.

Estoy buscando a Juan.   *I'm looking for Juan.*   **BUT**   Estoy buscando un taxi.   *I'm looking for a taxi.*

'Por' and 'para' are hard... but they're really useful to know.

Decide whether you need 'por', 'para' or 'a' in each of these sentences.

1. Esta revista es _____ ti.
2. Visito _____ mi abuelo.
3. _____ la tarde, vemos la tele.
4. Gracias _____ la carta.
5. Juego al fútbol dos veces _____ semana.
6. Lo quiero _____ el fin de semana.

Conjunctions

Conjunctions help you link your ideas together to make longer, more complex sentences.

Y — and

1) '<u>Y</u>' means '<u>and</u>' — you use it just like you would in English.

Me gusta jugar al fútbol.	Me gusta jugar al rugby.	Me gusta jugar al fútbol y al rugby.
I like playing football. **AND**	*I like playing rugby.* **=**	*I like playing football and rugby.*

2) '<u>Y</u>' changes to '<u>e</u>' <u>before</u> a word starting with '<u>i</u>' or '<u>hi</u>'.

Hablo español e inglés.   *I speak Spanish and English.*

O — or

1) '<u>O</u>' means '<u>or</u>'.

Juego al fútbol los sábados.	Juego al rugby los sábados.	Juego al fútbol o al rugby los sábados.
I play football on Saturdays. **OR**	*I play rugby on Saturdays.* **=**	*I play football or rugby on Saturdays.*

2) When '<u>o</u>' comes just <u>before</u> a word starting with '<u>o</u>' or '<u>ho</u>', it changes to '<u>u</u>'.

Cuesta siete u ocho euros.   *It costs seven or eight euros.*

Pero — but

1) '<u>Pero</u>' means '<u>but</u>'.

Me gusta el fútbol.	No me gusta el rugby.	Me gusta el fútbol, pero no me gusta el rugby.
I like football. **BUT**	*I don't like rugby.* **=**	*I like football, but I don't like rugby.*

2) When '<u>but</u>' means '<u>but rather</u>', it becomes '<u>sino</u>'.

No es español, sino francés.   *He isn't Spanish, but (rather) French.*

Porque — because

'<u>Porque</u>' helps you <u>give opinions</u>:

Me gusta porque es sabroso.   *I like it because it's tasty.*

There's more about 'porque' and opinions on p.9.

Other conjunctions you need to know

cuando	*when*	así que	*so, therefore*	como	*as, since*	
si	*if*	de manera que	*such that*	pues	*well, then*	
sin embargo	*however*	mientras	*while*	entonces	*then*	

Tiene hambre, así que va a comer.

He's hungry, so he's going to eat.

You don't want to sound like a robot, so start using conjunctions...

Translate these sentences into **Spanish**, deciding which conjunctions you need to use.

1. Geography is fun, but it's difficult.
2. I like history because it's easy.
3. As I'm ill, I'm staying at home.
4. I go to the park when it's hot.
5. I speak French and Italian.
6. Do you prefer blue or yellow?

Quick Questions

There was a lot to take in in that section — and it's all really important stuff. Use these quick questions to see how much you've remembered. You can always flick back through the pages if you get stuck.

Quick Questions

1) For each sentence, decide which verb you would need.
   a) Buenos días, señores! ¿Cómo .... ?   **está / están / estáis**
   b) ¡Hola Lily! ¿ .... visto a mi hermano?   **Habéis / Has / Ha**
   c) Julio y Carmen, ¿ .... ir de compras?   **queréis / quiere / quieres**
   d) Como presidente, usted .... hacer más por la gente. **debes / debe / deben**

2) Translate these sentences into Spanish using the correct indirect object pronouns.
   a) He gave me the book.
   b) I sent him a letter.
   c) I called you *(inf., pl.)* yesterday.
   d) Would you *(form., pl.)* like to go to the cinema?
   e) She showed us a photo.

3) Complete each sentence by circling the correct option.
   a) La tarta es para **tú / ti**.
   b) Ayer estaba pensando en **ella / su**.
   c) ¿Las zanahorias son para **me / mí**?
   d) ¿Ellas tienen que ir **contigo / con ti / con tú**?
   e) Estábamos hablando de **ti / tú** y de **su / él**.

4) Translate these sentences into Spanish using the correct interrogative pronouns.
   a) Whose is this car?
   b) What did you *(inf., sing.)* do last weekend?
   c) Who called you *(inf., sing.)*?
   d) What is your *(inf., sing.)* address?
   e) Which one do you (inf., sing.) prefer?
   f) Whose *(plural)* are these coats?

5) Translate these sentences into Spanish using the correct demonstrative pronouns.
   a) I don't want to buy this skirt — I want to buy that one.
   b) If you want to read a book, you can read that one over there.

6) Decide whether you need 'por' or 'para' to complete each of these sentences.
   a) El tren .... Madrid va a salir en diez minutos.
   b) Hice esta tarta .... Melissa, porque es su cumpleaños.
   c) Gracias .... el regalo.
   d) Pagué treinta euros .... los zapatos.

7) Fill in the gaps with the most appropriate conjunction.
   a) Comió tres peras .... dos piñas.   **porque / y / si**
   b) Quiero dar un paseo .... está lloviendo.   **así que / pero / con**
   c) Yo cocinaba la cena .... ellos iban al parque. **mientras / o / sino**
   d) Puedes hacerlo .... quieres.   **porque / entonces / si**

Verbs in the Present Tense

There's not a lot you can do without verbs — your Spanish won't make very much sense without them.

Verbs are actions

1) A verb is an action word — for example, 'speak', 'eat' and 'live'.

2) Verbs can be put into different tenses, such as the future or past, for example, 'Yesterday, I ate a pie'.

3) To use a verb, you need to know its infinitive — the form you find in a dictionary, e.g. 'hablar' (to speak).

Forming the present tense

1) Most regular verbs in Spanish end in '-ar', '-er' or '-ir'. To form the present tense of these regular verbs, you need to find the stem. To do this, remove the last two letters from the infinitive.

2) Then add the endings below to the stem.

Infinitive	Remove last two letters	Stem
hablar	ar	habl-

-ar verbs

I speak	hablo	hablamos	we speak
you (inf., sing.) speak	hablas	habláis	you (inf., pl.) speak
he/she/it/you (form., sing.) speak(s)	habla	hablan	they/you (form., pl.) speak

Cantan bien. *They sing well.*

Toca la viola. *He plays the viola.*

-er verbs

I eat	como	comemos	we eat
you (inf., sing.) eat	comes	coméis	you (inf., pl.) eat
he/she/it/you (form., sing.) eat(s)	come	comen	they/you (form., pl.) eat

Bebes té. *You (inf., sing.) drink tea.*

Vendemos uvas. *We sell grapes.*

-ir verbs

I live	vivo	vivimos	we live
you (inf., sing.) live	vives	vivís	you (inf., pl.) live
he/she/it/you (form., sing.) live(s)	vive	viven	they/you (form., pl.) live

Suben la torre. *They go up the tower.*

Kevin interrumpe. *Kevin interrupts.*

When to use the present tense

For another way to say what you're doing now, see p.150.

① Use the present tense for actions taking place now.

Hablo español. *I speak Spanish / I am speaking Spanish.*

② You also need the present tense for things that take place regularly.

Canto todos los días. *I sing every day.*

③ Use the present tense with 'desde hace' to say how long you've been doing something.

Toco el violín desde hace cuatro años. *I've been playing the violin for four years.*

④ You can also use the present tense for things that are about to happen.

Mañana vamos al cine. *Tomorrow we are going to the cinema.*

Get to grips with the present before you revise the other tenses...

Put each of the infinitives into the form given in brackets, and then translate Q8 into **Spanish**.

1. bailar (yo)
2. beber (nosotros)
3. nadar (vosotros)
4. correr (usted)
5. aprender (él)
6. visitar (ellos)
7. escribir (tú)
8. She has been living here for a year.

Irregular Verbs in the Present Tense

Unfortunately, not all Spanish verbs are regular — some of the worst offenders are really common verbs...

Radical-changing verbs

These are also known as 'stem-changing verbs'.

1) A <u>radical-changing verb</u> is a verb that <u>changes its spelling</u> in the <u>present tense</u>.

2) Usually, the '<u>e</u>' in their stem changes to '<u>ie</u>', or the '<u>o</u>' or '<u>u</u>' in their stem to '<u>ue</u>'. Some <u>verbs</u> like '<u>pedir</u>' (*to order / ask for*), '<u>repetir</u>' (*to repeat*) and '<u>vestirse</u>' (*to get dressed*) change the '<u>e</u>' in their stem to '<u>i</u>'.

3) Their stem <u>changes</u> in every form apart from the '<u>we</u>' and '<u>you (inf., pl.)</u>' forms.

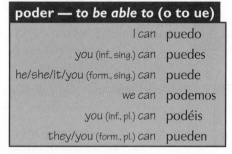

querer — to want (e to ie)	
I want	quiero
you (inf., sing.) want	quieres
he/she/it/you (form., sing.) want(s)	quiere
we want	queremos
you (inf., pl.) want	queréis
they/you (form., pl.) want	quieren

Even though their stems change, their endings are regular.

These verbs also change their '<u>e</u>' to '<u>ie</u>'...

cerrar	*to close*	preferir	*to prefer*
comenzar	*to begin*	sentarse	*to sit down*
despertarse	*to wake up*	sentir(se)	*to feel*
empezar	*to begin*	tener	*to have*
pensar	*to think*	venir	*to come*

'Tener' and 'venir' have irregular first person singular forms — 'tengo' and 'vengo'.

poder — to be able to (o to ue)	
I can	puedo
you (inf., sing.) can	puedes
he/she/it/you (form., sing.) can	puede
we can	podemos
you (inf., pl.) can	podéis
they/you (form., pl.) can	pueden

These verbs change their '<u>o</u>' or '<u>u</u>' to '<u>ue</u>'...

acostarse	*to go to bed*	encontrar	*to find*
almorzar	*to have lunch*	jugar	*to play*
costar	*to cost*	llover	*to rain*
doler	*to hurt*	morir	*to die*
dormir	*to sleep*	volver	*to return*

Some common irregular verbs

In Spanish, the verbs '<u>to go</u>', '<u>to give</u>', '<u>to do / make</u>' and '<u>to know</u>' are irregular.

To say you know a person, use 'conocer' instead. It also has an irregular 1st person — conozco.

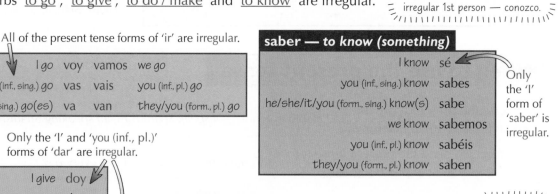

ir — to go   All of the present tense forms of 'ir' are irregular.

I go	voy	vamos	we go
you (inf., sing.) go	vas	vais	you (inf., pl.) go
he/she/it/you (form., sing.) go(es)	va	van	they/you (form., pl.) go

saber — to know (something)

I know	sé
you (inf., sing.) know	sabes
he/she/it/you (form., sing.) know(s)	sabe
we know	sabemos
you (inf., pl.) know	sabéis
they/you (form., pl.) know	saben

Only the 'I' form of 'saber' is irregular.

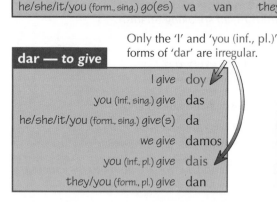

Only the 'I' and 'you (inf., pl.)' forms of 'dar' are irregular.

dar — to give

I give	doy
you (inf., sing.) give	das
he/she/it/you (form., sing.) give(s)	da
we give	damos
you (inf., pl.) give	dais
they/you (form., pl.) give	dan

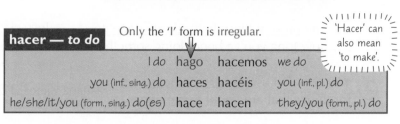

hacer — to do   Only the 'I' form is irregular.

I do	hago	hacemos	we do
you (inf., sing.) do	haces	hacéis	you (inf., pl.) do
he/she/it/you (form., sing.) do(es)	hace	hacen	they/you (form., pl.) do

'Hacer' can also mean 'to make'.

Practise saying these irregular verbs over and over again...

Find the mistake in each of these Spanish sentences. The subject of the verb is in brackets to help you.

1. Comenza a las tres. (ella)
2. Vís a la tienda. (vosotros)
3. Quieremos leche. (nosotros)
4. Do el libro a Lola. (yo)
5. Podes conducir. (tú)
6. Sabo tu nombre. (yo)

'Ser' and 'Estar' in the Present Tense | Present Tense

In Spanish, there are two verbs for 'to be' — 'ser' and 'estar'. They're used differently, so it's really important to know which you need in each situation. Oh, and one more thing — they're irregular too...

Use 'ser' for permanent things

The verb 'ser' means 'to be'. It's used for permanent things. You need it to...

ser — to be	
I am	soy
you are (inf., sing.)	eres
he/she/it/you (form., sing.) is/are	es
we are	somos
you are (inf., pl.)	sois
they/you (form., pl.) are	son

1) ...talk about nationalities.

> Somos galeses.   *We are Welsh.*

2) ...say someone's name or say who someone is in relation to you.

> Nerea es mi prima.   *Nerea is my cousin.*

3) ...talk about someone's job.

> Mi tío es profesor.   *My uncle is a teacher.*

4) ...describe the physical characteristics of a person or thing.

> Sois altos.   *You (inf., pl.) are tall.*

5) ...describe someone's personality.

> Son alegres.   *They are cheerful.*

> Eres muy amable.   *You are very kind.*

Use 'estar' for temporary things and locations

'Estar' also means 'to be'. You use it to...

1) ...talk about things that might change in the future.

> Estoy bastante enfermo.   *I'm quite ill.*
> (But you might not be ill next week.)

> Estás muy triste hoy.   *You are very sad today.*
> (But you might not be sad tomorrow.)

estar — to be	
I am	estoy
you are (inf., sing.)	estás
he/she/it/you (form., sing.) is/are	está
we are	estamos
you are (inf., pl.)	estáis
they/you (form., pl.) are	están

2) ...talk about where someone or something is.

> Madrid está en España.   *Madrid is in Spain.*

> Estamos en casa.   *We are at home.*

Always ask yourself whether you need 'ser' or 'estar'...

Decide whether you need 'ser' or 'estar' in each of these situations.

1. Es / Está muy hablador hoy.
2. Es / Está muy hablador en general.
3. Somos / Estamos de Escocia.
4. Soy / Estoy en Bradford.
5. Este es / está mi hermano.
6. Mi padre es / está médico.

Quick Questions

Now that you're knee-deep in verbs and tenses, it's time for us to proudly present... some more questions. Use these to find any gaps in your knowledge so you can sort them out before the exams.

1) Write each of these verbs in Spanish in their infinitive form.
   a) to have
   b) to want
   c) to live
   d) to sing
   e) to write
   f) to think

2) Complete each sentence by circling the correct form of escribir (a regular -ir verb).
   a) Sita y Raúl **escribe** / **escriben** muchas cartas.
   b) Alejandro, ¿ **escribes** / **escribimos** una novela?
   c) Yo **escribo** / **escribe** cerca del mar.
   d) ¿Usted **escribes** / **escribe** / **escribís** mucho?

3) Translate these sentences into Spanish using the present tense.
   a) I eat chicken every day.
   b) I have been coming here for four years.
   c) We have been waiting for an hour.

4) Tom has written these Spanish sentences, but he has made some mistakes with his radical-changing verbs. Write out the wrong sentences correctly.
   a) Yo penso que él tiene un perro.
   b) Almorzo a las once.
   c) Me duelen los dedos.
   d) Jugamos al baloncesto.
   e) No duermo bien cuando llove.

5) Translate these sentences into Spanish.
   a) I know that she has a sister.
   b) When he goes to the park, he plays football.
   c) I prefer to do my homework straightaway.

6) Complete these sentences with a form of 'ser'.
   a) Daniel y yo .... griegos.
   b) Mi padre .... bombero y mi madre .... traductora.
   c) Boris y John .... unos jóvenes muy inteligentes.
   d) Tú .... una persona muy amable.

7) Translate these sentences into Spanish using the verb 'estar'.
   a) The book is in my rucksack.
   b) I am very tired today.
   c) Bilbao is in Spain.
   d) Are you (inf., sing.) ill today?

8) Decide whether you need 'ser' or 'estar' in each of these sentences. Circle your answer.
   a) ¡Hola! **Soy** / **Estoy** George.
   b) No puedo venir a tu fiesta. Todavía **soy** / **estoy** de vacaciones en Escocia.
   c) No **somos** / **estamos** de Valencia, sino de Málaga.
   d) Hannah **es** / **está** una persona bastante trabajadora.
   e) Ethan **es** / **está** triste porque ha perdido su dinero.

Talking About the Past

The preterite tense ('I went' etc.) has quite a few tricky irregular forms — so pay close attention to this page.

I went — The preterite tense

To form the <u>preterite tense of regular verbs</u>, find the <u>stem</u> (see p.137) and then <u>add these endings</u>...

-ar verb endings

I	-é	-amos	we
you (inf., sing.)	-aste	-asteis	you (inf., pl.)
he/she/it/you (form., sing.)	-ó	-aron	they/you (form., pl.)

-er and -ir verb endings

I	-í	-imos	we
you (inf., sing.)	-iste	-isteis	you (inf., pl.)
he/she/it/you (form., sing.)	-ió	-ieron	they/you (form., pl.)

Habló con Marcela.
He spoke to Marcela.

Don't forget the accent — without it, you'd be saying 'I speak to Marcela'.

Nací en Japón.
I was born in Japan.

Bebisteis mucho.
You (inf., pl.) drank a lot.

Irregular verbs in the preterite tense

Here are four important <u>irregular verbs</u> in the <u>preterite tense</u>. 'Ser' and 'ir' are the <u>same</u> in the <u>preterite tense</u>.

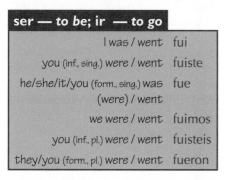

ser — to be; ir — to go

I was / went	fui
you (inf., sing.) were / went	fuiste
he/she/it/you (form., sing.) was (were) / went	fue
we were / went	fuimos
you (inf., pl.) were / went	fuisteis
they/you (form., pl.) were / went	fueron

estar — to be

I was	estuve
you (inf., sing.) were	estuviste
he/she/it/you (form., sing.) was (were)	estuvo
we were	estuvimos
you (inf., pl.) were	estuvisteis
they/you (form., pl.) were	estuvieron

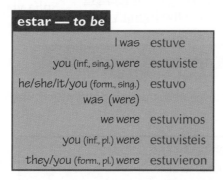

hacer — to do / make

I did / made	hice
you (inf., sing.) did / made	hiciste
he/she/it/you (form., sing.) did / made	hizo
we did / made	hicimos
you (inf., pl.) did / made	hicisteis
they/you (form., pl.) did / made	hicieron

Verbs ending in '-<u>car</u>' change from '<u>c</u>' to '<u>qu</u>' in the '<u>I</u>' form of the <u>preterite tense</u> — '<u>tocar</u>' becomes '<u>toqué</u>'.
Verbs ending in '-<u>zar</u>' change from '<u>z</u>' to '<u>c</u>' in the '<u>I</u>' form of the <u>preterite tense</u> — '<u>cruzar</u>' becomes '<u>crucé</u>'.

Even more irregular verbs

Some verbs <u>change their stem</u> in the <u>preterite tense</u>. If you know what the stem change is, you can predict what the verb is going to be in its other forms.

Infinitive	I	he/she/it
dar (*to give*)	di	dio
decir (*to say*)	dije	dijo
poder (*to be able to*)	pude	pudo
poner (*to put*)	puse	puso
querer (*to want*)	quise	quiso
tener (*to have*)	tuve	tuvo
traer (*to bring*)	traje	trajo
venir (*to come*)	vine	vino

The 'he/she/it/you (form., sing.)' form is sometimes different to what you might expect.

Le dimos un gato.   *We gave him a cat.*

Pero dijiste que te gustó.   *But you (inf., sing.) said you liked it.*

Tuvisteis una idea.   *You (inf., pl.) had an idea.*

Vinieron a mi fiesta.   *They came to my party.*

'Ser' and 'ir' are the same in the preterite tense...

Put these verbs into the preterite tense. The subject is given in brackets.

1. llorar (ellos)
2. comer (nosotros)
3. escribir (vosotros)
4. cenar (yo)
5. dar (tú)
6. poder (yo)
7. hacer (vosotros)
8. poner (usted)
9. venir (tú)
10. traer (nosotros)

| Imperfect Tense | **Talking About the Past** |

The imperfect tense is used to describe things in the past. It helps you say what you 'were doing', what 'was happening' and what you 'used to do'.

I was going / I used to go — The imperfect tense

To form the <u>imperfect tense</u>, find the <u>stem</u> (see p.137) and then <u>add these endings</u>. The 'I' form and the '<u>he/she/it/you (form., sing.)</u>' form look the <u>same</u>, so you'll have to use the <u>context</u> to tell which is which.

-ar verb endings

	I	-aba	-ábamos	we
you (inf., sing.)		-abas	-abais	you (inf., pl.)
he/she/it/you (form., sing.)		-aba	-aban	they/you (form., pl.)

Hablábamos por teléfono.
We were talking / used to talk on the phone.

-er and -ir verb endings

	I	-ía	-íamos	we
you (inf., sing.)		-ías	-íais	you (inf., pl.)
he/she/it/you (form., sing.)		-ía	-ían	they/you (form., pl.)

Hacía mucho deporte.
I was doing / used to do a lot of sport.

You can also say what you <u>used to do</u> using the <u>imperfect tense</u> of the verb '<u>soler</u>' ('<u>solía</u>') and then the <u>infinitive</u>.

Solía viajar mucho.   *I used to travel a lot.*

Irregular verbs in the imperfect tense

1) '<u>Ser</u>', '<u>ir</u>' and '<u>ver</u>' are the only three verbs which <u>don't</u> follow the pattern. '<u>Ser</u>' and '<u>ir</u>' are <u>irregular</u>...

ser — to be

	I was	era	éramos	we were
you (inf., sing.) were		eras	erais	you (inf., pl.) were
he/she/it/you (form., sing.) was (were)		era	eran	they/you (form., pl.) were

Mi padre era pintor.
My dad was / used to be a painter.

ir — to go

	I went	iba	íbamos	we went
you went (inf., sing.)		ibas	ibais	you went (inf., pl.)
he/she/it/you (form., sing.) went		iba	iban	they/you (form., pl.) went

Iba a muchos conciertos.
I went / used to go to lots of concerts.

2) ...but '<u>ver</u>' is <u>almost regular</u> — just add the '<u>-er</u>' endings onto '<u>ve-</u>', e.g. '<u>veía</u>'.

Veía la tele.   *I watched / used to watch TV.*

Había — There was / There were

In the <u>present tense</u> '<u>hay</u>' means '<u>there is</u>' or '<u>there are</u>'. The <u>imperfect</u> form of '<u>hay</u>' is '<u>había</u>', which means '<u>there was</u>' or '<u>there were</u>' — it <u>stays the same</u>, regardless of whether the noun is <u>singular</u> or <u>plural</u>.

Había un mono en el árbol.   *There was a monkey in the tree.*
Siempre había muchos niños allí.   *There were always lots of children there.*

'Hay' and 'había' come from the verb 'haber'.

Learning the imperfect — a perfect way to spend your time...

Put these verbs into the imperfect tense. The subject is given in brackets.

1. cantar (yo)	**3.** aprender (usted)	**5.** volver (ustedes)	**7.** nadar (tú)
2. ser (nosotros)	**4.** decir (él)	**6.** seguir (vosotros)	**8.** ir (ellos)

Talking About the Past

Choosing which past tense to use can be a tricky business — even for people who have been learning Spanish for ages. Here are some guidelines to get you started –– read them carefully.

Use the preterite tense to...

1) ...talk about a <u>single completed action</u> in the past.

> Fui al cine el jueves.   *I went to the cinema on Thursday.*

2) ...talk about events that happened during a <u>set period of time</u>.

> Ayer hizo calor.   *Yesterday it was hot.*

Remember to use 'hacer' with nouns such as 'calor', 'frío', 'viento' and 'sol' to say 'it's hot / cold / windy / sunny'. See p.66 for more weather vocabulary.

3) ...<u>interrupt a description of movement</u> taking place in the <u>imperfect tense</u>.

> Volvía del gimnasio cuando vi a Irene.   *I was coming back from the gym when I saw Irene.*

Use the imperfect tense to...

1) ...talk about what you <u>used to do repeatedly</u> in the past.

> Iba al cine cada jueves.   *I used to go to the cinema every Thursday.*

2) ...<u>describe something</u>, like the weather, in the past.

> Hacía calor, pero estaba nublado.   *It was hot, but it was cloudy.*

3) ...say <u>where you were going</u> when <u>something else happened</u>. You use the <u>imperfect</u> tense to describe the <u>background situation</u>.

> Volvía del gimnasio cuando vi a Irene.
> *I was coming back from the gym when I saw Irene.*

4) ...say <u>how long</u> something <u>had been happening for</u>. For this, you also need '<u>desde hacía</u>', which is the <u>imperfect</u> form of '<u>desde hace</u>' (see p.137).

> Leía desde hacía una hora cuando me llamó.
> *I had been reading for an hour when he called me.*

You only need to be able to recognise this structure — you don't need to be able to use it.

Ask yourself whether you need the preterite or the imperfect...

In each of the following sentences, choose whether you need the preterite or the imperfect tense.

1. Siempre hizo / hacía mucho viento.
2. Ayer volví / volvía de mis vacaciones.
3. ¿Fuiste / Ibas a la piscina ayer?
4. Fui / Iba al colegio cuando tuve / tenía una idea.

Perfect and Pluperfect

Talking About the Past

The perfect and pluperfect tenses allow you to say what you 'have done' or 'had done'.
They're pretty easy to learn and are a useful addition to your magic bag of grammatical tricks.

Finding the past participle

1) In the sentence 'I have done', 'done' is a past participle. You need to know how to form past participles before you get started on the perfect and pluperfect tenses.

2) For '-ar' verbs, remove the 'ar' and add '-ado'.

> esperar *(to wait)* ⟹ esperado *(waited)*

3) For '-er' and '-ir' verbs, remove the 'er' or 'ir' and add '-ido'.

> comer *(to eat)* ⟹ comido *(eaten)*
> elegir *(to choose)* ⟹ elegido *(chosen)*

4) There are some irregular participles that you also need to learn...

Infinitive	Past participle	Infinitive	Past participle
abrir	abierto *(opened)*	leer	leído *(read)*
cubrir	cubierto *(covered)*	poner	puesto *(put)*
decir	dicho *(said)*	romper	roto *(broken)*
escribir	escrito *(written)*	ver	visto *(seen)*
hacer	hecho *(done / made)*	volver	vuelto *(returned)*

In these tenses, the participle stays the same — you don't need to make it feminine or plural.

He hecho — I have done

'I have done' is the perfect tense.

To say what you 'have done', you need the present tense of the verb 'haber' and the past participle.

haber — to have...

I have...	he	hemos	we have...
you (inf., sing.) have...	has	habéis	you (inf., pl.) have...
he/she/it has... / you (form., sing.) have...	ha	han	they have... / you (form., pl.) have...

Han jugado al tenis. *They have played tennis.*
¡Ha roto la botella! *He has broken the bottle!*

Me gustaría ir a Pisa porque nunca he estado allí. *I'd like to go to Pisa because I've never been there.*

Había hecho — I had done

'I had done' is the pluperfect tense.

To say what you 'had done', you need the imperfect tense of the verb 'haber' and the past participle.

haber — to have...

Learn more about the imperfect tense on p.142.

I had...	había	habíamos	we had...
you (inf., sing.) had...	habías	habíais	you (inf., pl.) had...
he/she/it had... / you (form., sing.) had...	había	habían	they had... / you (form., pl.) had...

Había vuelto a casa. *He had returned home.*
Habían visto el coche. *They had seen the car.*

No pude ir porque no había hecho mis deberes. *I couldn't go because I hadn't done my homework.*

Using these compound tenses really makes you sound clever...

Translate these sentences into Spanish using the perfect and pluperfect tenses.

1. They had sung. **3.** You have (inf., pl.) learned. **5.** I had drunk. **7.** She has followed.

2. He has travelled. **4.** You have (form., sing.) seen. **6.** We had finished. **8.** You have (inf., sing.) lived.

Talking About the Future

You'll need to talk about things that are going to happen at some point in the future.
There are two ways you can do it — and the first one's a piece of cake...

I'm going to... — The immediate future

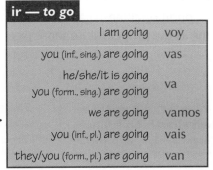

ir — to go

I am going	voy
you (inf., sing.) are going	vas
he/she/it is going you (form., sing.) are going	va
we are going	vamos
you (inf., pl.) are going	vais
they/you (form., pl.) are going	van

1) The <u>immediate future</u> tense can be used to talk about something that's <u>about to happen</u>, as well as something <u>further</u> on in the future.

2) To form the immediate future, take the <u>present tense</u> of '<u>ir</u>' (*to go*) that goes with the person you're talking about.

3) Then, add '<u>a</u>' and a verb in the <u>infinitive</u>.

voy *I am going* <u>Present tense</u> of '*ir*'.	+	a	+	comer *to eat* Another verb in the <u>infinitive</u>.	=	Voy a comer. *I am going to eat.* *A sentence about the <u>future</u>.*

Susana va a leer una revista.	*Susana is going to read a magazine.*

El sábado, vamos a ir a Francia.	*On Saturday, we are going to go to France.*

Put in phrases to say when you're going to do something (p.2-3).

I will... — The proper future tense

1) Use the proper <u>future tense</u> to say what will happen.

2) To form it, take the '<u>future stem</u>' of the verb — for most verbs, this is the <u>infinitive</u>.

3) Add the <u>ending</u> that matches the person you're talking about (the endings are the <u>same</u> for <u>all verbs</u>).

Future endings

I	-é	-emos	we
you (inf., sing.)	-ás	-éis	you (inf., pl.)
he/she/it/you (form., sing.)	-á	-án	they/you (form., pl.)

hablar *infinitive*	+	é *future ending*	=	hablaré *I will talk.*

Dormirás.	*You will sleep.*

There are a few verbs that have a special future stem, so you just have to learn them off by heart. These are the most important ones.

Jugaré al tenis.	*I will play tennis.*

Cogerá el autobús.	*He will take the bus.*

Venderemos el perro.	*We will sell the dog.*

Infinitive	'yo' form
decir (*to say*)	diré
haber (*to have...*)	habré
hacer (*to do / make*)	haré
tener (*to have*)	tendré
poner (*to put*)	pondré
querer (*to want*)	querré
saber (*to know*)	sabré
venir (*to come*)	vendré
salir (*to go out*)	saldré
poder (*to be able to*)	podré

Show off your skills by using <u>both</u> types of future tense...

Put these present tense verbs into the immediate and proper future tenses, keeping the subject the same.

1. como
2. tenemos
3. baila
4. doy
5. ponen
6. jugáis
7. puedes
8. canta
9. queremos
10. vivís

Would, Could and Should

Now it's time to talk about what could or would happen in the future.

Future stem + imperfect -er / -ir endings — The conditional

1) The conditional tense can be used for saying 'would'. It uses the same stems as the proper future tense (see p.145) and adds these endings:

comer	**+**	**comía**	**=**	**comería**	
to eat		*I was eating.*		*I would eat.*	
This is the infinitive. Not all verbs use the same future stem though (see p.145).		This is the -er / -ir ending of the imperfect tense.		A sentence in the conditional.	

Conditional endings

I	-ía
you (inf., sing.)	-ías
he/she/it/you (form., sing.)	-ía
we	-íamos
you (inf., pl.)	-íais
they/you (form., pl.)	-ían

Podría ayudarme?	*Could you (form., sing) help me?*

Using 'poder' (to be able to) in the conditional lets you say 'could', and 'deber' (to have to) helps you form sentences with 'should'.

Debería hacer mis deberes.	*I should do my homework.*

2) You can combine the conditional with other tenses to make more complicated sentences:

Bailaría, pero me duelen los pies.	*I would dance, but my feet hurt.*

Les gustaría ir a la playa, sin embargo no pueden ir porque está lloviendo. *They would like to go to the beach, however they can't go because it's raining.*

For more on conjunctions, check out p.135.

3) If you want to seriously wow the examiners, use the conditional tense of 'haber' (*to have...*) with the past participle (see p.144) to mean 'would have...'.

Habría comprado un libro, pero no tengo dinero.	*I would have bought a book, but I have no money.*

Quisiera — I would like

Two really common verbs sometimes get replaced in the conditional by a different form.

1) The conditional form of 'querer' (*to want*) is often replaced by 'quisiera' — it means '*I would like*'.

Quisiera un coche.	*I would like a car.*		Quisiera una manzana.	*I would like an apple.*

2) You can use 'quisiera' in polite requests.

Quisiera reservar una mesa para tres personas.	*I would like to reserve a table for three.*

3) The conditional of 'haber' (*to have...*) can also be replaced by 'hubiera'.

'Quisiera' and 'hubiera' are in the imperfect subjunctive. See p.154 for more.

Hubiera venido antes.	*I would have come earlier.*

It's your lucky day — the conditional only has one set of endings...

Write these verbs in the conditional. The subject has been given to you in brackets.

1. ir (tú)   **3.** venir (nosotros)   **5.** partir (yo)   **7.** hablar (usted)

2. cantar (él)   **4.** decir (vosotros)   **6.** salir (ellos)   **8.** tener (nosotros)

Quick Questions

Make sure you've got all those tenses clear before moving on. Some of them can be tricky, so take your time going through this set of quick questions. Remember to check the answers too.

Quick Questions

1) Finish these sentences by adding the correct ending to the verb.
   The sentences should all be in the preterite tense.
   a) Ishmael llor............ mucho.
   b) Javier y yo sal............ anoche.
   c) Tú suspend............ la prueba.
   d) El concierto dur............ una hora.
   e) Yo abr............ la puerta.
   f) Nosotros escrib............ un artículo interesante.
   g) Vosotros com............ todo el queso.
   h) Carla e Irene aprob............ el examen.
   i) Mi madre nac............ en 1971.
   j) Erica y Kate beb............ zumo de manzana.

2) Fill in the gaps by choosing the correct preterite verb.
   a) Mercedes, ¿tú .... a la pescadería?   fue / fuiste / fuisteis
   b) Mis primos y yo .... la caja en el coche.   pusisteis / puse / pusimos
   c) Yo .... mis libros.   traje / trajo / trajiste
   d) Vosotras .... al espectáculo.   vine / viniste / vinisteis
   e) Luis .... su maleta anteayer.   hice / hizo / hicieron
   f) Tus amigos te .... un sombrero.   diste / disteis / dieron
   g) Lia me .... que Joe estaba triste.   dijo / dije / dijeron

3) Translate these sentences into Spanish using the imperfect tense.
   a) We used to visit our grandmother.
   b) You (inf., sing.) used to be a cook.
   c) I used to watch movies on Fridays.
   d) He used to sing in the car.
   e) It was snowing in the countryside.
   f) They used to go to that supermarket.
   g) She used to talk a lot.
   h) You (inf., pl.) used to eat a lot of chocolate.

4) Fill in the gaps by choosing between the preterite and imperfect forms.
   a) Siempre .... en el coche.   cantaste / cantabas
   b) El lunes .... al colegio.   fui / iba
   c) Los jueves .... con su hermano.   cenaron / cenábamos
   d) .... las compras a menudo.   Hicimos / Hacíamos
   e) Ayer, Pedro .... la verdad a su madre.   dijo / decía
   f) De niña, Rita siempre .... habladora.   fue / era
   g) Anteayer, ... buen tiempo.   hizo / hacía
   h) .... nublado el día de mi cumpleaños.   Estuvo / Estaba

5) Translate the following sentences into Spanish.
   a) When I heard the noise, I was at home.
   b) It was very cold and it was raining too.
   c) They were going to York when they saw the cat.
   d) He used to have a green jacket.

6) You can use past participles with the verb 'haber' to say what you 'have done' or 'had done'. Write out the past participles for these verbs. Some of them might be irregular.
   a) hablar ....
   b) pedir ....
   c) abrir ....
   d) ver ....
   e) poner ....
   f) beber ....
   g) escribir ....
   h) nadar ....
   i) decir ....
   j) hacer ....
   k) volver ....
   l) romper ....

Quick Questions

7) Change these sentences from the present tense into the perfect tense.
   The perfect tense is the 'have done' tense.
   a) Como una ración de tortilla.
   b) Lucía escribe una historia interesante.
   c) Hacemos un viaje a Londres.
   d) Pones las tazas en el lavaplatos.

8) Change these sentences from the preterite tense into the pluperfect tense.
   The pluperfect tense is the 'had done' tense.
   a) El examen empezó.
   b) Elegiste estudiar arte dramático.
   c) Abrieron el monedero.
   d) Compré el collar en una tienda.

9) Translate these sentences into English.
   a) Habíais roto las ventanas.
   b) Federico ya había almorzado.
   c) Habíamos visto esa película.
   d) Habían dormido en el sofá.

10) Translate the words in brackets into Spanish to form regular future tense sentences.
   a) Mañana .... (we will learn) sobre las ventajas y las desventajas.
   b) Noelia te .... (will bring) el videojuego.
   c) El sábado tú .... (will sing) la canción que has escrito.
   d) .... (I will correct) los deberes cuando tenga tiempo.
   e) Pilar y Miguel .... (will lie) a su tío.

11) Translate these sentences into Spanish.
   a) I will look for the book tomorrow.
   b) We will have dinner at my father's restaurant.
   c) They will call us after the show.
   d) You (inf., pl.) will put the pencils on the table.
   e) You (form., sing.) will have an umbrella.

12) Señor Ramos has written a list of what he would do if he won the lottery. Complete the
   sentences by writing the verbs in brackets in the conditional tense in the 'yo' form.
   a) .... (viajar) por el mundo en mi barco.
   b) .... (tener) diez casas grandes con piscinas.
   c) .... (poder) comprar mi propia isla.
   d) .... (hacer) viajes a Australia para visitar a mis primos.
   e) .... (dar) dinero a mis amigos.
   f) .... (dejar) de trabajar.

13) Translate these sentences into Spanish.
   a) He would eat, but he isn't hungry.
   b) You (form., sing.) would help, but you can't drive.
   c) Could you (inf., sing.) give me that scarf?
   d) We should visit Sergio.
   e) I would buy a souvenir, but I don't have money.
   f) They wouldn't sell their house.

Reflexive Verbs

Sometimes you'll have to talk about things you do to yourself — like 'washing yourself' or 'getting yourself up' in the morning. It sounds weird in English, but in Spanish they do it all the time.

Me, te, se... — Reflexive pronouns

1) '<u>Se</u>' means '<u>oneself</u>'. Here are all the different ways to say 'self':

myself	me	ourselves	nos
yourself (inf., sing.)	te	yourselves (inf., pl.)	os
himself/herself/oneself yourself (form., sing.)	se	themselves, each other yourselves (form., pl.)	se

You can tell which verbs need 'self' by checking in the dictionary. 'To get washed' in the dictionary would be 'lavarse'.

2) Reflexive verbs follow a straightforward pattern, e.g. '<u>lavarse</u>' = to get washed (literally '<u>to wash oneself</u>'). The <u>reflexive pronoun</u> usually just goes in <u>front</u> of the normal <u>verb</u>.

I get washed	me lavo	we get washed	nos lavamos
you (inf., sing.) get washed	te lavas	you (inf., pl.) get washed	os laváis
he/she/it gets washed you (form., sing.) get washed	se lava	they get washed you (form., pl.) get washed	se lavan

¿Te sientes mal?	*Do you feel ill?*

No me despierto temprano.	*I don't wake up early.*

3) There are lots of these verbs, but here are the ones you really <u>should know</u>:

'acostarse', 'sentirse', 'despertarse' and 'vestirse' are all radical-changing verbs (see p.138).

acostarse	*to go to bed*	sentirse	*to feel*	despertarse	*to wake up*	vestirse	*to get dressed*
levantarse	*to get up*	llamarse	*to be called*	irse	*to go away*	ponerse	*to put on*

Putting reflexive verbs in the perfect tense

When you want to use reflexive verbs in the <u>perfect tense</u>, put the <u>reflexive pronoun</u> (e.g. 'me', 'se') in front of the <u>verb</u> as usual:

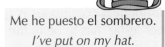

Me Stick the reflexive pronoun at the start.	+	he puesto Then put the whole of the perfect tense verb (see p.144).	=	Me he puesto el sombrero. *I've put on my hat.*

Use 'se' to make impersonal phrases

The reflexive pronoun '<u>se</u>' is often used in front of a verb that's not reflexive to make it <u>impersonal</u>. It's like saying '<u>one does something</u>' in English. The verb has to be in the '<u>he / she / it</u>' form.

¿Se puede comer afuera?	*Can one eat outside?*

For more about impersonal verbs, turn to p.152.

Make sure you know all the reflexive verbs on this page...

Write these reflexive verbs in the present and perfect tenses. The subject has been given to you in brackets.

1. llamarse (yo)   **3.** lavarse (él)   **5.** sentirse (nosotros)   **7.** vestirse (usted)

2. levantarse (ellos)   **4.** acostarse (tú)   **6.** irse (vosotros)   **8.** despertarse (tú)

Verbs with '-ing' and 'Just Done'

The continuous tenses are great if you want to specify that something is ongoing at a particular moment.

Use the present continuous for something happening right now

1) <u>Most</u> of the time you'd translate phrases such as 'I am doing' and 'I was doing' with <u>normal tenses</u> — those two would be 'hago' (present tense), and 'hacía' (imperfect tense).

2) If you want <u>to stress</u> that something <u>is happening</u> at the moment, use the <u>present continuous</u>.

> Estoy almorzando.   *I'm having lunch.*

3) To form the present continuous, you need the correct part of '<u>estar</u>' (*to be*) in the <u>present</u> tense...

4) ...and the '<u>-ing</u>' part — also called the <u>present participle</u> or <u>gerund</u>.

5) It's made up of the <u>stem</u> of the verb (p.137), plus the correct <u>ending</u>.

estar — to be	
I am	estoy
you (inf., sing.) are	estás
he/she/it is you (form., sing.) are	está
we are	estamos
you (inf., pl.) are	estáis
they / you (form., pl.) are	están

    a) if it's an -<u>ar</u> verb, add '-<u>ando</u>'.

estoy	+	hablar	+	-ando	=	estoy hablando
present of 'estar'		*'hablar' stem*		*-ar ending*		*I am speaking*

    b) if it's an -<u>er</u> or -<u>ir</u> verb, add '-<u>iendo</u>'.

estás	+	comer	+	-iendo	=	estás comiendo
present of 'estar'		*'comer' stem*		*-er ending*		*you (inf., sing.) are eating*

6) There are only a few <u>irregular</u> ones you need to <u>know</u>:

caer (*to fall*)	⟶	cayendo	servir (*to serve*)	⟶	sirviendo
leer (*to read*)	⟶	leyendo	pedir (*to ask for*)	⟶	pidiendo
oír (*to hear*)	⟶	oyendo	morir (*to die*)	⟶	muriendo
construír (*to build*)	⟶	construyendo	decir (*to say*)	⟶	diciendo

The imperfect continuous is for saying what was happening

1) If you want <u>to stress</u> that something <u>was happening</u> in the past, use the <u>imperfect continuous</u>.

2) The imperfect continuous is <u>similar</u> to the present continuous, except '<u>estar</u>' has to be in the <u>imperfect</u> tense.

> Estaba durmiendo cuando sonó el teléfono.
> *He / She was sleeping when the telephone rang.*

The preterite tense is used here to show that a sudden action — the telephone ringing — interrupted an ongoing action in the imperfect continuous — i.e. the person sleeping.

'Acabar de' — to say that something's just happened

'Acabar' is a regular -ar verb.

To say what's <u>just</u> happened, use the present tense of '<u>acabar</u>', followed by '<u>de</u>' and a verb in the <u>infinitive</u>.

> Acabo de ducharme.   *I have just taken a shower.*

> Acaba de salir.   *She has just left.*

The present continuous stresses what's going on at the moment...

Put these verbs in the present continuous, the imperfect continuous and the 'acabar de' forms.

1. caer (él)   **3.** saltar (ella)   **5.** correr (vosotros)   **7.** dar (tú)   **9.** servir (ustedes)

2. abrir (tú)   **4.** decir (ellos)   **6.** seguir (nosotros)   **8.** leer (yo)   **10.** bailar (nosotros)

Negative Forms

No, I'm not going to write anything here about negatives. Nothing at all... except that they're pretty useful.

'No' in front of the verb means 'not'

1) To change a sentence to mean the <u>opposite</u> in Spanish, you have to put '<u>no</u>' in front of the <u>action word</u>:

Soy profesor. *I'm a teacher.*	No soy profesor. *I'm not a teacher.*
Hablo español. *I speak Spanish.*	No hablo español. *I don't speak Spanish.*

2) You can do the <u>same</u> with <u>all of the tenses</u> — look at these examples:

No leerás el libro. *You will not read the book.*	No fui al parque. *I didn't go to the park.*

Sometimes you have to say 'no' twice...

1) 'No' in Spanish means both '<u>no</u>' and '<u>not</u>'.

2) This means that if you're answering a <u>question</u>, you may need to say 'no' <u>twice</u>:

No, no quiero sopa, gracias.   *No, I don't want soup, thanks.*

No, Juan no veía la tele.   *No, Juan wasn't watching TV.*

Even more negatives...

There are more negatives you need to <u>understand</u> — for top marks you should use them too.

ya no	*not any more*
no ... nadie	*not anybody (nobody)*
no ... nunca / jamás	*not ever (never)*
no ... nada	*not anything (nothing)*
no ... ni ... ni	*neither ... nor*
no ... ningún / ninguna	*none / not one / not a single (before noun)*
no .. ninguno / ninguna	*none / not one / not a single one (to replace noun)*

Ya no voy a York.
I don't go to York any more.

No hay nadie aquí.
*There isn't anybody here. /
There's nobody here.*

Julia no va nunca al cine.
Julia never goes to the cinema.

No hay nada. *There isn't anything. / There's nothing.*	Sam y Clara no van ni a Londres ni a Madrid. *Sam and Clara go to neither London nor Madrid.*

No hay ningún plátano. *There is not a single banana.*	No hay ninguna pera. *There is not a single pear.*
Jo no tiene ninguno/a. *Jo doesn't have a single one.*	

p.119 has more information on 'ningún'.

Remember 'no' in Spanish means 'no' <u>and</u> 'not'...

Translate these sentences using negative forms.

1. I didn't go to the cinema.
2. We don't go to the gym any more.
3. You (tú) go to neither Oslo nor Faro.
4. Sally doesn't have a single apple.
5. There's nothing here.
6. There's nobody in the car.

The Passive and Impersonal Verbs

Impersonal verbs and the passive come up occasionally, so it's important that you know a bit about them.

Ser + past participle — The passive voice

You don't need to use the passive, but you do need to be able to recognise it.

1) In an <u>active</u> sentence, the <u>subject does</u> something.

> Lavé la taza.   *I washed the cup.*

2) In the <u>passive</u> voice, something is <u>done to</u> the <u>subject</u>.

> La taza fue lavada.   *The cup was washed.*

3) This means you can say something is <u>happening</u> without always saying <u>who</u> is doing it.

4) The passive is formed using 'ser' (*to be*) and the <u>past participle</u> (see p.142).

fueron *they were* This is the <u>preterite tense</u> of 'ser' (see p.141). This changes depending on the tense and subject.	**+**	limpiado *cleaned* <u>past participle</u> of the verb '<u>limpiar</u>'	**=**	Las mesas fueron limpiadas. *The tables were cleaned.* A sentence in the <u>passive</u> voice.

In the passive, the past participle must always match the gender and number of the object that you're talking about. Here 'limpiadas' is used because 'las mesas' are feminine and plural.

5) If you want to add <u>someone</u> or <u>something</u> doing the action, add '<u>por</u>' (*by*) and <u>who / what</u> did it.

> El libro será leído por Jo.   *The book will be read by Jo.*

> Fue escrito por Adil.   *It was written by Adil.*

Se + 3rd person — Impersonal verbs

1) You can turn <u>any</u> Spanish verb into an <u>impersonal</u> <u>verb</u> (e.g. '*one does*' rather than '*I do*') by using '<u>se</u>' and the '<u>he / she / it</u>' form of the verb:

> ¿Se necesita un libro?   *Does one need a book?*

2) If there's a <u>subject</u> in the sentence, use the <u>singular</u> for a single subject, and the <u>plural</u> for plural subjects:

> El arroz se cocina durante quince minutos.   *The rice is cooked for fifteen minutes.*

> Las puertas se abren a las nueve.   *The doors are opened at nine.*

Some more important impersonal verbs...

1) '<u>Hay que</u>' is an impersonal way of saying that '*one has to do something*'.

> Hay que hacer los deberes.   *Homework has to be done.* ⟵ Literally: *One has to do homework.*

2) '<u>Parece que</u>' means '*it seems that*':   Parece que poco ha cambiado.   *It seems that little has changed.*

3) <u>Weather</u> verbs are <u>always impersonal</u> — they're written in the '<u>he / she / it</u>' form of the verb.

> Llueve.   *It rains.*   Está nevando.   *It's snowing.*   Truena.   *It thunders.*

Tronar (to thunder) is a radical-changing verb.

One has to learn this — it's nothing personal...

A) Decide which of these 4 sentences are in the passive voice.

1. Comimos la sopa.
2. El poema fue escrito.
3. La mesa es puesta.
4. Cierras la puerta.

B) Complete using the impersonal form.

1. .... la bufanda. (comprar)
2. .... los postres. (comer)

The Subjunctive

Time to learn how to form the Spanish subjunctive. It's easy to get mixed up, so it's a good idea to make sure you really understand the present tense (p.137-139) before you get started.

Forming the present subjunctive

1) Sometimes, the present subjunctive is needed instead of the normal present tense.

2) To form the subjunctive, use the same stem as the 'I' form of the normal present tense.

3) For -ar verbs, add the -er present tense endings. For -er or -ir verbs, add the -ar endings.

infinitive	hablar	comer	vivir
'yo form'	hablo	como	vivo
I	hable	coma	viva
you (inf., sing.)	hables	comas	vivas
he/she/it/you (form., sing.)	hable	coma	viva
we	hablemos	comamos	vivamos
you (inf., pl.)	habléis	comáis	viváis
they/you (form., pl.)	hablen	coman	vivan

Irregular verbs in the present subjunctive

1) Some verbs are irregular in the 'I' form of the present tense, so the subjunctive has to match this.

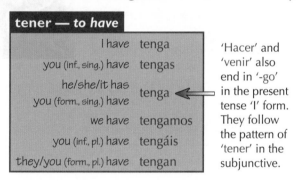

tener — to have

I have	tenga
you (inf., sing.) have	tengas
he/she/it has / you (form., sing.) have	tenga
we have	tengamos
you (inf., pl.) have	tengáis
they/you (form., pl.) have	tengan

'Hacer' and 'venir' also end in '-go' in the present tense 'I' form. They follow the pattern of 'tener' in the subjunctive.

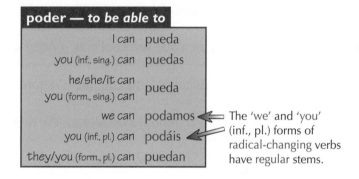

poder — to be able to

I can	pueda
you (inf., sing.) can	puedas
he/she/it can / you (form., sing.) can	pueda
we can	podamos
you (inf., pl.) can	podáis
they/you (form., pl.) can	puedan

The 'we' and 'you' (inf., pl.) forms of radical-changing verbs have regular stems.

2) But some verbs are completely irregular in the subjunctive. Here are some of them:

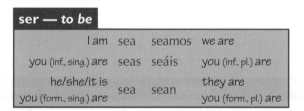

ser — to be

I am	sea	seamos	we are
you (inf., sing.) are	seas	seáis	you (inf., pl.) are
he/she/it is / you (form., sing.) are	sea	sean	they are / you (form., pl.) are

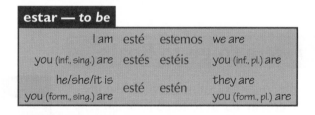

estar — to be

I am	esté	estemos	we are
you (inf., sing.) are	estés	estéis	you (inf., pl.) are
he/she/it is / you (form., sing.) are	esté	estén	they are / you (form., pl.) are

ir — to go

I go	vaya	vayamos	we go
you (inf., sing.) go	vayas	vayáis	you (inf., pl.) go
he/she/it goes / you (form., sing.) go	vaya	vayan	they go / you (form., pl.) go

dar — to give

I give	dé	demos	we give
you (inf., sing.) give	des	deis	you (inf., pl.) give
he/she/it gives / you (form., sing.) give	dé	den	they give / you (form., pl.) give

Don't confuse the present tense with the present subjunctive...

Write these verbs in the present subjunctive. The subject has been given to you in brackets.

1. saltar (tú)
2. escuchar (yo)
3. limpiar (nosotros)
4. abrir (ellos)
5. venir (él)
6. hacer (nosotros)
7. poder (ustedes)
8. tener (vosotros)

Subjunctive	# The Subjunctive

Now it's time to find out when you need to use the subjunctive. It's a tricky old page so take your time.

Use the present subjunctive...

1) ...to get <u>someone else</u> to do something:

> Ana quiere que lavemos los platos. *Ana wants us to wash the dishes.*

2) ...to express a <u>wish</u> or <u>desire</u>:

> Espero que haya fresas en el supermercado. *I hope that there are strawberries in the supermarket.*

3) ...after expressing an <u>emotion</u> or <u>opinion</u>:

> Es importante que estudiéis. *It's important that you (inf., pl.) study.*

4) ...to say that something's <u>unlikely</u> to happen:

> No creo que vaya a venir. *I don't believe he's going to come.*

'sepa' is from the verb 'saber' (to know). It's also irregular in the subjunctive — its stem is 'sep'.

5) ...when there's a <u>requirement</u>:

> Necesito a alguien que sepa cocinar. *I need someone who knows how to cook.*

6) ...after '<u>cuando</u>' ('*when*'), '<u>antes de que</u>' ('*before*') and '<u>aunque</u>' ('*even if*') when talking about the future:

> Vamos al teatro cuando llegue Marta. *We're going to the theatre when Marta arrives.*

7) ...after '<u>para que</u>' ('*so that*') to express purpose:

> Vamos al parque para que puedas jugar. *We're going to the park so that you (inf., sing.) can play.*

If I *were* to go to Spain...

1) The <u>imperfect subjunctive</u> is like the '<u>were</u>' in '*if I <u>were</u> to go to Spain*'. You <u>don't</u> need to use it, but you'll need to <u>recognise</u> it.

2) '<u>Quisiera</u>' ('*I would like*') is a <u>common example</u> of the imperfect subjunctive. See p.146 for more about using it in <u>polite requests</u>.

	hablar	comer	vivir
I	hablara	comiera	viviera
you (inf., sing.)	hablaras	comieras	vivieras
he/she/it/you (form., sing.)	hablara	comiera	viviera
we	habláramos	comiéramos	viviéramos
you (inf., pl.)	hablarais	comierais	vivierais
they/you (form., pl.)	hablaran	comieran	vivieran

Make sure you know how both types of subjunctive are used...

Decide which sentences use the present subjunctive and which use the imperfect subjunctive.

1. Quiere que le des el abrigo.

2. Si tuviera mucho dinero, compraría un coche.

3. Vamos a hacerlo cuando tengamos tiempo.

4. Mi madre pido que mi padre sacara la basura.

Giving Orders | Imperative

Learn what's on this page and you'll be giving out orders in no time...

Informal commands

1) To form a <u>singular informal</u> command, take the '<u>tú</u>' part of the <u>present tense</u> verb and <u>take off</u> the '<u>s</u>'.

> escribes *you write* ⟹ ¡Escribe! *Write!*

> escuchas *you listen* ⟹ ¡Escucha! *Listen!*

2) With commands, <u>pronouns</u> (e.g. *me*, *them*, *it*) are placed at the <u>end</u> of the word and you need to <u>add</u> an <u>accent</u> to show where the <u>stress</u> is.

> ¡Cómelo! *Eat it!*

3) To tell <u>two or more people</u> what to do in an <u>informal</u> way, take the <u>infinitive</u> and <u>change</u> the final '<u>r</u>' to a '<u>d</u>'.

> hablar (*to speak*) ⟹ ¡Hablad! *Speak!*

> leer (*to read*) ⟹ ¡Leed! *Read!*

> salir (*to go out*) ⟹ ¡Salid! *Go out!*

There are a few common irregular imperatives.

Infinitive	Informal Singular
decir (*to say*)	¡Di!
hacer (*to do / make*)	¡Haz!
ir (*to go*)	¡Ve!
poner (*to put*)	¡Pon!
salir (*to go out*)	¡Sal!
ser (*to be*)	¡Sé!
tener (*to have*)	¡Ten!
venir (*to come*)	¡Ven!

Formal commands

1) To <u>politely</u> tell someone what to do, use the <u>formal 'you'</u> form of the <u>present subjunctive</u>.

> ¡Hable! *Speak!*

For a reminder of the present subjunctive, head back to p.153.

> Siga todo recto. *Continue straight on.*

Infinitive	Present Subjunctive
dar (*to give*)	dé
haber (*to have...*)	haya
ir (*to go*)	vaya
saber (*to know*)	sepa
ser (*to be*)	sea

2) As always, there are some <u>irregular forms</u> that you just need to <u>learn</u>.

3) When politely telling <u>more than one</u> person what to do, use the <u>formal plural</u> of the <u>subjunctive</u>.

> ¡Entren! *Enter!*

> Cojan la primera calle a la derecha. *Take the first street on the right.*

Making commands negative

1) To tell someone <u>not</u> to do something, <u>always</u> use the <u>subjunctive</u>.

> ¡No escuches! *Don't listen!*

2) Watch out — any <u>pronouns</u> have to go before the verb:

> ¡Tócalo! *Touch it!* ⟹ ¡No lo toques! *Don't touch it!*

Learn how to use the imperative — go on...

Write these verbs as positive and negative commands. The type of command is in brackets.

1. cantar (inf., sing.)
2. bailar (form., pl.)
3. tener (inf., sing.)
4. dar (form., sing.)
5. abrir (inf., pl.)
6. venir (inf., pl.)
7. ser (form., sing.)
8. ir (form., pl.)

Quick Questions

You're almost there — just one last bunch of quick questions before you can declare yourself a Spanish grammar expert. Don't forget to keep going back over what you've learned so that it really sinks in.

Quick Questions

1) Put these reflexive verbs into the correct present tense form.
   a) llamarse *(tú)*
   b) sentirse *(yo)*
   c) levantarse *(nosotros)*
   d) dormirse *(vosotros)*
   e) acostarse *(usted)*
   f) irse *(ellos)*
   g) despertarse *(nosotros)*
   h) ponerse *(ella)*

2) Translate these sentences into Spanish using the '-ing' form.
   a) I am chatting with my friends.
   b) She is listening to music in the lounge.
   c) We are ordering some drinks.
   d) You *(form., sing.)* were reading the newspaper.

3) Using the words in brackets, make these sentences negative.
   You might need to change words or take some out too.
   a) Joe enseña química. **(ya no)**
   b) Vamos al parque. **(no ... nunca)**
   c) Llevo gafas y un collar azul. **(no ... ni ... ni)**

4) Underline the verbs written in the passive. Not every sentence contains the passive.
   a) El autobús partió a las tres y cuarto.
   b) La compañía fue fundada en 1986.
   c) La máquina hace mucho ruido.
   d) El salón está pintado por sus hermanos.
   e) El niño siguió al veterinario.
   f) Encontraron una llave en el jardín.
   g) El anillo será llevado por Juana.
   h) Los coches fueron comprados anteayer.

5) Match these Spanish sentences on the left with their English translations on the right.
   a) ¿Se venden casas aquí?
   b) Se puede reservar habitaciones.
   c) Se juega al fútbol en el parque.
   d) Se recicla el vidrio.

   i.   *Rooms can be reserved.*
   ii. *Football is played in the park.*
   iii. *Do you sell houses here?*
   iv. *Glass is recycled.*

6) Complete these sentences by putting the verbs in brackets into the present subjunctive.
   a) Quiero que mi madre me .... **(dejar)** ir al concierto.
   b) Vamos a esconder estos dulces antes de que .... **(venir)** nuestra amiga.
   c) Buscáis un piso pequeño que .... **(estar)** cerca de la biblioteca.

7) Underline the verbs written in the imperfect subjunctive.
   a) Pedí que me enviaras tu respuesta ayer.
   b) Si yo fuera tú, estaría de acuerdo con Mónica.
   c) Organizaría la fiesta, si tuviera más tiempo.

8) Write out the following verbs as singular informal commands.
   a) cantar   c) hacer   e) saltar   g) decir   i) correr   k) tener
   b) abrir   d) ser   f) poner   h) venir   j) mentir   l) salir

9) You are giving a tourist directions. Write the verbs in brackets as formal commands.
   a) .... *(Seguir)* todo recto.
   b) .... *(Girar)* a la izquierda.
   c) Luego, ... *(tomar)* la primera calle a la derecha.

Revision Summary for Section Eleven

By now you'll know that the only way to be sure you know your stuff is to practise over and over again. Now that you've done the Quick Questions, there shouldn't be much to trouble you. If there's something you don't understand, though, make sure you go back over it — it's the only way to improve.

Nouns and Articles (p.116-117) ☑

1) What gender are these words...?
   a) versión   b) algodón   c) ardilla   d) día
2) Predict the plural of 'el avestruz' (ostrich).
3) How would you say 'I'm a teacher' in Spanish?

Adjectives and Adverbs (p.118-126) ☑

4) Using the word 'blanco', translate these phrases into Spanish:
   a) the white bird   c) the white houses
   b) the white table   d) the white coats
5) When would 'bueno' become 'buen'?
6) How would you say 'that beach over there'?
7) Translate 'Camino muy despacio' into English.

Pronouns (p.129-132) ☑

8) Marisol loves mushrooms. How would you say this in Spanish?
9) Translate this sentence into Spanish: 'I live in Birmingham, which is a big city.'
10) You're looking at some mobile phones. Say 'I'd like this one please' in Spanish.

Prepositions (p.133-134) ☑

11) 'Las fresas están encima de las naranjas.' Where are the strawberries?
12) Give three uses of the preposition 'para'.
13) Translate 'Thank you for your letter' into Spanish.

Verbs in Different Tenses (p.137-146) ☑

14) How do you say...?   a) It closes at nine.   b) It begins at four.   c) I go to bed at ten.
15) Say all the preterite tense forms of 'hacer' out loud.
16) When would you use the imperfect tense?
17) Translate into Spanish: 'I can't come to your party because I'm going to go to Spain.'
18) Using the proper future tense, say that you will buy a present for your sister.
19) Translate into English: 'En un mundo ideal, comería patatas todos los días.'

The Subjunctive and Imperative Forms (p.153-155) ☑

20) 'Es importante que hagáis vuestros deberes.' How would you say this in English?
21) Martha says: 'I want you to wash the dishes.' Translate this into Spanish.
22) Translate this sentence into English: 'Sería mejor si no viviera en un pueblo tan pequeño.'
23) How would you use an imperative to tell your friend to open the door?
24) How would you use an imperative to tell two older people who you don't know to wait a minute?

Section Twelve — Exam Advice

The Listening Exam

Ah. Your reward for conquering all that grammar is a section about those pesky exams... Sorry about that. But there is some good news — these pages are crammed full of advice to help you tackle them head on.

There are four exams for GCSE Spanish

1) Your Spanish GCSE is assessed by four separate exams — Listening, Speaking, Reading and Writing.

2) Each exam is worth 25% of your final mark. You'll get a grade between 1 and 9 (with 9 being the highest).

3) You won't sit all of the papers at the same time — you'll probably have your speaking exam a couple of weeks before the rest of your exams.

The Listening Exam has two sections

1) For the listening paper, you'll listen to various recordings of people speaking in Spanish and answer questions on what you've heard.

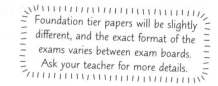
Foundation tier papers will be slightly different, and the exact format of the exams varies between exam boards. Ask your teacher for more details.

2) The paper is 45 minutes long (including 5 minutes reading time).

3) You'll get one section where the questions are in English, so you'll write these answers in English too. The questions in the other section will be in Spanish — you may need to answer these in Spanish.

Read through the paper carefully at the start of the test

1) Before the recordings begin, you'll be given five minutes to read through the paper.

2) Use this time to read each question carefully. Some are multiple choice, and others require you to write some short answers — make sure you know what each one is asking you to do.

3) In particular, look at the questions which are written in Spanish. Try to work out what the questions mean. There's a list of exam-style Spanish question words and phrases on the inside front cover of this book to help you prepare for this.

4) Reading the question titles, and the questions themselves, will give you a good idea of the topics you'll be asked about. This should help you predict what to listen out for.

5) You can write on the exam paper, so scribble down anything that might be useful.

Make notes while listening to the recordings

1) You'll hear each audio track twice, and then there'll be a pause for you to write down your answer.

2) While you're listening, it's a good idea to jot down a few details — e.g. dates, times, names or key words. But make sure you keep listening while you're writing down any notes.

3) Listen right to the end, even if you think you've got the answer — sometimes the person will change their mind or add an important detail at the end.

Listen to the speaker's tone, too — this will hint at their mood, e.g. angry or excited.

4) Don't worry if you can't understand every word that's being said — just listen carefully both times and try to pick out the vocabulary you need to answer the question.

Give an answer for every question, even if you're not sure about it...

If you've heard a track twice, and you're still not sure of the answer, scribble one down anyway — you never know, it might be the right one. You may as well write something sensible just in case — it's worth a shot.

The Speaking Exam

The Speaking Exam can seem daunting, but remember — no one is trying to catch you out, so try to stay calm.

There are three parts to the Speaking Exam

During your preparation time, you can make notes to take in with you for the first two tasks. You can't keep the notes for the conversation.

1) Your speaking exam will be conducted and recorded by your teacher.

2) The exam is in three parts. Before you start, you'll get 10-12 minutes to prepare for the first two sections:

① Role-play (2 min.)	② Photo Card (3 min.)	③ Conversation (5-7 min.)
You'll get a card with a scenario on it. It'll have five bullet points — most will have notes on what to say, in Spanish. The '!' means you'll be asked an unknown question, and '?' shows you have to ask a question about the words next to it. See p.5 for an example.	Before the exam, you'll receive a photo and some questions relating to it (look at the example on p.48). Your teacher will ask you the questions that are on the photo card, as well as some questions you haven't seen.	You and your teacher will have a conversation based on one or two themes that you've studied. You may get to choose one of the themes, and you may also have to ask your teacher a question during the conversation.

3) The role-play card will tell you if you need to use 'tú', but otherwise, use 'usted' to talk to your teacher.

Try to be imaginative with your answers

You need to find ways to show off the full extent of your Spanish knowledge. You should try to:

1) Use a range of tenses — e.g. for a question on daily routine, think of when something different happens.

| Pero mañana será diferente porque jugaré al tenis después del instituto. | *But tomorrow it will be different because I will play tennis after school.* |

If you can't remember a word, just say something suitable that you do know instead, e.g. swap in 'tennis' for 'rugby', or 'sister' for 'cousin'.

2) Talk about other people, not just yourself — it's fine to make people up if that helps.

| Me gusta el rugby, pero mi primo lo odia. | *I like rugby, but my cousin hates it.* |

3) Give loads of opinions and reasons for your opinions.

| En mi opinión, debemos reciclar más porque producimos demasiada basura. | *In my opinion, we must recycle more because we produce too much rubbish.* |

If you're really struggling, ask for help in Spanish

1) If you get really stuck trying to think of a word or phrase, you can ask for help — as long as it's in Spanish.

2) For example, if you can't remember how to say 'homework' in Spanish, ask your teacher. You won't get any marks for vocabulary your teacher's given you though.

| ¿Cómo se dice 'homework' en español? | *How do you say 'homework' in Spanish?* |

3) If you don't hear something clearly, just ask:

| ¿Puede repetir, por favor? | *Can you repeat, please?* |

You could also ask this if you're desperately in need of time to think of an answer.

Don't speak too soon — wait for the teacher to tell you to start...

Given that you're only human, you're bound to have a few slip-ups in the speaking exam. Don't panic — it's completely natural. What's important is how you deal with a mistake — just correct yourself and move on.

The Reading Exam

The Reading Exam is split up into three sections. Make sure you know what you'll need to do in each one.

Read the questions and texts carefully

1) The <u>higher tier</u> reading paper is around <u>1 hour long</u>.

2) You'll be given a <u>variety of Spanish texts</u> and then asked questions about them. The texts could include blog posts, emails, newspaper reports, adverts and literary texts. Some questions will be in <u>English</u> and some will be in <u>Spanish</u>. You need to write your <u>answers</u> in the <u>same language</u> as the question.

3) <u>Scan through the text</u> first to <u>get an idea</u> of what it's about. Then read the <u>questions</u> that go with it carefully, making sure you understand <u>what information</u> you should be looking out for.

4) Next, <u>go back through the text</u>. You're not expected to understand every word, so don't get distracted by trying to work out what everything means — <u>focus</u> on finding the <u>information you need</u>.

> *The inside front cover of this book has a list of common Spanish question words, phrases and instructions.*

5) The <u>last</u> question is a <u>translation</u> question — you'll have to translate a short passage of text from Spanish <u>into English</u>. See p.162 for more tips on tackling translation questions.

Don't give up if you don't understand something

1) Use the <u>context</u> of the text to help you understand what it might be saying. You might be able to find some clues in the <u>title of the text</u> or the <u>type of text</u>.

2) Knowing how to spot <u>different word types</u> (e.g. nouns, verbs) can help you work out what's happening in a sentence. See the <u>grammar section</u> (p.116-157) for more.

3) You can <u>guess</u> some Spanish words that look or sound the <u>same as English</u> words, e.g. el problema — *problem*, la música — *music*, el color — *colour*.

> *Look for words that look like ones you know, e.g. 'la comida basura'. 'La comida' means 'food', and 'basura' means 'rubbish', so you can guess it means 'junk food'.*

4) Be careful though — you might come across some '<u>false friends</u>'. These are Spanish words that look like an English word, but have a <u>completely different meaning</u>:

la nota	*mark*	la carpeta	*folder, file*	la arena	*sand*	la librería	*bookshop*	actual	*present*
el pie	*foot*	la dirección	*address*	el éxito	*success*	sensible	*sensitive*	fatal	*awful*
el campo	*countryside*	el pariente	*relative*	la ropa	*clothes*	largo	*long*	embarazada	*pregnant*

Keep an eye on the time

1) There are quite a few questions to get through in the reading exam, so you need to work at a <u>good speed</u>.

2) If you're having trouble with a particular question, you might want to <u>move on</u> and <u>come back to it later</u>.

3) Don't forget that the <u>last question</u> in the paper is a <u>translation</u> — this is worth <u>more marks</u> than any other question, so you should leave <u>plenty of time</u> to tackle it.

4) Make sure you put an answer down for <u>every question</u> — lots of the questions are multiple choice, so even if you can't work out the answer, it's always worth putting down one of the options.

Make sure you're up to speed with the structure of the exam...

Don't forget, some of the questions will be in Spanish. Don't panic if you don't understand them — search for any familiar vocabulary and use any answer lines or boxes to help you guess what you have to do.

The Writing Exam

The writing exam is a great way of showing off what you can do — try to use varied vocabulary, include a range of tenses, and pack in any clever expressions that you've learnt over the years.

There'll be three tasks in the Writing Exam

1) The higher tier writing paper is about 1 hour and 15 minutes long and has three tasks.

① Structured Task

You'll be asked to write about 90 words in Spanish, based on some bullet points. Make sure you write about each bullet point and give some opinions. There may be a choice of two questions.

② Open-ended Task

There will be a choice of tasks. You'll need to write about 150 words in Spanish, based on some bullet points. This task is more creative — make sure you include some opinions with reasons.

③ Translation

You'll be given an English passage to translate into Spanish. The passage could be on any topic you've studied. There's more advice for doing translations on p.162.

2) Each task is worth a different number of marks, so you should spend more time on the higher-mark tasks.

Read the instructions carefully, and spend some time planning

1) Read the instructions for questions 1 and 2 carefully — you'll need to make sure you cover all of the bullet points. You can often use words from the question in your answer too.

Try to use varied vocab and a range of tenses.

2) Spend a few minutes for each question planning out your answer. Decide how you're going to cover everything that's required and in what order you're going to write things.

3) Write the best answer you can, using the Spanish that you know — it doesn't matter if it's not true.

Check through your work thoroughly

Checking your work is really important — even small mistakes can cost marks. Take a look at this checklist:

- Are all the verbs in the right tense?
  Mañana, trabajé en el jardín. ✘   Mañana, trabajaré en el jardín. ✓

- Are the verb endings correct?
  ¿No te gusta las fresas? ✘   ¿No te gustan las fresas? ✓

- Do your adjectives agree with their nouns?
  La camisa es amarillo. ✘   La camisa es amarilla. ✓

All of the points on this checklist are covered in the grammar section — see p.116-157.

- Are your adjectives in the right place?
  Una blanca falda. ✘   Una falda blanca. ✓

- Do your reflexive verbs and pronouns agree?
  A las siete, me levantamos. ✘   A las siete, me levanto. ✓

- Have you spelt everything correctly, including using the right accents?
  El toca la guitar con su tio. ✘   Él toca la guitarra con su tío. ✓

Write something for every bit of the task...

When you're nervous and stressed, it's dead easy to miss out something the question has asked you to do. For tasks one and two, try to write about the bullet points in order, and tick them off as you go along.

The Translation Tasks

When you're studying Spanish, you do little bits of translation in your head all the time. For the translation questions, you just need to apply those skills — one sentence at a time — to a couple of short passages.

In the Reading Exam, you'll translate from Spanish to English

1) The final question of the reading paper will ask you to translate a <u>short Spanish passage</u> (about 50 words) <u>into English</u>. The passage will be on a <u>topic you've studied</u>, so most of the vocabulary should be familiar.

2) Here are some <u>top tips</u> for doing your translation:

   • Read the whole text <u>before you start</u>. Make some <u>notes in English</u> to remind you of the main ideas.

   • Translate the text <u>one sentence at a time</u>, rather than word by word — this will avoid any of the Spanish word order being carried into the English.

Ella compra la manzana roja.	*She buys the apple red.* ✖	*She buys the red apple.* ✔
Salma lo comió.	*Salma it ate.* ✖	*Salma ate it.* ✔

   • Keep an eye out for <u>different tenses</u> — there will definitely be a variety in the passage.

   • <u>Read through</u> your translation to make sure it sounds <u>natural</u>. Some words and phrases don't translate literally, so you'll need to make sure that your sentences sound like <u>normal English</u>:

   Watch out for adverbs that might suggest a change in tense, e.g. en el futuro — in the future, mañana — tomorrow, ayer — yesterday.

La semana pasada, Irene hizo su maleta.	*The week last, Irene made her suitcase.* ✖	*Last week, Irene packed her suitcase.* ✔

3) Make sure you've translated <u>everything</u> from the original text — you'll lose marks if you miss something.

In the Writing Exam, you'll translate from English to Spanish

1) In the writing paper, you will have to translate <u>a short English passage</u> (about 50 words) <u>into Spanish</u>.

2) Here are <u>some ideas</u> for how you could approach the translation:

   • <u>Read</u> through the <u>whole text</u> before you get started so you know exactly what the text is about.

   • Tackle the passage <u>one sentence at a time</u> — work slowly and carefully through each one.

   • <u>Don't</u> translate things <u>literally</u> — think about what each English sentence means and try to write it in the <u>most Spanish way</u> you know. Don't worry — the translation is likely to include similar sentences to the ones you've learnt.

   • Work on the <u>word order</u> — remember that most Spanish <u>adjectives</u> follow the noun. If you need a <u>double negative</u>, remember to include both bits.

   Don't try to write a perfect translation first time — do it roughly first, and then write it up properly, crossing out any old drafts. Remember to keep an eye on the time.

3) Once you've got something that you're happy with, go back through and <u>check that you've covered everything</u> that was in the English.

4) Now <u>check</u> your Spanish text thoroughly using the <u>list from p.161</u>.

Thankfully, none of that got lost in translation...

Congratulations — you've made it through 162 pages. That's no mean feat, so give yourself a pat on the back. Once you've taken all the advice on board, test your knowledge and skills using the practice exam.

Practice Exam

Once you've been through all the questions in this book, you should be starting to feel prepared for the final exams. As a last piece of preparation, here's a practice exam for you to have a go at. It's been designed to give you the best exam practice possible for the Higher Tier papers. Good luck!

General Certificate of Secondary Education

GCSE Spanish
Higher Tier

Listening Paper

Centre name	Parth					CGP
Centre number	I	D	O	N	^T	**Practice Exam Paper**
Candidate number		K	N	O	W	**GCSE Spanish**
Surname	Patel					
Other names	N/A					
Candidate signature	Paru					

Time Allowed: 40 minutes approximately
+ 5 minutes reading before the test.

Instructions:
- Write in black ink.
- You have 5 minutes at the start of the test during which you may read through the questions and make notes. Then start the recording.
- Answer **all** questions in the spaces provided.
- Answer the questions in Section A in **English**.
- Answer the questions in Section B in **Spanish**.
- Give all the information you are asked for, and **write neatly**.

Advice:
- Before each new question, read through all the question parts and instructions carefully.
- Listen carefully to the recording. There will be a pause to allow you to reread the question, make notes or write down your answers.
- Listen to the recording again. There will be a pause to allow you to complete or check your answers.
- You may write at any point during the exam.
- Each item on the recording is repeated once.
- You are **not** allowed to ask questions or interrupt during the exam.

Information:
- The maximum mark for this paper is **50**.
- The number of marks for each question is shown in brackets.
- You are **not** allowed to use a dictionary.

Turn over

Section A   Questions and answers in **English**

School Subjects

Whilst in a small café in Guatemala, you overhear a group of students talking about the subjects they study at school.

What is their attitude towards the subjects?

Write **P** for a **positive** attitude. Write **N** for a **negative** attitude.
Write **P+N** for a **positive** and a **negative** attitude.

1

Maths	Geography

[2 marks]

2

English	Business Studies

[2 marks]

3

History	Biology

[2 marks]

Free Time

You listen to a podcast about what a politician does in her free time.

Answer the questions in **English**.

4   What does she always do in the evenings?

.... *[1 mark]*

5   What does she like to do when she has the time?

Give **two** details.

1. ....

2. .... *[2 marks]*

Eating Out

You're on a bus in Seville and you hear Blanca talking about her birthday meal.

Answer the questions in **English**.

6 Give **one** detail about the restaurant that Blanca went to.

.... *[1 mark]*

7 Does Blanca think she chose the right starter? Why / why not?

....

.... *[2 marks]*

8 Why did Blanca decide against the chef's speciality?

.... *[1 mark]*

9 Why does Blanca think it would be better to go to the restaurant later? Give **two** details.

....

.... *[2 marks]*

Weather

While listening to Spanish radio, you hear this announcement.

Answer the questions in **English**.

10   The increased temperatures are being caused by ....

        .... *[1 mark]*

11   You should avoid...

A	doing any sort of physical exercise.
B	using the oven during the warmest times of the day.
C	spending too much time in warm places.

        [1 mark]

12   What are people advised to do if they're suffering from a headache?
        Give **two** details.

        1. ....

        2. .... *[2 marks]*

Healthy Lifestyle

Listen to this advice from a personal trainer.

Choose the two correct answers for each question and write the letters in the boxes.

13   According to the personal trainer, alcoholic drinks...

A	are unhealthy because of their ingredients.
B	dehydrate you.
C	are fine in moderation.
D	are linked to weight problems.
E	have health benefits.

        [2 marks]

14   She says that doing regular exercise will help you...

A	expand your lung capacity.
B	keep your organs healthy.
C	stop smoking.
D	make new friends.
E	feel more energetic.

        [2 marks]

Travel

You are listening to some Spanish-speaking exchange students talking about where they're going on holiday.

Complete the sentences in **English**.

Example   Danilo is going to ......New Zealand...... with his parents.

He is excited because ......he loves flying...... .

15   Galia's father enjoys ....

The disadvantage of holidays is that .... *[2 marks]*

16   Gorka has decided to go to Nepal because ....

When he returns, ... *[2 marks]*

17   For Irene, short trips are good because ....

She thinks the highlight of her trip will be .... *[2 marks]*

School Pressures

You are on a train and overhear two Spanish people talking about their friend, Elena.

Answer the questions in **English**.

Example   When did Elena's parents separate?

     <u>During the summer term.</u>

18   What was the worst effect on Elena?

     ....   *[1 mark]*

19   What did the school suggest Elena should do?

     ....   *[1 mark]*

20   What does one of the girls decide to do?

     ....   *[1 mark]*

Voluntary Work

You've asked your Argentinian classmate, Omar, about his experience of voluntary work.

Answer both parts of the question.

21.1   What does Omar say about the people who come into the shop? Write the correct letter in the box.

A	They are mostly teenagers.
B	They don't have a lot of money.
C	They come from different backgrounds.

[1 mark]

21.2   What attitude do all the charity shop's customers share? Answer in **English**.

     ....   *[1 mark]*

22   What did the man give to the charity shop? Write the correct letter in the box.

A	Old, battered furniture.
B	Furniture that he no longer wanted.
C	Furniture made of glass.

[1 mark]

A Story

Your teacher has asked you to listen to an extract from *Dos días en Salamanca*
by Pedro Antonio de Alarcón as part of a group project.

Choose the correct answer and write the letter in the box.

23   Salamanca...

A	is home to lots of historical buildings.
B	is a small city.
C	has enough to keep you busy for a few days at most.

[1 mark]

24   Why were they so worn out?

A	They had done a lot of walking.
B	The sun was too hot.
C	They hadn't had time to rest.

[1 mark]

Las Fallas

Listen to this tourist advert for the Las Fallas festival in Valencia.

Choose the correct answer and write the letter in the box.

Answer **both** parts of the question.

25.1   In winter, the carpenters had to...

A	use more electricity.
B	use oil lamps to see.
C	stop working.

[1 mark]

25.2   In spring, the carpenters burnt things to...

A	mark the start of the new season.
B	keep warm.
C	remind them of the Middle Ages.

[1 mark]

Now answer this question.

26   'Ninots' are...

A	very rare.
B	constructed in the squares.
C	made of cardboard.

[1 mark]

Section B — Questions and answers in **Spanish**

Los medios sociales

Escucha este anuncio que trata de las desventajas de los medios sociales.

27 Según el anuncio, ¿cuántas veces al día es aceptable usar los medios sociales?

A	dos o tres veces
B	más de tres veces
C	nunca

[1 mark]

28 ¿Por qué es importante saber comunicarse con la gente?

....

.... *[1 mark]*

La música

Escuchas una entrevista en la radio con una persona famosa que promociona su nuevo programa televisivo en el que se busca talento musical.

Selecciona las **dos** frases correctas y escribe las letras correctas en las casillas.

29 ¿Qué dice Gerardo sobre las habilidades musicales de los concursantes?

A	La mayoría de los concursantes tiene una voz perfecta.
B	Unos tienen mucho talento.
C	Los concursantes solo pueden participar si cantan bien.
D	Hay unos que tocan un instrumento, y otros que no saben.
E	Dependen de la edad del concursante.

[2 marks]

30 ¿Cuáles son los aspectos de participar en el programa que menciona Gerardo?

A	Puedes hablar con la gente sobre sus sueños.
B	Hay la oportunidad de conocer a mucha gente.
C	Es posible cambiar la vida de alguien.
D	No es posible decir 'sí' a todo el mundo.
E	Hay que elegir tus palabras con cuidado.

[2 marks]

Turn over

Planes para el futuro

Escucha a la directora de un colegio que da consejos a sus estudiantes sobre las carreras.

31   Selecciona las **dos** frases correctas de la lista.

A	Todos los jóvenes saben lo que quieren ser de mayores.
B	Elegir una carrera no es fácil.
C	Hay que hablar con los demás.
D	No es la decisión del individuo.

[2 marks]

32   ¿Qué consejo ofrece la directora? Selecciona las **dos** frases correctas de la lista.

A	Es importante trabajar duro.
B	No es posible tener éxito sin buenas notas.
C	Lo mejor es elegir una carrera ahora.
D	Hay que prepararse ahora.

[2 marks]

END OF QUESTIONS

General Certificate of Secondary Education

GCSE Spanish
Higher Tier

Centre name						
Centre number						
Candidate number						

CGP
Practice Exam Paper
GCSE Spanish

Surname	
Other names	
Candidate signature	

Speaking Paper

Time Allowed: 10-12 minutes
 + 12 minutes of supervised preparation time.

Instructions to candidates

- Find a friend or parent to read the teacher's part for you.
- You will have **12 minutes** to prepare the Role-play and Photo Card tasks.
- You may make notes on a separate piece of paper during the preparation time.
- You must not use any notes during the General Conversation.
- The General Conversation will be on the following themes: Local, national, international and global areas of interest; Current and future study and employment.
- You must ask at least one question in the General Conversation.

Instructions to teachers

- It is essential that you give the student every opportunity to use the material they have prepared.
- You may alter the wording of the questions in response to the candidate's previous answers. However you must remember **not** to provide students with any key vocabulary.
- The candidate **must** ask you at least **one** question during the General Conversation.
- Candidates who have not yet asked you a question towards the end of the test must be prompted in **Spanish** with the following question: 'Is there anything you want to ask me?'

Information

- The test consists of **3** tasks.
- You may only prepare the Role-play and Photo Card tasks during the preparation time.
- The Role-play task will last approximately 2 minutes.
- The Photo Card task will last approximately 3 minutes.
- The General Conversation will last between 5 and 7 minutes.
- You are **not** allowed to use a dictionary at any time during the preparation time or the test.

In the actual exam, you will nominate one theme to be asked about in the General Conversation.
This will determine your Photo Card theme and the remaining theme for the General Conversation.
For this practice paper, you don't need to nominate a theme as there's only one Photo Card,
so the General Conversation will use the two themes not covered by the Photo Card.

Turn over

ROLE-PLAY
CANDIDATE'S MATERIAL

Instructions to candidate

- Your teacher will play the role of your Spanish friend. They will speak first.

- You should use *tú* to address your friend.

- **!** – means you will have to respond to something you have not prepared.

- **?** – means you will have to ask your friend a question.

Estás hablando con tu amigo/a español/a en una cafetería.

- La frecuencia con que practicas deporte.

- Tu opinión de jugar en equipo (**dos** razones).

- **!**

- **?** Practicar deporte.

- Llevar una vida más sana — cómo (**dos** detalles).

PHOTO CARD
CANDIDATE'S MATERIAL

Instructions to candidate

- You should look carefully at the photo during the preparation time.

- You can make notes on a separate piece of paper.

- Your teacher will ask you questions about the photo and about topics related to **customs and festivals**.

You will be asked the three questions below and then **two more questions** which you haven't seen in the preparation time.

- ¿Qué hay en la foto?

- ¿Te gustaría pasar la Navidad en España? ¿Por qué (no)?

- ¿Cuál es tu fiesta preferida? ¿Por qué?

ROLE-PLAY
TEACHER'S MATERIAL

Instructions to teacher

- You begin the role-play.

- You should address the candidate as *tú*.

- You may alter the wording of the questions in response to the candidate's previous answers.

- Do not supply the candidate with key vocabulary.

Begin the role-play by using the introductory text below.

Introductory text: *Estás hablando con tu amigo/a español/a en una cafetería. Yo soy tu amigo/a.*

1 Ask the candidate how often they do sport.

¿Con qué frecuencia practicas deporte?

2 Allow the candidate to say how often they play sport.

Ask the candidate whether they like playing in a team and why. (Elicit **two** reasons.)

¿Te gusta jugar en equipo? ¿Por qué?

3 Allow the candidate to say whether or not they like playing in a team and why.

Ask the candidate what their opinion of sport was when they were little.

! *¿Qué pensabas del deporte cuando eras pequeño/a?*

4 Allow the candidate to say what their opinion of sport was when they were little.

Muy bien.

? Allow the candidate to ask you about playing sport.

Give an appropriate answer.

5 Ask the candidate what they could do to have a healthier lifestyle. (Elicit **two** details.)

¿Qué podrías hacer para llevar una vida más sana?

PHOTO CARD & GENERAL CONVERSATION
TEACHER'S MATERIAL

Photo Card

Theme: Identity and culture   **Topic**: Customs and festivals in Spanish-speaking countries

This part of the test should last for a maximum of **three minutes**. It may be less than that for some candidates. Candidates can use any notes they made during the preparation time.

Begin the conversation by asking the candidate the first question from the list below. Then ask the remaining four questions in order. You can adapt the questions, but make sure they still have the same meaning. You can repeat or reword any questions that the candidate does not understand. Allow the candidate to develop their answers as much as possible.

- ¿Qué hay en la foto?

- ¿Te gustaría pasar la Navidad en España? ¿Por qué (no)?

- ¿Cuál es tu fiesta preferida? ¿Por qué?

- ¿Cómo celebraste tu cumpleaños el año pasado?

- ¿Crees que gastamos demasiado dinero en las fiestas? ¿Por qué (no)?

General Conversation

The General Conversation follows the Photo Card task. It should last between **five** and **seven minutes**, and a similar amount of time should be spent on each theme. Sample questions for a range of topics within each theme have been provided below, but these lists are not exhaustive.

Themes and sample questions for the General Conversation:

Local, national, international and global areas of interest

1) ¿Cómo es tu casa?

2) ¿Dónde te gustaría vivir en el futuro? ¿Por qué?

3) ¿Cuál es el problema medioambiental que más te preocupa?

4) ¿Qué podemos hacer para los sin techo?

5) ¿Te gustaría ir de vacaciones con tus amigos?

6) ¿Cuáles son tus planes para el verano que viene?

Current and future study and employment

1) ¿Cómo es tu colegio?

2) ¿Cuáles son tus asignaturas preferidas? ¿Por qué?

3) ¿Estás de acuerdo con las reglas en tu colegio?

4) ¿Te gustaría continuar con tus estudios?

5) ¿Qué trabajo querías tener cuando eras pequeño/a?

6) ¿Crees que es una buena idea tomar un año sabático?

Remember — the candidate must ask you at least one question during the General Conversation. If, towards the end of the task, the candidate has not asked you a question, you must prompt them by asking, «¿Hay algo que quieres preguntarme?»

General Certificate of Secondary Education

GCSE Spanish
Higher Tier

Centre name					
Centre number					
Candidate number					

CGP

**Practice Exam Paper
GCSE Spanish**

Surname	
Other names	
Candidate signature	

Reading Paper

Time Allowed: 1 hour

Instructions
- Write in black ink.
- Answer **all** questions in the spaces provided.
- Answer the questions in Section A in **English**.
- Answer the questions in Section B in **Spanish**.
- In Section C, translate the passage into **English**.
- Give all the information you are asked for, and **write neatly**.
- Cross out any rough work that you do not want to be marked.

Information
- The maximum mark for this paper is **60**.
- The number of marks for each question is shown in brackets.
- You are **not** allowed to use a dictionary.

Section A — Questions and answers in **English**

1   **Directions**

Your Spanish friend, Oria, has sent you directions to the youth club in the town centre.

Read her message and answer the questions in **English**.

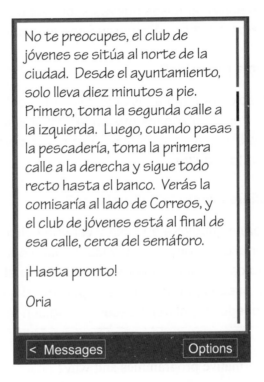

No te preocupes, el club de jóvenes se sitúa al norte de la ciudad. Desde el ayuntamiento, solo lleva diez minutos a pie. Primero, toma la segunda calle a la izquierda. Luego, cuando pasas la pescadería, toma la primera calle a la derecha y sigue todo recto hasta el banco. Verás la comisaría al lado de Correos, y el club de jóvenes está al final de esa calle, cerca del semáforo.

¡Hasta pronto!

Oria

< Messages   Options

1.1   How long does it take to get to the youth club using the route Oria has suggested?

.... *[1 mark]*

1.2   When should you turn right?

.... *[1 mark]*

1.3   Name **one** other building which is on the same street as the youth club.

.... *[1 mark]*

2   TV

While flicking through a magazine, you see an interview with Manu Olivarez, a Spanish celebrity.

Answer the questions in **English**.

¿Te gustan más las telenovelas o los documentales?

Es una pregunta facilísima. Prefiero los documentales porque puedo aprender cosas nuevas sobre varios temas interesantes. Detesto las telenovelas porque son muy aburridas.

¿Cuál es tu programa preferido?

¡Es imposible elegir solo uno! Me apasionan las series policíacas porque son muy emocionantes. Pero también me gustan los dibujos animados porque puedo verlos con mis hijos. A veces hay bromas que los niños no entienden, pero que hacen reír a los adultos.

Y finalmente, ¿prefieres ver la tele o ir al cine?

Sin duda, es más barato quedarse en casa y ver una película en la tele. Para mí, no vale la pena ir al cine porque si instalas un buen equipo de audio y una pantalla grande en tu casa, puedes disfrutar de la misma atmósfera que hay en el cine. Además, puedes poner pausa a la película si quieres ir a por algo de comer e incluso puedes repetir una escena si alguien te interrumpe.

2.1   What does Manu think of informative programmes and why?

....

....   *[2 marks]*

2.2   What does Manu say about the humour in cartoons?

....   *[1 mark]*

2.3   According to Manu, what can you do to recreate the experience of going to the cinema at home?

Write the correct letter in the box.

A	You can buy snacks such as popcorn.
B	You can buy special equipment.
C	You can pause the film.

[1 mark]

3 **Vocational training**

You are on holiday in Spain and you read this article in a newspaper.

Write the correct letter in each box.

Hace unos meses, el Ministerio de Educación de España reveló planes para iniciar cursos de formación profesional en tauromaquia, el arte de cuidar y matar toros. Los cursos durarán dos años escolares y serán para jóvenes entre 15 y 17 años que pueden tener dificultades para terminar sus estudios básicos.

En aulas especiales, los participantes aprenderán sobre la historia de la tauromaquia, incluso hasta cómo limpiar la chaqueta especial que llevan los toreros. Además, tendrán que seguir estudiando asignaturas más ordinarias como matemáticas, español, biología e inglés. Para conseguir el título al final del curso, harán una práctica en la que aplicarán todo lo que han aprendido.

Sin embargo, hay mucha gente que está en contra de la tauromaquia y que opina que el gobierno no debería apoyar a una industria que mata animales. Marta Gómez, madre de dos hijos, nos dijo: — Yo no dejaría que mis hijos participaran en tal curso. Preferiría que se hicieran aprendices o que estudiaran en la universidad después de hacer el bachillerato.

3.1 The courses are for students who...

A	are likely to get good marks in their exams.
B	are at least 15 years old.
C	have experience in looking after bulls.

[1 mark]

3.2 During the course, the participants...

A	will learn about the origins of bullfighting.
B	will only have to learn about the theory of bullfighting.
C	will spend the majority of their time outdoors with the bulls.

[1 mark]

3.3 Marta Gómez wants her children to...

A	carry on studying.
B	enrol on one of the new bullfighting courses.
C	support the bullfighting industry.

[1 mark]

Turn over

4 **Healthy Living**

You are in Spain and you read this article in a lifestyle magazine.

> **El yoga: un billete para una vida mejor.**
>
> Practicar el yoga no es nada nuevo. De hecho, la práctica existe desde hace más de dos mil años. Sin embargo, se está haciendo cada vez más popular en España y ahora se estima que un 12% de los españoles lo practican.
>
> Yashira, una instructora de yoga, me explica los beneficios del ejercicio. — Tiene muchas ventajas relacionadas con la salud física. Por ejemplo, practicar el yoga mejora la coordinación y la flexibilidad y algunos expertos creen que reduce el riesgo de sufrir un ataque cardíaco. Hay beneficios para el sistema respiratorio también. Pero el yoga no solo contribuye a la salud física, sino también al bienestar mental. Para mí, hacer yoga es una buena manera de relajarme, luchar contra el estrés de la vida moderna y recargar las pilas.
>
> Debo admitir que todo me parece muy interesante. La semana que viene se celebra el Día Internacional del Yoga. Habrá clases de yoga gratis en Madrid para que todo el mundo pueda aprovecharse de los beneficios que trae este antiguo ejercicio. ¿Quién viene conmigo?

4.1 Which two of the following statements are true?

Write the correct letters in the boxes.

A	About 2000 Spanish people do yoga.
B	For Yashira, the physical benefits of yoga are more important than the mental ones.
C	Yoga helps Yashira cope with the problems of everyday life.
D	Yashira says that according to some people, yoga helps to prevent some illnesses.
E	The number of people who do yoga in Spain has decreased recently.

[2 marks]

4.2 Why have the organisers of International Yoga Day decided not to charge for the classes? Answer in **English**.

.... [1 mark]

5 Customs and Festivals

Whilst on holiday in Spain, you read this article about how Carnival is celebrated in Cádiz.

Durante por lo menos diez días en febrero o marzo, los habitantes de Cádiz salen a la calle para celebrar el Carnaval. Lo que realmente distingue esta fiesta de las otras que hay en España y por el mundo es que al pasear por las calles, se ven 'chirigotas'. Estos grupos de músicos cantan coplas, canciones graciosas cuya letra habla de políticos o de gente famosa. Cádiz tiene fama de ser una de las ciudades más divertidas de toda España, y esta música forma parte de su imagen.

La tradición de celebrar el Carnaval en Cádiz no es nada nuevo. Hace unos quinientos años, Cádiz era un puerto muy importante y de esta manera llegaban muchas influencias extranjeras, sobre todo de Venecia. El estilo de música, los disfraces y la atmósfera de alegría tienen sus orígenes en las festividades venecianas, pero las celebraciones en Cádiz ahora tienen un carácter muy español.

5.1 What is a 'chirigota'?

A	A funny song about politicians or celebrities.
B	An area where groups of musicians sing songs.
C	A group of singers who perform for the passers-by.

[1 mark]

5.2 What reputation does the city have? Answer in **English**.

.... *[1 mark]*

5.3 How has the festival changed over the years?

A	It has become more 'Spanish' over time.
B	It has been increasingly influenced by foreign traditions.
C	It hasn't changed much — it's the same as it used to be.

[1 mark]

6   Education post-16

Your Spanish friend has sent you an email about his plans for after his exams.

Read what he has to say, and write the correct letter in each box.

From: gonzalogarcia@esmail.es

Reply   Subject: Planes

¡Hola!

Por fin he terminado mis exámenes, ¡no me lo puedo creer! Pienso que la mayoría de ellos me han salido bien, pero es difícil saber, sobre todo cuando hablas con los amigos sobre lo que has escrito y resulta que algunos han puesto algo completamente distinto. La última vez que te vi, me preguntaste qué quería hacer después de los exámenes. Mi respuesta entonces fue que no lo sabía, y ¡todavía no lo sé! Estoy pensando en hacer una práctica durante las vacaciones, pero según mis padres, sería mejor conseguir un trabajo a tiempo parcial y luego volver a mi instituto para hacer el bachillerato, como han hecho mis primos.

¿Qué piensas?

Un saludo,

Gonzalo

6.1   How does Gonzalo say his exams went?

A	He's pleased because they all went very well.
B	He thinks most of them were alright.
C	He's worried because his friends all wrote different things.

[1 mark]

6.2   What did Gonzalo think he wanted to do when he last saw you?

A	He wanted to do some work experience.
B	He didn't know.
C	He wanted to get a part-time job.

[1 mark]

6.3   What do Gonzalo's parents want him to do?

A	They want him to go to a different school.
B	They want him to do an apprenticeship.
C	They think he should follow in his cousins' footsteps.

[1 mark]

7 Marriage

In this extract from *El paraíso de las mujeres* by Vicente Blasco Ibáñez, Margaret is contemplating getting married to Gillespie.

> Margaret le amaba; pero el amor de una señorita de buena familia y excelente educación, acostumbrada a las comodidades que proporciona una gran fortuna, debe tener sus límites forzosamente*. No iba ella a abandonar a su madre y a reñir** con todas las familias amigas para casarse con un novio pobre, dedicado por completo a su amor e ignorante del camino que debía seguir en el presente momento. Estas resoluciones desesperadas sólo se ven en las novelas.
>
> *forzosamente — out of necessity   **reñir — to fall out with

Put a cross in the correct box.

7.1 Margaret's family is...

☐	**A** small.
☐	**B** rich.
☐	**C** dedicated to her.
☐	**D** loving.

[1 mark]

7.2 A marriage between Margaret and Gillespie wouldn't be considered suitable because...

☐	**A** Gillespie is too old for her.
☐	**B** it would cause conflict with Gillespie's family.
☐	**C** Gillespie doesn't know what he wants to do in the future.
☐	**D** people think that he doesn't love her.

[1 mark]

8 **Contributing to Society**

Some young people are talking about how and why they started volunteering with a charity.

Identify the people and write **A** (Aimar), **P** (Paula) or **A+P** (Aimar and Paula) in the boxes.

 Aimar	El año pasado estaba esperando el autobús cuando unos chicos me robaron. Nadie me ayudó, menos un hombre que estaba dando un paseo. Cuando hablé con él, resultó que estaba sin techo y que dormía en las calles desde hacía dos años. Esta experiencia me animó a hacer algo por los sin techo, porque son personas exactamente como nosotros y ahora son mis amigos. Lavo la ropa de la gente que vive en las calles, sobre todo cuando alguien tiene una entrevista para un trabajo. Creo que todos deberíamos pensar en lo difícil que es vivir así.
 Paula	No conocía a ninguna persona sin techo antes de empezar a trabajar con la organización. Decidí ofrecerme como voluntaria hace nueve meses porque un amigo mío me dijo que si no hubiera suficiente gente para ayudar, la organización tendría que cerrar. Ha sido una experiencia muy gratificante y tengo muchos amigos entre los voluntarios y los sin techo. Intento organizar cursos de formación profesional para que los que reciben nuestro apoyo puedan entrar en el mundo laboral.

8.1   Who had met a homeless person before they started volunteering?   [1 mark]

8.2   Who makes it easier for homeless people to get a job?   [1 mark]

8.3   Who has made friends through volunteering?   [1 mark]

8.4   Who says that the charity has been in some difficulty recently?   [1 mark]

9   **Film reviews**

While on holiday in Spain, you decide to go to the cinema.

You read these film reviews in a magazine.

El castillo	Generalmente, me gustan las películas de terror. Sin embargo, esta película me aburrió un montón. La trama cuenta la historia de un castillo en un bosque casi inaccesible que hace desaparecer a las personas que tocan los árboles. No hay ni suspenso ni tensión, solo una serie de eventos estúpidos.
Los hombros del enemigo	Para los que les gustan las películas históricas, les recomiendo esta obra maestra. Se trata de dos ejércitos que luchan por conquistar una isla en medio de una tierra desconocida. La actuación de los protagonistas crea una atmósfera increíble. ¡No hay otra película que pueda ofrecer una experiencia igual!
No dejes de ser loca	Tenía muchas ganas de ver esta película, pero me siento verdaderamente decepcionada. Se trata de dos amigas que se enamoran en circunstancias inusuales. A pesar de que se describa como una comedia, hay algunos aspectos muy tristes, lo que me fastidió.
Botas de papel	Prepárate para dos horas llenas de emoción. Basada en hechos reales, esta película presenta la historia de un viudo que debe afrontar las dificultades de vivir sin la mujer que ama. Aunque sea una película encantadora, no menciona ningún detalle de lo que pasó con su mujer, lo que me decepcionó bastante.

Complete the grids below in **English** to indicate whether the opinions of the films were positive or negative (or both) and why.

Example

	Opinion	Reason
El castillo	negative	no suspense or tension

9.1

	Opinion	Reason
Los hombros del enemigo		

[2 marks]

9.2

	Opinion	Reason
No dejes de ser loca		

[2 marks]

9.3

	Opinion	Reason
Botas de papel		

[2 marks]

Turn over

Section B   Questions and answers in **Spanish**

10   **Doña Perfecta**

Lee este extracto de *Doña Perfecta*, una novela escrita por Benito Pérez Galdós.

Rellena los espacios blancos en el texto usando las palabras de la lista.

Escribe la letra correcta en cada casilla.

Poco después Pepe se presentaba en el comedor.

—Si almuerzas fuerte—le dijo doña Perfecta con cariñoso acento, — se te va a quitar la gana

de comer. Aquí comemos a la una. Las modas del [B] no te gustarán.

—Me [ ] , señora tía.

—Pues di lo que prefieres: ¿almorzar fuerte ahora o [ ] una cosita ligera para que

resistas hasta la hora de comer?

—Escojo la cosa ligera para tener el gusto de comer con ustedes; y si en Villahorrenda hubiera

encontrado algún alimento, nada tomaría a esta hora.

—Por supuesto, no necesito decirte que nos trates con [ ] franqueza. Aquí puedes

mandar como si [ ] en tu casa.

—Gracias, tía.

A	estuvieras	E	encantan
B	**campo**	F	como
C	muy	G	tomar
D	toda	H	vivir

[4 marks]

11   La tecnología

Lee este correo que Aleix ha escrito a su amigo inglés.

Contesta a las preguntas en **español**.

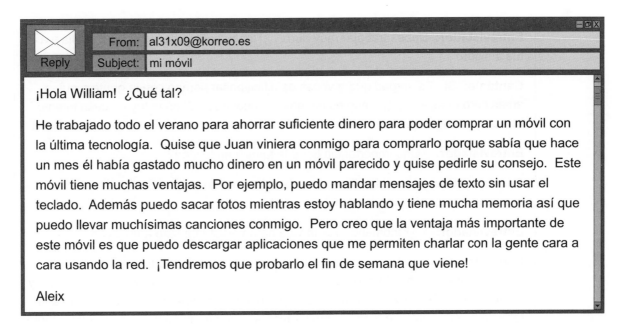

11.1   ¿Cómo pudo Aleix permitirse gastar tanto dinero en este móvil?

.... *[1 mark]*

11.2   ¿Por qué quiso Aleix que Juan le ayudara con la compra del móvil?

.... *[1 mark]*

11.3   ¿Qué se puede hacer en medio de una conversación por teléfono?

.... *[1 mark]*

11.4   ¿Qué van a hacer pronto?

.... *[1 mark]*

Turn over

12 La familia

En un programa de radio, escuchas esta conversación entre un entrevistador y una cantante.

Contesta a las preguntas en **español**.

> **Entrevistador:** Debes trabajar muy duro. ¿Tienes tiempo para ver a tu familia y a tus amigos?
>
> **Cantante:** Sí. Es verdad que a veces es difícil pasar tiempo con la gente a quien amas pero le aseguro que eso es mi máxima prioridad. Si no estoy en casa intento llamar a mis hijos por Internet para decirles 'buenas noches'. ¡Eso es una maravilla!
>
> **Entrevistador:** ¿Qué importancia tiene la familia en tu vida?
>
> **Cantante:** Claro que mi familia es lo más importante de todo. Si algo pasara con mis hijos, cambiaría mis planes de inmediato.
>
> **Entrevistador:** Y ¿recomendarías la vida de un artista famoso a un joven?
>
> **Cantante:** ¡Sí y no! Lo bueno de mi vida es que me da la oportunidad de ser creativa. Además, he viajado por todo el mundo y he conocido a unas personas muy interesantes. Pero por otro lado, es casi imposible mantener amistades debido a la falta de tiempo libre que tengo. Otra desventaja es que no puedo saber exactamente quién es un verdadero amigo; a veces parece que la gente solo quiere dinero.

12.1 ¿Cómo se comunica con sus hijos cuando está fuera de casa?

.... *[1 mark]*

12.2 ¿Cuáles son las ventajas de la vida que lleva la cantante?
Menciona **dos** cosas.

1. ....

2. .... *[2 marks]*

12.3 ¿Cuáles son los problemas que tiene en cuanto a los amigos?
Menciona **dos** cosas.

1. ....

2. .... *[2 marks]*

13   El medio ambiente

Unos jóvenes están participando en un debate sobre el medio ambiente.

Contesta a las preguntas en **español**.

Elena	A mí me importa muchísimo el medio ambiente. Es imprescindible protegerlo porque si no lo hacemos, la generación que viene va a sufrir. Mi hermano opina que la culpa la tiene el gobierno, porque si hubiera hecho algo hace treinta años, no tendríamos tantos problemas ahora. Sin embargo, desde mi punto de vista, echar la culpa al gobierno no es una solución adecuada. Todos deberíamos ayudar a salvar la Tierra.
Silvio	Se habla de la necesidad de proteger el planeta por todas partes: en el colegio y en las noticias, en los periódicos y en casa. El tema del calentamiento global me aburre mucho porque, claro, no es mi problema. Apago las luces y voy al colegio en autobús, así que creo que ya hago suficiente por el medio ambiente. ¡Déjame en paz!

13.1   Según Elena, ¿por qué deberíamos hacer más por el medio ambiente?

.... *[1 mark]*

13.2   Según el hermano de Elena, ¿quién no ha hecho suficiente para cambiar la situación?

.... *[1 mark]*

13.3   ¿Qué piensa Silvio sobre el tema del medio ambiente?

.... *[1 mark]*

13.4   ¿Qué piensa Silvio sobre su contribución a la protección del planeta?

.... *[1 mark]*

Turn over

14   **Ir de compras**

Estás mirando los folletos en una oficina de turismo y lees esta información sobre las tiendas que hay en Valencia.

Escribe la letra correcta en cada casilla.

¿Te apetece ir de compras en nuestro barrio?

Mercado Tecnicolor

Si buscas una experiencia que representa el sabor auténtico de España, visita Mercado Tecnicolor. Prueba los productos artesanos o encuentra un recuerdo único de tu viaje.

Zona Girasol

La Zona Girasol ofrece una gran selección de tiendas de lujo y las mejores cafeterías y restaurantes de la región. Da un paseo por los jardines preciosos y disfruta del día bajo el sol mediterráneo.

Playa Albaricoque

A un paso de la playa, estos grandes almacenes tienen todo lo que deseas. Explora las tiendas especializadas como la juguetería mundialmente famosa 'Juega a la noruega' y aprovéchate de las otras instalaciones tales como el cine y la bolera.

14.1   Si quieres comprar algo tradicional que te recordará a tus vacaciones, deberías ir a...

A	Mercado Tecnicolor.
B	Zona Girasol.
C	Playa Albaricoque.

[1 mark]

14.2   Si te apetece ir de compras y hacer otras actividades de ocio también, la mejor opción sería...

A	Mercado Tecnicolor.
B	Zona Girasol.
C	Playa Albaricoque.

[1 mark]

14.3   Si prefieres estar al aire libre cuando vas de compras, visita...

A	Mercado Tecnicolor.
B	Zona Girasol.
C	Playa Albaricoque.

[1 mark]

Section C   Translation into **English**

15   You're considering booking a trip to Spain and you read this review online.

Translate it into **English**.

> Acabamos de pasar una semana increíble en Granada. Nos alojamos en un hotel moderno en el centro. La comida estaba rica y la habitación tenía un balcón enorme. Si pudiera volver a Granada mañana, lo haría en seguida, especialmente porque no tuvimos tiempo para visitar la catedral. ¡Tendremos que volver el año que viene!

[9 marks]

....

....

....

....

....

....

....

....

....

....

....

END OF QUESTIONS

General Certificate of Secondary Education

GCSE Spanish
Higher Tier

Centre name					
Centre number					
Candidate number					

CGP

Practice Exam Paper
GCSE Spanish

Surname	
Other names	
Candidate signature	

Writing Paper

Time Allowed: 1 hour 15 minutes

Instructions
- Write in black ink.
- Give all the information you are asked for, and **write neatly**.
- You must answer **three** questions.
- Answer **either** Question 1.1 **or** Question 1.2. Do **not** answer both questions.
- Answer **either** Question 2.1 **or** Question 2.2. Do **not** answer both questions.
- You **must** answer Question 3.
- All questions must be answered in **Spanish**.
- In the actual exam, you must write your answers in the spaces provided. Do **not** write on blank pages.
- You may plan your answers in the exam booklet. Make sure you cross through any work you do not want to be marked.

Information
- This paper contains **3** writing tasks.
- The maximum mark for this paper is **60**.
- The number of marks for each question is shown in brackets.
- For Questions 1 and 2, the highest marks will be awarded for answers that make reference to each bullet point and include a variety of vocabulary, structures and opinions with reasons.
- You are **not** allowed to use a dictionary.

Answer **either** Question 1.1 **or** Question 1.2

1.1   Tienes que escribir un artículo para tu revista escolar sobre el trabajo voluntario que haces.

Menciona :

- qué haces
- por qué decidiste hacerlo
- si crees que es importante ayudar a otras personas
- algo más que podrías hacer para contribuir a la sociedad.

Escribe aproximadamente **90** palabras en **español**. Responde a todos los aspectos de la pregunta.

[16 marks]

1.2   Acabas de volver de vacaciones y vas a escribir algo para tu blog sobre tus experiencias.

Menciona :

- adónde fuiste y con quién
- si prefieres irte de vacaciones en verano o en invierno
- si te gusta pasar las vacaciones con tu familia
- cómo serían tus vacaciones ideales.

Escribe aproximadamente **90** palabras en **español**. Responde a todos los aspectos de la pregunta.

[16 marks]

Answer **either** Question 2.1 **or** Question 2.2

2.1   Vas a escribir un email a tu amigo/a español/a sobre una película que viste ayer.

Menciona :

- qué pasa en la película
- si la película te gustó o no y por qué.

Escribe aproximadamente **150** palabras en **español**. Responde a todos los aspectos de la pregunta.

[32 marks]

2.2   Estás trabajando en España durante las vacaciones. Escribe una carta a tu amigo/a sobre tus experiencias.

Menciona :

- las ventajas de trabajar en el extranjero
- qué vas a hacer en el futuro.

Escribe aproximadamente **150** palabras en **español**. Responde a todos los aspectos de la pregunta.

[32 marks]

You **must** answer Question 3

3   Translate the following passage into **Spanish**.

I like recycling. At home, we recycle bottles and paper. I used to think it was boring but now I think it's essential. I believe it will be more important in the future because if we don't recycle, there will be more rubbish in the streets. Do you agree with me?

[12 marks]

Vocabulary

Section One — General Stuff

Numbers (p.1)

cero	zero
uno (un) / una	one
dos	two
tres	three
cuatro	four
cinco	five
seis	six
siete	seven
ocho	eight
nueve	nine
diez	ten
once	eleven
doce	twelve
trece	thirteen
catorce	fourteen
quince	fifteen
dieciséis	sixteen
diecisiete	seventeen
dieciocho	eighteen
diecinueve	nineteen
veinte	twenty
veintiuno	twenty-one
veintidós	twenty-two
treinta	thirty
treinta y uno	thirty-one
cuarenta	forty
cincuenta	fifty
sesenta	sixty
setenta	seventy
ochenta	eighty
noventa	ninety
ciento (cien)	hundred
ciento setenta y siete	one hundred and seventy-seven
doscientos/as	two hundred
quinientos veintiocho	five hundred and twenty-eight
novecientos noventa y tres	nine hundred and ninety-three
mil	thousand
mil cuatrocientos cincuenta y tres	one thousand four hundred and fifty-three
millón	million
primero / primera	first
segundo/a	second
tercero/a	third
cuarto/a	fourth
quinto/a	fifth
sexto/a	sixth
séptimo/a	seventh
octavo/a	eighth
noveno/a	ninth
décimo/a	tenth
una docena	dozen
el número	number

un par	pair / couple
unos (diez)	about (10)

Times and Dates (p.2-3)

el lunes	Monday
el martes	Tuesday
el miércoles	Wednesday
el jueves	Thursday
el viernes	Friday
el sábado	Saturday
el domingo	Sunday
enero	January
febrero	February
marzo	March
abril	April
mayo	May
junio	June
julio	July
agosto	August
septiembre	September
octubre	October
noviembre	November
diciembre	December
la estación	season
el invierno	winter
el otoño	autumn
la primavera	spring
el verano	summer
a diario	daily / everyday
a eso de ...	at about ...
a fines de ...	at / to the end of ...
a mediados de ...	around the middle of ...
a menudo	often
a partir de	from
a veces	sometimes
ahora	now / nowadays
al mismo tiempo	at the same time
algunas veces	sometimes
anoche	last night
el año	year
anteayer	the day before yesterday
antes (de)	before
ayer	yesterday
breve	brief / short
cada (...) días / horas	every (...) days / hours
casi	nearly
de momento	at the moment / right now
de nuevo	again
de repente	suddenly
de vez en cuando	now and then / from time to time
dentro de (...) días / horas	within (...) days / hours
desde	since

desde hace	since
despacio	slowly
después (de)	after / afterwards
el día	day
durante	during / for
durar	to last
en seguida / enseguida	straightaway
esta noche	tonight
la fecha	date
el fin de semana	weekend
hace (un mes) que	it's been a month since
hace (un mes)	a month ago
hoy	today
lento	slow
los lunes etc.	(on) Mondays etc.
luego	then / afterwards
mañana	tomorrow
la mañana	morning
el mes	month
mientras tanto	meanwhile
mucho tiempo	a long time
la noche	night
otra vez	again
el pasado	past
pasado (adj)	past / last
pasado mañana	the day after tomorrow
pocas veces	seldom / a few times
por año	per year
por fin	at last
por lo general	generally
el porvenir	future
al principio	at the beginning
pronto	soon
próximo	next
que viene (el mes etc.)	next (month etc.)
quince días	fortnight
el rato	while / short time
la semana	week
siempre	always
el siglo	century
siguiente	next / following
sobre	on / around
solo (sólo)	only
tardar	to take time
tarde	late
la tarde	afternoon / evening
la temporada	period / spell / season
temprano	early
tener prisa	to be in a hurry
el tiempo	time
todas (las semanas)	every (week)
todavía	still / yet

todos (los días / meses)	every (day / month)
último	last
una vez	once
dos veces	twice

Questions (p.4-5)

¿(a)dónde?	where (to)?
¿a qué hora?	at what time?
¿cómo?	how?
¿cuál(es)?	which?
¿cuándo?	when?
¿cuánto?	how much?
¿cuánto cuesta(n)?	how much does it / do they cost?
¿cuánto es?	how much is it?
¿cuánto vale(n)?	how much does it / do they cost?
¿cuántos...?	how many?
¿cuántos años tiene(s)?	how old are you?
¿de dónde?	where from?
¿de qué color (es)?	what colour (is it)?
¿de quién?	whose?
¿es...?	is it...?
¿por cuánto tiempo?	for how long?
¿por dónde?	through where?
¿por qué?	why?
¿qué?	what?
¿qué día?	what day?
¿qué fecha?	what date?
¿qué hora es?	what time is it?
¿quién?	who?

Being Polite (p.6-7)

¡Adiós!	Goodbye!
así así	so-so
¡Basta ya!	That's enough!
¡Bienvenido/a!	Welcome!
¡Buen viaje!	Have a good trip!
¡Buena suerte!	Good luck!
¡Buenas noches!	Good night!
¡Buenas tardes!	Good afternoon! / Good evening!
¡Buenos días!	Good morning! / Good day!
¡Claro!	Of course!
¿Cómo está(s)?	How are you?
con permiso	excuse me
¡Cuidado!	Careful! Watch out!
de nada	you're welcome / don't mention it
¿De veras?	Really?
encantado/a	pleased to meet you
¡Enhorabuena!	Congratulations!
Este/a es...	This is...
fatal	terrible
¡Felices vacaciones!	Have a good holiday!
¡Felicidades!	Best wishes! Congratulations!
¡Felicitaciones!	Congratulations!
hasta el (lunes)	till / see you (Monday)
hasta luego	see you later

hasta mañana	see you tomorrow
hasta pronto	see you soon
¡Hola!	Hello!
Le presento a...	May I introduce...?
lo siento	I'm sorry
mucho gusto	pleased to meet you
(muy) bien	(very) well
no muy bien	not very well
¡Ojo!	Watch out! Careful!
perdón	sorry / excuse me
perdone	sorry / excuse me
por favor	please
¿Puedo...?	May I...?
¡Qué (+ adjective)!	How ...!
¡Qué (+ noun)!	What a ...!
¿Qué hay?	What's happening? What's the matter?
¡Que lo pase(s) bien!	Have a good time!
¿Qué pasa?	What's happening? What's the matter?
¿Qué tal?	How are you? How's ...?
¡Qué va!	Come on! Rubbish! Nonsense!
Quisiera...	I would like...
saludar	to greet / say hello
saludos	regards / greetings
¡Socorro!	Help!
vale	ok

Opinions (p.8-10)

aburrido	boring / bored
aburrirse	to get bored
adorar	to adore / to love
afortunado	lucky
agradable	pleasant
alegrar	to cheer up
alegrarse (de)	to be happy (about)
amable	nice / kind / friendly
antiguo	old
apreciar	to appreciate
apropiado	correct / appropriate
aprovechar	to make the most of
aprovecharse (de)	to take advantage (of)
barato	cheap
bonito	pretty
bueno	good
la calidad	quality
caro	expensive
creer	to believe
dar igual	to be all the same / to make no difference
decepcionante	disappointing
decir	to say
desagradable	unpleasant
desear	to wish
la desventaja	disadvantage
disfrutar	to enjoy
distinto	different
divertido	amusing / fun / entertaining

divertirse	to have a good time
dudar	to doubt
duro	hard
emocionante	exciting / thrilling / moving
encantador	charming
encantar	to delight
entretenido	entertaining / amusing
esperar	to hope
espléndido	fantastic / terrific
estar a favor de	to be in favour of
estar de acuerdo	to agree
estar en contra de	to be against
estar harto de	to be fed up of
estupendo	fantastic
fabuloso	fabulous
fácil	easy
fastidiar	to annoy / to bother
fatal	awful / fatal
fenomenal	great / fantastic
feo	ugly
genial	brilliant / great
guay	cool
hermoso	beautiful
horroroso	horrible
impresionante	impressive / striking
increíble	incredible
inseguro	unsafe / uncertain
interesante	interesting
interesar(se)	to interest / to be interested in
inútil	useless
malo	bad
maravilloso	marvellous
nuevo	new
odiar	to hate
opinar	to think / to give an opinion
parecer	to seem
pasarlo bien	to have a good time
pensar	to think
perfecto	perfect
ponerse de acuerdo	to agree
porque	because
precioso	precious / beautiful
preferir	to prefer
profundo	deep / profound
quedar en	to agree
querer decir	to mean
raro	strange / rare
la razón	reason
reconocer	to recognise
ridículo	ridiculous
seguro	safe / certain
sencillo	simple / plain / straightforward
sentir(se)	to feel
sorprendido	surprised
tener ganas de hacer algo	to feel like doing something
tener razón	to be right
tonto	silly

Vocabulary

tranquilo	*peaceful / quiet*
único	*unique / only / single*
útil	*useful*
valer la pena	*to be worth the trouble*
la ventaja	*advantage*
viejo	*old*

Access

abierto	*open*
abrir	*to open*
cerrado	*closed*
cerrar	*to close*
gratis / gratuito	*free (of charge)*
libre	*free / unoccupied*
ocupado	*engaged / occupied*
permitir	*to allow*
prohibido	*forbidden*

Colours and Shapes

amarillo	*yellow*
azul	*blue*
blanco	*white*
claro	*light*
cuadrado	*square*
el color	*colour*
la forma	*shape*
gris	*grey*
marrón	*brown*
morado	*purple*
naranja	*orange*
negro	*black*
oscuro	*dark*
pálido	*pale*
redondo	*round*
rojo	*red*
rosa / rosado	*pink*
verde	*green*
vivo	*vivid / bright*

Common Abbreviations

Sr (señor)	*Mr*
Sra (señora)	*Mrs*
Srta (señorita)	*Miss*
Sta (santa)	*Saint*
c/ (calle)	*street*
1° / primero (2°, 3° etc.)	*1st (2nd, 3rd etc.)*
1ª / primera (2ª, 3ª etc.)	*1st (2nd, 3rd etc.)*
Dr (doctor)	*Dr*
Dra (doctora)	*Dr*
el AVE	*high-speed train*
Renfe / RENFE	*Spanish railways*
IVA	*VAT*
Avda (avenida)	*avenue*
EEUU (Estados Unidos)	*USA*

Connectives

además	*moreover / besides*
aparte de	*apart from*
claro que	*of course*
dado que	*given that*

es decir	*in other words / that is to say*
por un lado / por otro lado	*on the one hand / on the other hand*
por una parte / por otra parte	*on the one hand / on the other hand*
sin duda	*obviously / certainly*

Correctness

cierto	*certain / sure / true*
corregir	*to correct*
equivocado	*wrong*
la falta	*error*
mal	*badly*
mentir	*to lie*
la mentira	*lie / untruth*
mentiroso	*liar*
tener razón	*to be right*
la verdad	*truth*
verdadero	*true*

Materials

el algodón	*cotton*
la cerámica	*pottery*
el cristal	*glass / crystal*
el cuero	*leather*
la lana	*wool*
la madera	*wood*
el oro	*gold*
el papel	*paper*
la piel	*leather / skin*
la plata	*silver*
la seda	*silk*
la tela	*fabric / material*
el vidrio	*glass*

Comparisons (p.121 & 126)

bastante	*sufficient / enough / quite*
comparar	*to compare*
demasiado	*too, too much*
igual que	*same as*
más (que)	*more (than)*
mayor	*main / larger / bigger / greater / older*
la mayoría	*most / majority*
mejor	*better / best*
menor	*smaller / less / least / younger*
menos (que)	*less (than)*
mismo	*same*
muy	*very*
parecido a	*like / similar to*
peor	*worse / worst*
poco (e.g. poco ruidoso)	*not very*
tan ... como	*as ... as*
tanto ... como	*as much ... as*

Prepositions (p.133)

a	*to / at*
de	*from / of*
en	*in / at*
hacia	*towards*
hasta	*until*

para	*for*
por	*through / by / in / for / per*
según	*according to*
sin	*without*

Conjunctions (p.135)

a pesar de	*in spite of / despite*
así que	*so / therefore*
aun (si)	*even (if)*
aunque	*although / (even) though*
como	*as / since*
cuando	*when*
de manera que	*in such a way that*
entonces	*then*
incluso	*even*
mientras (que)	*while, meanwhile*
o / u	*or*
pero	*but*
por eso	*for that reason / therefore*
por lo tanto	*therefore*
porque	*because*
pues	*then / since*
si	*if*
sin embargo	*however*
tal vez	*maybe / perhaps*
también	*also*
y / e	*and*
ya (que)	*as / since*

Negative Forms (p.151)

jamás	*never*
ni ... ni	*neither ... nor*
nada	*nothing*
nadie	*nobody*
ninguno	*none / no-one*
nunca	*never*
sino	*but (rather) / except*
tampoco	*neither / not ... either ...*
ya no	*not any more*

Important Verbs

acabar de + infinitive	*to have just (done something)*
comenzar	*to begin*
continuar	*to continue*
dar	*to give*
darse cuenta (de)	*to realise*
deber	*must / have to*
decidir	*to decide*
dejar de (hacer algo)	*to stop (doing something)*
echar	*to throw*
empezar	*to begin*
estar	*to be*
hace(n) falta	*to need / to be necessary*
hacer	*to do / to make*
hacerse	*to become*
hay	*there is / there are*

hay que	one must / one has to
ir	to go
ir a (hacer algo)	to be going to (do something)
irse	to go away / to leave
necesitar	to need
ocurrir	to happen
pasar	to happen / to spend (time)

poder	to be able / can
poner	to put
ponerse a (hacer algo)	to start (doing something)
querer	to want / to love
quisiera...	I'd like...
saber	to know (a fact / how to do something)
seguir	to continue / to follow

ser	to be
soler	to usually do something
tener	to have / to own
tener lugar	to take place
tener que	to have to do something
volver a hacer algo	to do something again
volverse	to become

Section Two — Me, My Family and Friends

You and Your Family (p.16-17)

el/la abuelo/a	grandfather / grandmother
el apellido	last name
el apodo	nickname
el bebé	baby
cuidar	to look after
el cumpleaños	birthday
cumplir años	to have a birthday
la edad	age
el/la gemelo/a	twin
la gente	people
el/la hermanastro/a	stepbrother/sister
el/la hijo/a (único/a)	(only) child
los hijos	children
el hogar	home
llamarse	to be called
la madrastra	stepmother
la madre	mother
el miembro	member
nacer	to be born
el nacimiento	birth
la nacionalidad	nationality
el/la nieto/a	grandchild
el/la niño/a	child
el nombre	name
el padrastro	stepfather
el padre, los padres	father, parents
los parientes	relatives
el/la primo/a	cousin
el recuerdo	memory
la reunión	get-together
el/la sobrino/a	nephew / niece
tener ... años	to be ... years old
el/la tío/a	uncle / aunt
el/la vecino/a	neighbour

Describing People (p.18-19)

el/la adolescente	teenager
alegre	happy
alto	tall
(de) altura mediana	(of) medium height
amistoso	friendly
anciano	elderly
el/la anciano/a	old person
animado	lively

antipático	unpleasant
el aspecto	appearance / looks
atrevido	daring / cheeky
bajo	short (height)
la barba	beard
el bigote	moustache
callado	quiet / reserved
calvo	bald
la cara	face
cariñoso	affectionate / tender
castaño	chestnut / brown
celoso	jealous
cobarde	coward
comprensivo	understanding
cortés	polite
corto	short (length)
delgado	slim
deportivo	sporty
educado	polite
egoísta	selfish
feliz	happy
fuerte	strong
las gafas	glasses
gordo	fat
gracioso	funny
guapo	good-looking
hablador	chatty / talkative
honrado	honest
joven	young
el/la joven	young person
jubilado	retired
el/la jubilado	OAP / pensioner
la juventud	youth / young people
largo	long
liso	straight (hair)
maduro	mature
maleducado	rude
moreno	dark (-haired / -skined)
el ojo	eye
la oreja	ear
orgulloso	proud
parecerse a	to look like
las pecas	freckles
pelirrojo	red-haired
el pelo	hair

perezoso	lazy / idle
rico	wealthy / rich
rizado	curly
rubio	blonde
sensible	sensitive
serio	serious / responsible
simpático	kind / nice / pleasant
torpe	clumsy
travieso	naughty / mischievous
triste	sad
valiente	brave / bold
viejo	old
el/la viudo/a	widow(er)

Pets (p.20)

el animal doméstico	pet
el cobayo / el conejillo de Indias	guinea pig
el conejo	rabbit
fiel	loyal
el gato	cat
el hámster	hamster
mandón	bossy / demanding
la mascota	pet
el olor	smell
el perro	dog
el pez de colores	goldfish
el pez tropical	tropical fish
la serpiente	snake
la tortuga	tortoise

Style and Fashion (p.21)

el abrigo	coat
afeitarse	to shave
ajustado	tight
el anillo	ring
anticuado	old-fashioned
la barra de labios	lipstick
el bolso	handbag
las botas	boots
la bufanda	scarf
los calcetines	socks
la camisa	shirt
la chaqueta	jacket
la chaqueta de punto	cardigan (knitted)
el cinturón	belt

el collar	necklace
cortarse el pelo	to have your hair cut
de estilo retro	vintage style
de lunares	spotty
de rayas / rayado	striped
elegante	smart / elegant
estar de moda	to be in fashion (thing)
estar en la onda	to be fashionable (person)
el estilo	style
la falda	skirt
el/la famoso/a	celebrity
la gorra	cap
los guantes	gloves
holgado	loose / baggy
ir vestido a la moda	to dress fashionably
el jérsey	jumper
las joyas	jewellery
el maquillaje	make-up
maquillarse	to put make-up on
la marca	brand
el/la modelo	model
el paraguas	umbrella
pasado de moda	out of fashion
los pendientes	earrings
el piercing	body piercing
pintarse	to put make-up on
el polo	poloshirt
la pulsera	bracelet
la rebeca	cardigan
el reloj	watch
la ropa de deporte	sports kit
el sombrero de paja	straw hat
la sudadera	sweatshirt
suelto	loose

el tatuaje	tattoo
tatuarse	to get a tattoo
teñido	dyed
el traje	suit
el traje de baño	swimming costume / trunks
los vaqueros	jeans
vestido de	dressed in
la zapatería	shoe shop
las zapatillas	slippers
las zapatillas de deporte	trainers

Relationships (p.22-24)

acordar	to agree on
aguantar	to bear / to put up with
la amistad	friendship
el amor	love
el anillo	ring
la barrera generacional	generation gap
la boda	wedding
besar	to kiss
casado	married
casarse	to get married
el/la compañero/a	classmate / colleague
comprometerse	to get engaged
el compromiso	engagement
confiar en	to trust
conocer	to know / be familiar with / get to know
el/la conocido	acquaintance
de buen humor	in a good mood
disculpar(se)	to apologise
discutir	to discuss / argue

la disputa	argument
divorciarse	to get divorced
echar de menos	to miss (someone)
enamorado	in love
enamorarse	to fall in love
el/la esposo/a	husband / wife
el estado civil	marital status
fastidiar	to annoy / to bother
hacer amigos	to make friends
el hombre	man
juntos	together
llevarse bien / mal con	to get on well / badly with someone
el marido	husband
el matrimonio	marriage / married couple
mimado	spoilt
el modelo de conducta	role model
molestar	to bother
la mujer	wife / woman
el/la novio/a	boyfriend / girlfriend
optimista	optimistic
la pandilla	gang
la pareja	couple / partner
pelear(se)	to fight
perdonar	to forgive
reírse	to laugh
relacionarse con	to be in contact with
romper	to break
roto	broken
salir	to go out
el sentimiento	feeling
solo	alone
soltero	single (not married)
sonreír	to smile

Section Three — Technology in Everyday Life

Technology (p.30-33)

acceder	to access
adjuntar	to attach
el archivo	file
arroba	@
el blog	blog
borrar	to erase / delete
el buscador	search engine
el buzón	inbox / mailbox
cargar	load
charlar	to chat
colgar	to post (photos on social media, etc.)
la contraseña	password
el correo basura	spam
el correo electrónico	email
la cuenta	account
crear	to create
desactivar	to deactivate / block
descargar	to download

el disco duro	hard drive
enviar	to send
funcionar	to work / function
grabar	to burn (a disk)
guardar	to save
el guión	hyphen
el guión bajo	underscore
hablar	to speak / talk
la herramienta	tool
inalámbrico	wireless
el/la internauta	Internet user
mandar	to send
el mensaje (de texto)	(text) message
el móvil	mobile phone
el muro	wall
el navegador	browser
navegar	to surf
el ordenador	computer
la pantalla	screen
la portada	home page

el portátil	laptop
publicar	to publish
punto	dot / full stop
puntocom	.com
el ratón	mouse
recibir	to receive
la red	network / Internet
la red social	social network
el riesgo	risk
la sala de chat	chat room
el sitio web	website
el servidor de seguridad	firewall
el teclado	keyboard
usar	to use
el/la usuario/a	user
utilizar	to use
el videojuego	video game

Section Four — Free-Time Activities

Books and Reading (p.39)

el lector de libros electrónicos	e-reader
la lectura	reading
leer	to read
el libro	book
el libro electrónico	e-book
la novela	novel
la novela de suspense	thriller
el periódico	newspaper
la prensa	the press
la revista	magazine
el tebeo	comic strip

Music, Cinema and TV (p.40-42)

el/la artista	artist
el actor	actor
la actriz	actress
la actuación	performance
el anuncio (publicitario)	advert
la banda sonora	soundtrack
la batería	drums
la cadena	channel
la canción	song
el/la cantante	singer
cantar	to sing
la ciencia ficción	science fiction
el concurso	game show / contest
los dibujos animados	cartoons
divertir(se)	to have a good time
el documental	documentary
en directo	live
la entrada	ticket
el espectáculo	show
la estrella	star
el género	genre
la grabación	recording
el grupo	band
hacer cola	to queue
la historia	story
la letra	song lyrics
el/la músico/a	musician
la música pop	pop music
la música rap	rap music
la música rock	rock music
la música clásica	classical music
las noticias	news
el papel	role
la película	film
la película de acción	action film
la película de aventuras	adventure film
la película romántica	romantic film
la película de terror	horror film
policíaco	detective (adj.)
el programa	programme
el reality show	reality show
el reparto	cast
ser aficionado a	to be very keen on / fond of (activity)
la taquilla	box office
la telenovela	soap opera
tocar	to play (an instrument)
la trama	plot

Food and Eating Out (p.43-44)

a la plancha	grilled
el aceite	oil
el agua mineral (con / sin gas) (f)	(fizzy / still) mineral water
el ajo	garlic
la alimentación	food / nutrition
el alimento	type of food
almorzar	to have lunch
el almuerzo	lunch
apetecer	to fancy / to feel like
el arroz	rice
asado	roast(ed)
el atún	tuna
el azúcar	sugar
el bacalao	cod
la barra (de pan)	loaf (of bread)
beber	to drink
la bebida	drink
el bistec	steak
el bocadillo	sandwich
los calamares	squid
el caramelo	boiled sweet
la carne	meat
de cerdo	pork
de cordero	lamb
de ternera	veal
de vaca	beef
la carta	menu
la cebolla	onion
la cena	dinner
cenar	to have the evening meal
la cerveza	beer
los champiñones	mushrooms
el chorizo	Spanish sausage
la chuleta	chop
los churros	fritters
la cocina	cuisine / cooking
cocinar	to cook
la col	cabbage
comer	to eat
la comida (basura / rápida)	junk / fast food
la comida	meal / lunch
la copa	wine glass
la cuchara	spoon
el cuchillo	knife
la cuenta	bill
desayunar	to have breakfast
el desayuno	breakfast
dulce	sweet
elegir	to choose
escoger	to choose
el filete	steak
la fresa	strawberry
frito	fried
la galleta	biscuit
las gambas	prawns
el gazpacho	cold soup
la grasa	fat
los guisantes	peas
la heladería	ice cream parlour
el helado	ice cream
hervido	boiled
el hielo	ice
el huevo	egg
incluido	included
el jamón	ham
las judías verdes	string beans
la leche	milk
la lechuga	lettuce
las legumbres	vegetables / pulses
la mantequilla	butter
la manzana	apple
los mariscos	seafood
el melocotón	peach
merendar	to have an afternoon snack / picnic
la merienda	afternoon snack / picnic
la mermelada	jam
nada más	nothing else
la naranja	orange
la nata	cream
el pastel	cake / pie
la patata	potato
pedir	to order / ask for
la pera	pear
el pescado	fish
picante	spicy
la pimienta	pepper (seasoning)
el pimiento	pepper (vegetable)
la piña	pineapple
el plátano	banana
el plato (combinado)	(set) dish
el pollo	chicken
el postre	dessert
el primer plato	starter
probar	to taste / to try
la propina	tip
el queso	cheese
rico	tasty
sabroso	tasty
la sal	salt
salado	salty
la salchicha	sausage
la salsa	sauce

el segundo plato	main meal / course	andar	to walk	jugar	to play
los servicios	toilets	bailar	to dance	marcar (un gol)	to score (a goal)
la sopa	soup	el baile	dancing	el monopatín	skateboard
las tapas	nibbles / bar snacks	el baloncesto	basketball	montar	to ride
el té	tea	la bicicleta / bici	bicycle / bike	(a caballo / en bici)	(horse / bike)
el tenedor	fork	el campeón	champion	nadar	to swim
tener hambre	to be hungry	la campeona		la natación	swimming
tener sed	to be thirsty	el campeonato	championship	el partido	match
tomar	to have / to take	la carrera	race	el patinaje	skating
la tortilla	omelette	el concurso	contest / competition	patinar	to skate
la tostada	toast	la copa	cup / trophy	la pelota	ball
traer	to bring	correr	to run	perder	to lose
las uvas	grapes	el deporte	sport	la pesca	fishing
el vaso	glass	los deportes de	adventure sports	pescar	to fish
las verduras	vegetables	riesgo		el piragüismo	canoeing
el vino (blanco /	(white / rosé / red)	el/la deportista	sportsperson	la pista	track / court / run /
rosado / tinto)	wine	el equipo	team / equipment		slope / rink
la zanahoria	carrot	la equitación	horse riding	la pista de hielo	ice rink
el zumo (de fruta)	(fruit) juice	el estadio	stadium	el premio	prize
		ganar	to win	el/la socio/a	member
		el gol	goal	el torneo	tournament
		el juego	game	la vela	sail / sailing
		el/la jugador/a	player		

Sport (p.45-46)

al aire libre	outdoors
el alpinismo	mountain climbing

Section Five — Customs and Festivals

Customs and Festivals (p.52-54)

el Año Nuevo	New Year	disfrazarse de	to dress up as	Nochevieja	31 December
la bandera	flag	el Eid al-Fitr	Eid al-Fitr	Papá Noel	Father Christmas
la broma	joke / trick	la fecha patria	national day to	la Pascua	Easter
las castañuelas	castanets		commemorate	el paso	statue paraded at
celebrar	to celebrate		historic event		Easter
la corrida	bullfight	¡Feliz Año Nuevo!	Happy New Year!	la plaza de toros	bullring
la costumbre	custom / way	¡Feliz cumpleaños!	Happy Birthday!	la procesión	procession
cristiano	Christian	¡Feliz Navidad!	Merry Christmas!	los Reyes Magos	the Three Kings
el Día de los	28 December	la feria	fair	el santo	saint's day
Inocentes	(equivalent of April	festejar	to celebrate	la Semana Santa	Easter week
	Fools' Day)	la fiesta	festival / party	la tradición	tradition
el Día de los	All Souls' Day	el Hannukah	Hannukah	la Tomatina	tomato-throwing
Muertos		judío	Jewish		festival
el Día de Reyes	Epiphany /	el juguete	toy	tener suerte	to be lucky
	6 January	el mariachi	Mexican musician	el/la torero/a	bullfighter
el día festivo	public holiday	el/la muerto/a	dead (person)	el toro	bull
el disfraz	fancy dress	musulmán	Muslim	el turrón	Spanish nougat
		Navidad	Christmas	el villancico	Christmas carol
		Nochebuena	Christmas Eve		

Section Six — Where You Live

Where You Live (p.60-61)

las afueras	outskirts	el baño	bathroom / bath	la casa (adosada)	(semi-detached)
la aldea	village	el barrio	neighbourhood		house
la alfombra	rug	la biblioteca	library	el centro	town centre
alquilar	to rent / to hire	la bolera	bowling alley	el centro comercial	shopping centre
el alquiler	rent	el bosque	forest / woods	el chalet / chalé	bungalow / house
el aparcamiento	parking	la butaca	armchair	el cine	cinema
el árbol	tree	la calefacción	heating	la ciudad	city
el armario	wardrobe / cupboard	la calle	street	el club (de jóvenes)	(youth) club
el ascensor	lift	la cama	bed	la cocina	cooker / kitchen
el aseo	toilet	el campo	countryside /	el comedor	dining room
el ayuntamiento	town hall		grounds	la comisaría	police station
bajar	to go down	la cancha (de tenis)	(tennis) court	cómodo	comfortable /
		la carnicería	butcher's		convenient / handy

Vocabulary

compartir	to share	las persianas	blinds, shutters	**Shopping (p.63-64)**	
la comunidad	community	la pescadería	fishmonger's	a mitad de precio	half-price
concurrido	busy / crowded	el piso	flat / floor (of room)	el agujero	hole
construir	to build	la planta baja	ground floor	Aquí lo tienes.	Here you are.
Correos	Post Office	la planta	floor / plant	bastante	enough
la cortina	curtain	la población	population	la bolsa	paper / plastic bag
el cuarto de baño	bathroom	el polideportivo	sports centre	la caja	box / till
dar a	to look onto	propio	own	cambiar	to change
de lujo	luxury	el pueblo	town / village /	la cantidad	quantity
la dirección	address		people / nation	el cartón	carton
el domicilio	address / home	el puente	bridge	el centro comercial	shopping centre
el dormitorio	bedroom	la puerta	door	el chándal	tracksuit
la ducha	shower	el puerto	port / harbour	el/la cliente	customer
el edificio	building	el río	river	la corbata	tie
la entrada	entrance	el ruido	noise	el/la dependiente/a	sales assistant
entrar	to go in / enter	ruidoso	noisy	el descuento	discount
los electrodomésticos	electrical appliances	el salón	lounge	devolver	to return
		la segunda planta	second floor	el dinero	money
la escalera	stairs	el semáforo	traffic lights	en efectivo	(in) cash
el espacio	space	la sierra	mountain range	el escaparate	shop window
el espejo	mirror	la silla	chair	exactamente	exactly
la esquina	corner	el sillón	armchair	el gramo	gram
el estanco	tobacconist's	el sótano	basement / cellar	los grandes almacenes	department store
el estante	shelf	subir	to go up		
la estantería	shelves	el suelo	floor	el hipermercado	hypermarket
la fábrica	factory	el teatro	theatre	el kilo	kilogram
el fregadero	kitchen sink	la terraza	terrace	la lata	tin
los grandes almacenes	department store	la tienda de comestibles	grocery shop	el litro	litre
				lleno	full
la granja	farm	la tienda de ropa	clothes shop	el número (de zapato)	shoe size
la habitación	room	la ventana	window		
el/la habitante	inhabitant	el vestíbulo	entrance hall / lobby	pagar	to pay
el horno	oven		/ foyer	el paquete	packet
la iglesia	church	la vivienda	dwelling / housing /	el pedazo	piece
la joyería	jeweller's		accommodation	pesar	to weigh
la juguetería	toy shop	la zona peatonal	pedestrian zone	los probadores	changing rooms
el lavabo	washbasin			quejarse	to complain
la lavadora	washing machine	**What You Do at Home (p.62)**		la ración	portion
el lavaplatos	dishwasher	acostarse	to go to bed	rasgado	ripped
la librería	bookcase / bookshop	arreglar	to tidy / to fix	las rebajas	the sales
		ayudar	to help	la rebanada	slice
la llave	key	cortar el césped	to mow the lawn	el recibo	receipt
la luz	light	despertarse	to wake up	reembolsar	to refund
la máquina	machine	dormirse	to go to sleep	reemplazar	to replace
el mercado	market	ducharse	to have a shower	roto	broken
la mesa	table	hacer la cama	to make the bed	el servicio de reparto a domicilio	home delivery service
la mezquita	mosque	hacer las compras	to do the shopping		
el microondas	microwave oven	lavar los platos	to do the washing-up		
mudarse (de casa)	to move (house)	lavarse la cara	to wash your face	suficiente	enough
los muebles	furniture	levantarse	to get up	la talla	size (clothes)
el museo	museum	limpiar	to clean	la tarjeta de crédito	credit card
el negocio	business	limpio	clean	el tarro	jar
la nevera	fridge	la paga	pocket money	el tercio	third
el paisaje	landscape / scenery	pasar la aspiradora	to do the vacuuming	la tienda de comestibles	grocery shop
la panadería	bakery	pasear al perro	to walk the dog		
la papelera	wastepaper basket	poner la mesa	to lay the table	el trozo	slice, piece
la papelería	stationery shop	quitar la mesa	to clear the table	vacío	empty
la pared	wall	sacar la basura	to take out the rubbish	varios/as	several
el parque	park				
el parque infantil	playground	sentarse	to sit down		
el pasillo	corridor	la tarea doméstica	chore		
la pastelería	pastry shop	vestirse	to get dressed		
la peluquería	hairdresser's				

Directions (p.65)

a un paso (de)	a few steps away (from)
abajo (de)	under / below
afuera (de)	outside
ahí	(just) there
aislado	isolated
al final (de)	at the end (of)
allá	(over) there
allí	(over) there
alrededor (de)	around
aquí	here
arriba (de)	above / on top (of)
atrás	behind
cerca (de)	near
cercano	nearby
contra	against
cruzar	to cross
debajo (de)	under
delante (de)	in front of
dentro (de)	inside
a la derecha	on / to the right
(todo) derecho	straight ahead
detrás (de)	behind
en / por todas partes	everywhere
en la esquina	on the corner
en las afueras	in the outskirts
encima (de)	above / on top / overhead
encontrarse	to be situated
enfrente (de)	opposite
entre	between
estar situado	to be situated
el este	east
en el / al fondo	at the back / at the bottom
fuera (de)	outside
a la izquierda	on / to the left
al lado (de)	next to
lejano	far away / distant / remote
lejos (de)	far (from)
el lugar	place
en (el) medio (de)	in the middle of
el norte	north
el oeste	west
seguir	to follow / continue
el sitio	place
el sur	south
todo recto	straight ahead
tomar	to take (a road)

Weather (p.66)

buen / mal tiempo	good / bad weather
caliente	hot
caluroso	hot / warm
el chubasco	shower
el cielo	sky
el clima	climate
despejado	clear (skies)
estable	stable / unchanged
fresco	fresh
el grado	degree
hacer (frío / calor etc.)	to be (cold / hot etc.)
helar	to freeze
el hielo	ice
húmedo	humid
llover	to rain
la lluvia	rain
mojar(se)	to get wet
nevar	to snow
la niebla	fog
la nieve	snow
la nube	cloud
nublado / nuboso	cloudy
el pronóstico	forecast
el relámpago	lightning
seco	dry
el sol	sun
la sombra	shade / shadow
templado	mild / temperate
tener (frío / calor)	to feel (cold / hot)
el tiempo	weather
la tormenta	storm
tormentoso	stormy
el trueno	thunder
el viento	wind

Section Seven — Social and Global Issues

Environmental Problems (p.72-73)

agotar	to exhaust / use up
el agujero	hole
amenazar	to threaten
apagar	to turn off (lights etc.)
arruinar	to ruin / destroy
el atasco	traffic jam
aumentar	to increase
beneficiar	to benefit
el beneficio	benefit
el calentamiento global	global warming
el cambio climático	climate change
la capa de ozono	ozone layer
el cartón	cardboard
el combustible	fuel
el consumo	consumption
contaminar	to pollute
el contenedor	container
cultivar	to grow / cultivate
el cultivo	crop
dañar	to harm / damage
el daño	harm / damage
desaparecer	to disappear
el desperdicio	waste / rubbish / squandering
ducharse	to have a shower
el efecto invernadero	greenhouse effect
encender	to turn on (lights etc.)
ensuciar	to make dirty / soil / make a mess
el envase	wrapping / packaging / container
la escasez	shortage / lack
escaso	scarce / meagre
estropear	to ruin / spoil
la falta	lack
faltar	to be missing
el fuego	fire
los gases de escape	exhaust fumes
el huracán	hurricane
el incendio	fire
la inundación	flood
la lluvia ácida	acid rain
malgastar	to waste / misuse / squander
la marea negra	oil spill
el medio ambiente	environment
medioambiental	environmental
mundial	global / worldwide
el mundo	world
la naturaleza	nature
nocivo	harmful
el pájaro	bird
el petróleo	oil
la pila	battery
la preocupación	worry
preocupado	worried / anxious
preocupante	worrying
los productos químicos	chemicals
proteger	to protect
químico (adj)	chemical
recargable	rechargeable
el recurso	resource
la selva	jungle / tropical forest
la sequía	drought
solucionar	to solve / resolve
sucio	dirty
la Tierra	Earth
tirar	to throw (away)
utilizar	to use
la ventaja	advantage
el vertedero	rubbish dump / tip

Problems in Society (p.74-75)

la belleza	beauty
combatir	to fight / combat
cometer	to commit
la culpa	fault / blame / guilt
el desarrollo	development
el desempleo	unemployment

los derechos	rights	la pobreza	poverty	la residencia (para ancianos)	(old people's) home
la desigualdad	inequality	el prejuicio	prejudice		
la discriminación	discrimination	el/la refugiado/a	refugee	los residuos	refuse / waste / rubbish
echar la culpa	to blame	robar	to steal		
estar en paro	to be unemployed	el robo	theft / burglary	reutilizar	to reuse
el/la extranjero/a	foreigner	los "sin techo"	homeless people	salvar	to save
el/la gamberro/a	hooligan / lout / troublemaker	el/la testigo	witness	la tienda con fines benéficos	charity shop
		la violencia	violence		
el gobierno	government			la tienda solidaria	charity shop
grave	serious			voluntario	voluntary

Contributing to Society (p.76)

la basura	rubbish / garbage	el/la voluntario/a	volunteer
los desechos	rubbish / waste		

Global Events (p.77)

grave	serious

la guerra	war	la encuesta	poll / survey	a beneficio de	in aid of
la igualdad	equality	la obra benéfica	charity	asistir a	to attend
injusto	unjust / unfair	la ONG	NGO (non-governmental organisation)	la campaña	campaign
inquietante	worrying / disturbing			estar en desventaja	to be disadvantaged
inquietar(se)	to worry			el evento	event
justo	just / fair	la organización benéfica	charitable organisation	el festival (de música)	(music) festival
el ladrón / la ladrona	thief				
la ley	law	organizar	to organise	los Juegos Olímpicos	Olympic Games
la libertad	liberty / freedom	la participación	participation		
luchar	to fight / struggle	el reciclaje	recycling	llamar la atención	to attract attention
matar	to kill	reciclar	to recycle	el Mundial	World Cup (football)
la multa	fine	recoger	to collect / gather / pick up	la organización caritativa	charitable organisation
los necesitados	needy people				
el peligro	danger	renovable	renewable	recaudar dinero	to raise money
peligroso	dangerous				
pobre	poor				

Section Eight — Lifestyle

Health (p.83-84)

activo	active	el/la fumador/a (pasivo/a)	(passive) smoker	**Illnesses (p.85)**	
advertir	to warn			el ataque cardíaco	heart attack
el asco	disgust	fumar	to smoke	el brazo	arm
asqueroso	disgusting	hacer daño	to injure / harm	la cabeza	head
el aviso	warning / notice	el humo	smoke	el cerebro	brain
el azúcar	sugar	malsano	unhealthy	el corazón	heart
borracho	drunk	mantenerse en forma	to keep fit / in shape	el dedo	finger
el botellón	drinking party in the street			doler	to hurt
		morir	to die	el dolor	pain / ache
caer(se)	to fall down	muerto	dead	el dolor de oídos	earache
cansado	tired / tiring	la necesidad	need	encontrarse bien / mal	to feel well / ill
cansar(se)	to get tired	oler	to smell		
el cigarrillo	cigarette	el olor	smell	la enfermedad	illness
contribuir	to contribute	el porro	joint	enfermo	ill
el cuerpo	body	la posibilidad	possibility	la espalda	back
dedicar(se)	to do / to go in for / to devote oneself	el propósito	aim / purpose / objective	estar bien / mal	to be well / ill
				el estómago	stomach
la dieta	diet	provocar	to cause / provoke	el estrés	stress
dormir	to sleep	respirar	to breathe	la garganta	throat
la droga (blanda / dura)	(soft / hard) drug	respiratorio	respiratory	el hígado	liver
		la salud	health	el/la médico/a	doctor
drogarse	to take drugs	saludable	healthy	mejorar(se)	to get better
el ejercicio (físico)	(physical) exercise	sano	healthy / wholesome	el pie	foot
emborracharse	to get drunk	el síndrome de abstinencia	withdrawal symptoms	la pierna	leg
el entrenamiento	training			los primeros auxilios	first aid
entrenar(se)	to train	el sobrepeso	overweight / obesity		
equilibrado	balanced	el tabaquismo	addiction to tobacco	los pulmones	lungs
el esfuerzo	effort	tener sueño	to feel sleepy	la receta	prescription
estar en forma	to be fit	la tentación	temptation	sentirse	to feel
evitar	to avoid	la vida	life	seropositivo	HIV-positive
formar parte (de)	to be part (of)	vivo	alive	el sida	AIDS
				tener dolor (de)...	to have a pain (in)...

Section Nine — Travel and Tourism

Where to Go (p.91)

alemán	German
Alemania	Germany
Argentina	Argentina
Australia	Australia
Brasil	Brazil
británico	British
las Islas Canarias	Canary Islands
Canadá	Canada
castellano	Castilian, Spanish spoken in Spain
Chile	Chile
Colombia	Colombia
Cuba	Cuba
escocés	Scottish
Escocia	Scotland
España	Spain
español	Spanish
los Estados Unidos	United States
Europa	Europe
europeo	European
francés	French
Francia	France
Gales	Wales
galés	Welsh
Gran Bretaña	Great Britain
Grecia	Greece
griego	Greek
la India	India
Inglaterra	England
inglés	English
Irlanda	Ireland
irlandés	Irish
Irlanda del Norte	Northern Ireland
la isla	island
Italia	Italy
italiano	Italian
latinoamericano	Latin American
Londres	London
el mar	sea
el mar Mediterráneo	Mediterranean Sea
México	Mexico
la montaña	mountain
el mundo	world
norirlandés	Northern Irish
norteamericano	North American
el país	country
Perú	Peru
Portugal	Portugal
portugués	Portuguese
la playa	beach
Rusia	Russia
sudamericano	South American

Preparation (p.92-93)

la agencia (de viajes)	(travel) agent's
el aire acondicionado	air conditioning

el albergue juvenil	youth hostel
el alojamiento	accommodation
alojarse	to lodge / stay
el ambiente	atmosphere
buscar	to look for
la cama de matrimonio	double bed
cambiar	to change
el camping	campsite
la caravana	caravan
el carnet de conducir	driving licence
el carnet de identidad	identity card
el cheque (de viaje)	traveller's cheque
la crema solar	sun cream
la dirección	management
disponible	available
DNI	ID card
el equipaje	luggage
el formulario	registration form
la ficha	registration form
el folleto	leaflet / pamphlet
(no) fumador	(non) smoking
el/la guía	guide
la guía	guidebook
la habitación (doble / individual)	(double / single) room
informarse	to find out
irse de camping	to go camping
las instalaciones	facilities
libre	available
llevar	to take
el lugar	place
la maleta	suitcase
la máquina (de fotos)	camera
media pensión	half board
el papel higiénico	toilet paper
el parador	state-owned hotel (in Spain)
el pasaporte	passport
pensión completa	full board
la pensión	boarding house / B&B
perder	to lose
el permiso de conducir	driving licence
quedarse	to stay
la queja	complaint
quejarse	to complain
la recepción	reception
recordar	to remember
la reserva	reservation
reservar	to book / reserve
el sitio	space / room / place / site
la tienda	tent
las vacaciones	holidays
la vista	view

How to Get There (p.94)

a mano derecha / izquierda	on the right- / left-hand side
a pie	on foot / walking
el aeropuerto	airport
el andén	platform
aparcar	to park
el autocar	coach
la autopista	motorway
el avión	aeroplane
el barco	boat
el billete (de ida / de ida y vuelta)	(single / return) ticket
la carretera	highway
el casco	helmet
el cinturón de seguridad	seat belt
el coche	car
coger	to take / catch
conducir	to drive / lead
el/la conductor/a	driver
la consigna	left luggage office
el cruce	crossroads / intersection
el crucero	cruise
cruzar	to cross
detener(se)	to stop
doblar	to turn
esperar	to wait
la estación (de autobuses / autocares / trenes)	(bus / coach / train) station
la estación de servicio	service station
el ferrocarril	railway system
la gasolina (sin plomo)	(unleaded) petrol
hacer transbordo	to change / transfer
la llegada	arrival
llegar	to arrive
el metro	underground
la parada	stop
parar	to stop
el/la pasajero/a	passenger
pasar (por)	to go (through) / pass
el paso subterráneo	underpass / subway
perder (vuelo etc.)	to miss (flight etc.)
perderse	to get lost
regresar	to go back
el retraso	delay
la rueda	wheel
la sala de espera	waiting room
la salida	exit
la señal	sign / signal
tardar	to take (time)
torcer	to turn
el tranvía	tram
venir	to come

la vía	track / lane
viajar	to travel
el viaje	trip / journey
el/la viajero/a	traveller
volver	to return
el vuelo	flight

What To Do (p.95)

el abanico	fan
bañarse	to bathe / swim
broncearse	to get a tan
caminar	to walk
el camino	path / route / road
los deportes acuáticos	water sports
descansar	to rest
el descanso	rest / pause
el esquí	skiing
esquiar	to ski
estar de vacaciones	to be on holiday

la excursión	trip / excursion
el lago	lake
la montaña	mountain
el museo	museum
la naturaleza	nature
el parque de atracciones	fairground
el parque temático	theme park
pasar (tiempo)	to spend (time)
la playa	beach
la postal	postcard
el recuerdo	souvenir
relajarse	to relax
el río	river
sacar fotos	to take photos
la tarjeta (postal)	card / (post)card
tomar el sol	to sunbathe

Practical Stuff (p.96)

asegurar	to insure
la avería	breakdown

el cajero automático	ATM / cashpoint
el camión	lorry
la cartera	wallet
chocar	to crash
la colisión	crash
la comisaría	police station
confirmar un billete	to validate a ticket
la consigna automática	left luggage locker
el desvío	diversion
la factura	bill (invoice)
el garaje	garage
la gasolina	petrol
el monedero	purse
perder	to lose
el/la revisor/a	ticket inspector
robar	to steal / rob

Section Ten — Current and Future Study and Employment

School Subjects (p.102)

el alemán	German
el arte dramático	drama
la asignatura	school subject
la biología	biology
las ciencias económicas	economics
las ciencias	science
la cocina	food technology
el comercio	business studies
el curso	school year
el dibujo	art
la educación física	PE
enseñar	to teach
el español	Spanish
la física	physics
el francés	French
la geografía	geography
la gimnasia	gymnastics
la historia	history
el idioma	language
la informática	IT
el inglés	English
la lengua	language / tongue
las matemáticas	maths
la música	music
optar	to choose / opt for
optativo	optional
la química	chemistry
la religión	RE
riguroso	severe / harsh
sencillo	simple / easy
los trabajos manuales	handicrafts

School Life (p.103-105)

el acoso (escolar)	(school) bullying
la agenda	diary
el/la alumno/a	pupil / student
apoyar	to support / help
el apoyo	support / help
aprender	to learn
aprobar	to approve / pass (an exam)
los apuntes	notes
el aula (f)	classroom
ausente	absent
la ayuda	help
el bolígrafo	pen
callar(se)	to shut up
el campo de deportes	sports field
la cantina	canteen
la carpeta	folder / file
castigar	to punish
el castigo	punishment
la clase	lesson
el colegio mixto	mixed school
el colegio privado	private school
el colegio público	state school
el colegio religioso	religious school
el comportamiento	behaviour
comportarse	to behave
la conducta	behaviour / conduct
contestar	to answer
charlar	to chat
el chicle	chewing gum
el cuaderno	exercise book
los deberes	homework
el despacho	office
dibujar	to draw
el/la director/a	head teacher

diseñar	to design
educativo	educational
la enseñanza	teaching / education
entender	to understand
entregar	to hand in
escribir	to write
la escuela (primaria)	(primary) school
esforzarse	to make an effort
estresante	stressful
el estuche	pencil case
la evaluación	assessment
el examen	exam
el éxito	success
la explicación	explanation
explicar	to explain
la falta	mistake / absence
faltar	to be absent
fracasar	to fail
el gimnasio	gymnasium
la hora de comer	lunchtime
el horario	timetable
el instituto	secondary school / institute
el intercambio	exchange
la intimidación	bullying
los lápices de colores	colour pencils
la lección	lesson
la letra	letter of the alphabet
levantar la mano	to put your hand up
el libro	book
mirar	to look
la mochila	rucksack / school bag
molestar	to annoy / bother
el nivel	level
la nota	mark

obligatorio	compulsory
oír	to listen / hear
olvidar	to forget
la página	page
la palabra	word
pasar (la) lista	to call the register
pedir prestado	to borrow
el permiso	permission
la pizarra interactiva	smart board
la pregunta	question
preguntar	to ask a question
la presión	pressure
privado	private
prometer	to promise / show promise
la prueba	test / proof
el recreo	break
la regla	rule / ruler
repartir	to hand out
repasar	to revise
la respuesta	answer
la rutina	routine
sacar buenas / malas notas	to get good / bad marks
la sala de profesores	staffroom
el salón de actos	hall / assembly room
sobresaliente	outstanding
suspender	to fail (exam / subject)
el taller	workshop
la tarea	task / piece of homework
el tema	topic / theme
tener miedo	to be afraid
terminar	to finish
las tijeras	scissors
trabajador	hard-working
el trabajo	work
el trimestre	(school) term
el uniforme	uniform

School Events (p.106)

el/la amigo/a por correspondencia	penfriend
el autobús escolar	school bus
el día de disfraces	fancy dress day
la entrega de premios	prize-giving
la excursión (del colegio)	school trip
(al) extranjero	abroad
el grupo escolar	school group
el intercambio	exchange
participar en	to participate in
el rendimiento	achievement / performance
la reunión de padres	parents' evening
la venta de pasteles	cake sale

la visita guiada	guided tour
la vuelta al colegio	first day back at school

Education Post-16 (p.107)

la academia	academy / school post-16 (for certain careers)
el/la aprendiz/a	apprentice
el aprendizaje	apprenticeship / training / learning
el bachillerato	school leaving exam (e.g. A-levels)
calificado	competent / skilled
la carrera	career / profession
el comienzo	beginning / start
los conocimientos	knowledge
conseguir	to get / achieve
Derecho	law (at university)
esperar	to hope / expect
la experiencia laboral	work experience
la formación (profesional)	vocational training
lograr	to achieve
las perspectivas laborales	employment prospects
la práctica	work placement
tomarse un año libre / sabático	to take a gap year
la universidad	university
útil	useful

Career Choices (p.108)

a tiempo completo	full time
a tiempo parcial	part time
el/la abogado/a	lawyer / solicitor
el arquitecto/a	architect
el/la bombero/a	firefighter
el/la cajero/a	bank-teller / cashier
el/la carnicero/a	butcher
el/la cocinero/a	cook
el/la constructor/a	builder
el/la contable	accountant
desafiante	challenging
el/la electricista	electrician
el/la empleado/a	employee / worker
el empleo	job / employment
la empresa	company
encontrar	to find
el/la enfermero/a	nurse
el/la escritor/a	writer
estar en paro	to be unemployed
estimulante	stimulating
el/la fontanero/a	plumber
el/la funcionario/a	civil servant
ganar	to earn
el/la gerente	manager
el/la granjero/a	farmer
gratificante	rewarding
el hombre / la mujer de negocios	businessman/ woman
el/la ingeniero/a	engineer

el/la jefe	boss
laboral	working
llegar a ser	to become
el/la mecánico/a	mechanic
el objetivo	aim / objective
obtener	to get / obtain
el/la oficial de policía	police officer
el/la orientador/a	careers adviser
parado	unemployed
el paro	unemployment
el/la peluquero/a	hairdresser
el periodismo	journalism
el/la periodista	journalist
probar	to have a go / try
el sueldo	salary
trabajar	to work
el trabajo	work / job
el/la traductor/a	translator
triunfar	to triumph / succeed
variado	varied
el/la veterinario/a	veterinary surgeon

Languages for the Future (p.109)

el/la auxiliar de lengua	language assistant
el/la azafato/a	flight attendant
comunicarse	to communicate
expresarse	to express yourself
el idioma	language
internacional	international
el laboratorio de idiomas	language lab
la lengua	language
multicultural	multicultural
pronunciar	to pronounce
traducir	to translate
viajar por el mundo	to travel the world

Applying for Jobs (p.110)

adjuntar	to attach
el anuncio de trabajo	job advertisement
bien pagado	well-paid
la carta de solicitud	application letter
la cita	appointment
con experiencia	experienced
las condiciones de empleo	terms of employment
despedir	to dismiss
el/la director/a	boss
la entrevista	interview
la habilidad	skill
por hora	per hour
las posibilidades de promoción	promotion prospects
rellenar	to fill in
solicitar un puesto de trabajo	to apply for a job
la solicitud	appliciation form
el sueldo	salary
la vacante	vacancy

Answers

The answers to the translation questions are sample answers only, just to give you an idea of one way to translate them. There may be different ways to translate these passages that are also correct.

Section One — General Stuff

Page 1: Numbers

1) Tiene diecisiete años.
2) Tiene ochenta y ocho años.
3) Vive en la segunda calle a la derecha.

Page 3: Times and Dates

1) the day before yesterday   2) London   3) Friday

Page 9: Opinions

1) Luis prefers watching films at home.
2) No, he doesn't. He thinks they're boring.
3) Elena thinks sometimes they're ridiculous.

Page 10: Putting it All Together

1)   F   2)   T   3)   F   4)   T   5)   F

Page 11: Listening Questions

1 a) 2003   b) about 190   c) 27
2 a) loves   b) doesn't like   c) hates   d) loves   e) likes

Page 13: Reading Questions

1 a) 48   b) second floor   c) 25
2   A & D

Page 14: Writing Questions

1 a) a las nueve   d) a las tres menos veinte
   b) a las diez y media   e) a las cuatro menos diez
   c) a la una menos cuarto
2   — ¿Qué piensas de este artículo en el periódico?
     — Pienso/Creo que el periodista tiene unas buenas ideas.
     — No estoy de acuerdo. Pienso/Creo que el otro artículo es
       mejor.
     — ¿Cuál es tu opinión del libro que ha leído?
     — Lo encuentro estupendo.

Section Two — Me, My Family and Friends

Page 17: My Family

I live with my mother, my older sister and my two younger sisters. They are twins. For me, it's important to have brothers and sisters because you always have someone to go out with. At the weekend, I visit my father, his wife and my stepbrother. He was born last year and he is only six months old. I would like to spend more time there with them because it's great fun / entertaining.

Page 18: Describing People

Descripción 1 = foto b   Descripción 3 = foto a
Descripción 2 = foto d   Descripción 4 = foto c

Page 20: Pets

I have a bird as a pet. He has always been very chatty — he repeats what you say and it's very funny when he says rude things. The good thing about birds is that they eat fruit, vegetables and cereals, so their food doesn't cost much. However, next weekend I have to take him to the vet and I think it will cost a lot of money.

Page 21: Style and Fashion

1)   A   2)   C

Page 24: Partnership

1 a) False   b) True   c) False
2   Jerez

Page 25: Listening Questions

1 a) glasses
   b) brown eyes; black hair; curly hair
   c) short hair; curly hair
2 a) A & C   b) B & D

Page 27: Reading Questions

1   I have a black hamster called Elvis. I bought him two years ago. Elvis makes me laugh a lot because he's a bit silly. He sleeps in his house during the day and comes out at night to eat and play. Sometimes he makes a lot of noise and doesn't let me sleep. In an ideal world, I would have several hamsters, but at the moment I don't have enough space.
2 a) toda la vida
   b) Les critican por su mal comportamiento.
   c) Siempre piensa antes de actuar.

Page 28: Writing Questions

2   Cuando era pequeño/a, me llevaba bien con mis padres, pero ahora prefiero hablar con mis abuelos. Son más comprensivos. Por eso, preferiría vivir con ellos. Creo que me llevaré mejor con mis padres en el futuro. No nos pelearemos tanto y serán más sensibles.

Section Three — Technology in Everyday Life

Page 31: Technology

No podría vivir sin la tecnología porque es muy útil. Me gusta jugar a los videojuegos en la red con mi hermano. Hablamos con internautas en otros países. Ayer, jugué con un chico en Chile, pero para proteger mi identidad, no uso nunca mi nombre. Lo mejor de los móviles es que no tienes que estar en casa para usar la red. En el futuro, pienso que los niños tendrán móviles cuando tengan dos o tres años.

Page 32: Social Media

1)   V   2)   V   3)   F   4)   F

Page 34: Listening Questions

1 a) homework / studying
   b) shopping
   c) organise her bank accounts
   d) people can steal your information / passwords
   e) there are many dangerous people (who can lie to you)
2 a) P   b) P+N   c) N

Page 36: Reading Questions

1   "Have you seen Luisa's wall recently?" asked Naiara.
     "No, why?" said Sara.
     "Because she's just posted some very silly photos and I think there's a photo of you."
     "Really? I will have to ring her right now to ask her why she did it."
     "Yes, of course. Luisa never thinks before she posts things on social networks."
2   My friend loves social networks. I'm fed up with not seeing him, so I said to him:
     "Why don't you come and have a coffee with us? You spend all your time on your laptop! It's important to do other things once in a while, Fernando! I know that social networks have advantages, but you're obsessed!"

Page 37: Writing Questions

2   Mis padres odian la tecnología. El año pasado, compraron un ordenador, pero solo lo usan para mandar correos electrónicos. Creo que es esencial saber cómo navegar por la red. Uso Internet para descargar música. No podría vivir sin Internet porque es una parte de mi vida muy grande.

Section Four — Free-Time Activities

Page 40: Music
1) the saxophone
2) It's very quick to get songs.
   It's cheaper than going to a shop and buying a CD.
3) Live music is always very exciting.

Page 41: Cinema
Me encantan las películas. En mi opinión, las películas policíacas son las mejores. Son las películas más divertidas porque tienes que pensar en la trama. La semana pasada, vi una película muy divertida. Me gusta ver películas con mis amigos los fines de semana. En el futuro, me encantaría ser actriz.

Page 42: TV
1) False   2) False   3) True   4) True

Page 43: Food
The correct sentences are 2 and 3.

Page 47: Listening Questions
1 a) Two from: una limonada; grande; con hielo
  b) el filete
  c) el filete con verduras y patatas fritas
  d) un helado de fresa
2 a) el tenis
  b) el atletismo, la natación
  c) el fútbol, el rugby, la natación

Page 49: Reading Questions
1   B & E
2   "Why wouldn't you like to go canoeing? It's an exciting and fun sport."
     "It seems like a very difficult and dangerous sport to me."
     "It's true that you can hurt yourself. A friend of mine broke his arm a year ago. If you prefer, you could go to the sports centre to play basketball or badminton."

Page 50: Writing Questions
2   Me encantan las novelas policíacas. Cuando era más pequeño/a / más joven me daban miedo pero ahora me gustan mucho. Cuando sea mayor, me gustaría escribir novelas. Creo que sería divertido pasar todo el día pensando en ideas para libros. Sin embargo, no soy muy paciente, así que solo escribiría libros cortos.

Section Five — Customs and Festivals

Page 52: Customs and Festivals
1) F   2) F   3) T   4) T

Page 54: Customs and Festivals
1) A   2) C   3) C   4) B

Page 55: Listening Questions
1 a) D   b) H   c) G   d) C   e) F
2 a) A   b) C   c) B

Page 57: Reading Questions
1 a) La fecha exacta cambia cada año.
  b) solemnes, impresionantes
  c) Habrá mucha gente por las calles.
2   A & C

Page 58: Writing Questions
2   Ayer aprendimos sobre algunas fiestas españolas. El Día de los Inocentes tiene lugar el 28 de diciembre en España. Es un evento religioso, pero es divertido también. Me encantaría ir a Buñol con mis amigos para participar en La Tomatina. Pienso/Creo que sería muy interesante pero no tengo suficiente dinero para ir este año.

Section Six — Where You Live

Page 61: The Home
1) False   4) False
2) False   5) True
3) True

Page 62: What You Do at Home
I believe it's important to help at home, but I don't think it's fair if I do a lot and my younger brother does very little. I love walking the dog. My dad gives me money if I mow the lawn, so I will do it next Sunday. Last week I had to clean the bathroom. How disgusting!

Page 64: Shopping
1) half a kilo   3) he's just sold the last bottle
2) salt   4) €6.50

Page 65: Giving and Asking for Directions
1) F   2) F   3) V   4) F

Page 66: Weather
1) the south   4) The temperatures will drop.
2) in the west (near Portugal) 5) There might be storms.
3) It'll be good weather.

Page 67: Listening Questions
1 a) A, E & F   b) B, C & D
2 a) No hace nada. / No ayuda en casa.
  b) porque su padre no vive en casa
  c) Any two from: quita la mesa; arregla su dormitorio; saca la basura.
  d) Prepara la cena.

Page 69: Reading Questions
1   O; A; L; B; F; K; J; D
2   Today I have a long list of things to do. First, I have to go to the department store to return some black socks. My grandmother needs a new coat, but I'm going to buy it online and make the most of the home delivery service. Finally, I have to take a dozen cakes to my aunt and uncle's house. I should start right now!

Page 70: Writing Questions
2   Hoy hace buen tiempo. La semana pasada, hubo tormenta y llovió durante tres días. Lo peor fue que no pude salir con mis amigos. Vi el pronóstico anoche y dijeron que mañana hará sol y viento aquí en el norte.

Section Seven — Social and Global Issues

Page 73: Environmental Problems
El cambio climático me preocupa mucho. Las fábricas y los coches contribuyen al efecto invernadero. Para mí, lo peor es que la gente en algunos países pobres sufre debido a las inundaciones y las sequías. No es justo. Creo que deberíamos trabajar juntos para reducir los efectos del cambio climático, pero será muy difícil.

Page 75: Problems in Society
1) economic problems   4) lazy
2) very difficult   5) work together
3) prejudice

Page 77: Global Events
Este año, hemos trabajado con una organización caritativa que ayuda a niños en desventaja en Asia. Organizamos un concierto y escribimos a unos cantantes para preguntarles si nos apoyarían. Tres de ellos vinieron y todo el mundo lo pasó bien. En el futuro, me encantaría ir al Mundial. Creo que sería muy divertido.

Page 78: Listening Questions
1 a) C   b) B   c) A
2 a) social inequality
  b) Any two from: buy food; buy clothes; heat their homes
  c) prejudice
  d) violence (among young people)

Page 80: Reading Questions

1 "I hope you're not going to go out with those boys! I think they're very rude, Pedro."

"Don't worry, I'm not going to go out with them. Now I know that they're violent. The other day, they bullied a woman in the street. They were very aggressive and she believed that they were going to hurt her. I didn't like that at all, and now we're not friends."

2 a) inactiva   b) acoger   c) buenas oportunidades

Page 81: Writing Questions

2 En mi opinión, hay muchos problemas con el medio ambiente. Debido al efecto invernadero, las temperaturas han aumentado mucho. Mi abuela me dijo que cuando ella era más joven, nevaba cada invierno, pero ahora no nieva mucho. En el futuro, creo que habrá más sequías.

Section Eight — Lifestyle

Page 85: Illnesses

I feel very ill. Last week, I went to the countryside, but unfortunately it was raining and I hadn't brought my umbrella. My throat hurts a lot and I can hardly speak. I have had to drink lots of liquids for a few days and I don't feel like eating. I will have to go to the doctor if I don't get better soon. The worst thing is that if I'm still ill on Saturday, I won't be able to go to my friend's party.

Page 86: Listening Questions

1 a) C   b) B   c) Algunos cereales contienen mucho azúcar.
2 a) B   b) C   c) E   d) G

Page 88: Reading Questions

1 "Do you know anyone who takes drugs?"

"No, but my mother's a doctor, and she has worked a lot with people who are addicted to drugs."

"Well, what did your mother say to them about drugs?"

"She told them that it's not worth the trouble taking drugs because they make you feel awful. What's more, they cost lots of money and they can even kill you."

"It's true. I would never take drugs."

2 "Hello, madam. How can I help you today?"

"I feel ill. My throat hurts a lot and I have stomach ache."

"Let's see... I recommend that you try to rest and take this medicine. I'm going to give you a prescription. Apart from this, I can't do anything else. If you want to get better, you need to relax."

"Okay, thank you for your help, Doctor. Goodbye."

Page 89: Writing Questions

2 Pienso que es importante mantenerse en forma. Cuando era joven, era muy perezoso/a. Nunca hacía ejercicio y comía comida basura. Ahora corro o nado al menos tres veces por semana y me siento mejor. Sin embargo, todavía tengo que comer una dieta más equilibrada. Intentaré comer cinco frutas cada día y beberé más agua.

Section Nine — Travel and Tourism

Page 91: Where to Go

1) Está en la costa del océano Atlántico en el norte de España.
2) Es famosa por su catedral y sus peregrinaciones.
3) Se puede nadar en uno de los ríos.

Page 92: Accommodation

1) A   2) 3   3) modern, elegant   4) B

Page 94: How to Get There

My city has many types of transport. The underground, which opened in 1924, is very clean and fast. Moreover, there is a tram network by which you can visit the majority of the neighbourhoods of the city. From the airport, it is possible to fly to all the important cities in Europe and it's not very far from the centre. Soon, they're going to improve the bus network, which will be great.

Page 97: Listening Questions

1 a) A, B & E   b) F, H & I
2 a) February
  b) because her husband doesn't like to travel far by plane
  c) get a tan
  d) Rome / the capital of Italy
  e) €495 per person

Page 99: Reading Questions

1 The most stressful journey of my life was last year. We had to go to the airport by bus, but unfortunately, there was a traffic jam on the motorway, so we arrived quite late. Then they told us that the flight had been cancelled due to snow and that we would have to wait for some seven or eight hours. How awful!

2 a) She found it really funny.
  b) There are lots of activities / you can choose what to do.
  c) Two from: there weren't any arguments; they didn't have to come out of the staffroom to look after the students; everyone's still friends.

Page 100: Writing Questions

2 Mi país preferido es Gales porque hay muchas montañas y los galeses son muy simpáticos. Otra ventaja es que es fácil visitar algunos pueblos en tren. Me encantaría ir a Conwy en el futuro. Sin embargo, la última vez que fuimos a Gales, ¡llovió la semana entera!

Section Ten — Current and Future Study and Employment

Page 103: School Routine

1) el comercio   2) el dibujo   3) la música

Page 104: School Life

Statements 2, 5 and 6 are true.

Page 107: Education Post-16

Cuando era joven, pensaba que me gustaría ser profesor/a. Mis padres son profesores y aunque encuentran el empleo interesante, mi padre dice que es bastante estresante. Ahora he decidido que voy a ir a una academia para estudiar fotografía. ¡Me encantaría sacar fotos de bodas!

Page 108: Career Choices and Ambitions

"When I was fifteen, it was difficult to get a job," said my mother. "Yes, but a lot has changed in recent years," I replied.

"I want to be a lawyer. They earn a good salary and I would like to help people. The work would be so varied!"

Page 109: Languages for the Future

1) know at least three languages
2) start going to German evening classes
3) it will have language labs
4) the pronunciation

Page 111: Listening Questions

1 a) a teacher dedicated to supporting the victims of bullying
  b) He can't go to the toilet during lessons.
  c) one hour per day
  d) Two from: more time for sport; more time to relax; they'd be less stressed; they'd find subjects more interesting.
2 a) P — big salary; N — stressful
  b) P — working with numbers; N —boring to be in an office all day
  c) P — helping people / rewarding; N — working at night / weekends

Page 113: Reading Questions

1 I didn't have the opportunity to learn any languages in school. When I started working in an Italian restaurant, the chef/cook taught me a bit of his language. I'm going to look for an Italian course because it would be very interesting. I think it's essential that everyone learns at least one foreign language.

2 a) una agencia de viajes
  b) en casa
  c) Two from: un ordenador; tiempo; experiencia en cuanto a la creación de sitios web.

Page 114: Writing Questions

2   Después de mis exámenes, me gustaría ser aprendiz. El verano pasado, tuve dos semanas de experiencia laboral en una empresa pequeña. Fue muy interesante y aprendí mucho. No quiero hacer el bachillerato porque los exámenes son muy estresantes para mí y no me gusta hacer los deberes.

Section Eleven — Grammar

Page 116: Words for People and Objects
1) el; los sombreros
2) el; los problemas
3) la; las tradiciones
4) el; los viernes
5) el; los porcentajes
6) el; los franceses
7) la; las tensiones
8) la; las dificultades
9) la; las ciudades
10) el; los mapas

Page 117: 'The', 'A', 'Some' and Other Little Words
1) Me gusta el chocolate.
2) No tengo agua.
3) Es profesora.
4) Quiere unas patatas.
5) Quiero hablar con la señora López.
6) Cada persona tiene dos perros.

Page 118: Words to Describe Things
1) el perro feliz
2) siete faldas rojas
3) los coches azules
4) dos mujeres bajas
5) cinco gatos pequeños
6) nueve sillas violeta
7) cuatro libros beis
8) una persona triste

Page 119: Words to Describe Things
1) Hay muchos gatos.
2) el primer día
3) el mismo perro
4) los otros alumnos
5) Algunas personas creen que... / Alguna gente cree que...
6) Es un gran profesor.

Page 120: Words to Describe Things
1) Sus libros son nuevos. / Los libros suyos son nuevos.
2) Quiero esa manzana.
3) Aquel león está comiendo.
4) Estas peras son buenas.
5) Ese hombre, cuya mujer es española, es alto.
6) Lucas es el chico cuyos padres son simpáticos.

Page 121: Words to Compare Things
1) Mi gato es el más gordo.
2) Soy tan alto/a como mi padre.
3) El perro es mayor que el/la niño/a.
4) Fue el peor día de la semana.
5) La película es mejor que el libro.
6) Nuestra novela es la más interesante.

Pages 122-123: Quick Questions
1 a) m c) f e) m g) f i) m k) f m) f o) f
  b) m d) m f) f h) m j) m l) f n) m p) f
2 a) las fresas
  b) los sábados
  c) los conejos
  d) los peces
  e) los meses
  f) los jardines
  g) las edades
  h) las narices
  i) las mujeres
  j) los relojes
  k) las luces
  l) los limones
  m) los jueves
  n) los exámenes
  o) las camisas
3 a) las d) las
  b) El e) Los
  c) el

4 a) un, una, unas b) un, una c) un, unos
5 a) Nos gustan el jamón y el queso.
  b) Los sábados, me levanto tarde.
  c) En el futuro, quiero ser camarero.
  d) Quisiera unos tomates, por favor.
  e) La señora García es mi profesora.
  f) No tengo ordenador.
  g) Lo aburrido es que no podemos salir.
6 a) fáciles e) emocionante
  b) vieja f) mucha
  c) Tantas g) fenomenal
  d) castaño, largo, liso h) estupenda
7 a) grande f) felices
  b) gordo g) difícil
  c) delgadas h) bonitas
  d) fáciles i) peligroso
  e) alto j) hermosa
8 a) Vi tres casas **grandes**.
  b) Compró tres blusas **naranja**.
  c) Quisiera un abrigo **lila**.
  d) Las paredes son **azules**.
  e) Conocí a cuatro personas **tristes**.
9 a) Vivo en un piso pequeño.
  b) Maria es una niña feliz.
  c) Mis profesores son simpáticos.
  d) El fútbol es fácil.
  e) Compra tres libros interesantes.
  f) Ben y Adam son jóvenes.
10 a) Hace **buen** tiempo.
  b) No había **ningún** coche.
  c) Es un **mal** profesor.
  d) Probé un **buen** zumo.
  e) **Alguna** gente cree que es una **mala** idea.
11 a) Mis c) Nuestros e) Sus
  b) vuestro d) tus f) su
12 a) mías b) vuestra c) tuyos d) nuestro
13 a) Vivo en esta calle. c) Quisiera esas patatas.
  b) Viven en aquella calle. d) ¿Os gustaría este libro?
14 a) Las fresas son más deliciosas que las uvas.
  b) Barcelona es tan interesante como Madrid.
  c) El bádminton es menos aburrido que el hockey.
  d) Mi padre es tan estricto como mi madre.

Page 124: Words to Describe Actions
1) Lloran ruidosamente.
2) Vive saludablemente.
3) Habla claramente.
4) Hablamos inteligentemente.
5) El bebé duerme bien.
6) Corro rápidamente / deprisa.
7) Bailas / Bailáis mal.
8) Leo lentamente / despacio.

Page 125: Words to Describe Actions
1) Mis zapatos están aquí.
2) Quiero hacerlo de nuevo. / Lo quiero hacer de nuevo.
3) Lo hice con paciencia.
4) Vivimos lejos.
5) Lo hizo en seguida.
6) Bailó con entusiasmo.

Page 126: Words to Compare Actions
1) Carmen come más rápidamente.
2) Luis canta tan bien como Adela.
3) Selina es la que mejor conduce.
4) Estudio mejor que mis amigos.
5) Andamos / Caminamos más lentamente / más despacio que Rob.
6) Ed es el que peor corre.

Page 127: Words to Say How Much

1) Hay demasiados gatos aquí.
2) Es bastante interesante.
3) Tengo muchos amigos.
4) Hablan demasiado lentamente / despacio.
5) Hay tantas playas en España.
6) El libro es buenísimo.

Page 128: Quick Questions

1 a) lentamente   e) simplemente
  b) normalmente   f) obviamente
  c) ruidosamente   g) completamente
  d) claramente   h) honestamente

2 a) Hablan muy tristemente.
  b) Tenemos que escuchar cuidadosamente.
  c) Conduce peligrosamente.
  d) Canta dulcemente.

3 a) Voy a hacer mis deberes **en seguida**.
  b) Me despierto y **después** me levanto.
  c) Mi primo **siempre** ha comido así.
  d) **A veces** es difícil saber la respuesta.
  e) Haz las compras, y **mientras tanto**, iré allí.
  f) **Ahora** estoy listo.

4 a) Claudia habla más rápidamente **que** Irene.
  b) A Ian le encanta trabajar. Trabaja **más** alegremente que sus colegas.
  c) Mi hijo menor no duerme tan **tranquilamente** como su hermano.
  d) Corro más **despacio** que mis amigas. ¡No voy a ganar nunca!
  e) Yo canto bien, pero ella canta **mejor**.
  f) Él baila **peor** que sus hermanos.

5 a) Elisa studies the most diligently.
  b) Julia sings the most happily.
  c) José and Luna speak the most clearly.
  d) They celebrate the most frequently.

6 a) Para mí, el inglés es bastante difícil.
  b) Creo que el rugby es muy aburrido.
  c) Normalmente es demasiado honesto.
  d) Jodie estuvo muy enferma el lunes.

7 a) El campo es **hermosísimo**.
  b) Mi casa es **pequeñita**.
  c) Creo que los patos son **feísimos**.

Page 129: I, You, We

1) ellos   3) nosotros   5) él   7) ellas
2) ella   4) vosotros   6) ustedes   8) ellos

Page 130: Me, You, Them

1) La rompe.
2) La bebo.
3) Le compró una falda.
4) Le envío / mando un correo electrónico.
5) Quiero hacerlo. / Lo quiero hacer.
6) Nos lo dijo.

Page 131: More Pronouns

1) Mi hermana, que tiene siete años, es baja.
2) Fui a Madrid, que es la capital de España.
3) ¿Cuál es tu dirección?
4) ¿Con quién vives?
5) ¿De quién es este perro?
6) ¿Cuál prefieres?

Page 132: More Pronouns

1) Son los míos.
2) ¿Qué es aquello?
3) Esta cama es más grande que aquella.
4) Este libro es más interesante que ese.
5) ¿Es el vuestro?
6) Alguien está hablando tranquilamente.

Page 133: Prepositions

1) La casa está enfrente del banco.
2) El tren va hasta Italia.
3) Lo escuché en la radio.
4) Entro en el supermercado.
5) Soy de Hull, pero vivo en Crewe.
6) A partir de septiembre, tendré un trabajo.

Page 134: Por, Para and the Personal 'a'

1) para   3) Por   5) por
2) a   4) por   6) para

Page 135: Conjunctions

1) La geografía es divertida, pero es difícil.
2) Me gusta la historia porque es fácil.
3) Como estoy enfermo/a, me quedo en casa.
4) Voy al parque cuando hace calor.
5) Hablo francés e italiano.
6) ¿Prefieres azul o amarillo?

Page 136: Quick Questions

1 a) ¡Buenos días, señores! ¿Cómo **están**?
  b) ¡Hola Lily! ¿**Has** visto a mi hermano?
  c) Julio y Carmen, ¿**queréis** ir de compras?
  d) Como presidente, usted **debe** hacer más por la gente.

2 a) Me dio el libro.
  b) Le mandé una carta.
  c) Os llamé ayer.
  d) ¿Les gustaría ir al cine?
  e) Nos mostró una foto.

3 a) La tarta es para **ti**.
  b) Ayer estaba pensando en **ella**.
  c) ¿Las zanahorias son para **mí**?
  d) ¿Ellas tienen que ir **contigo**?
  e) Estábamos hablando de **ti** y de **él**.

4 a) ¿De quién es este coche?
  b) ¿Qué hiciste el fin de semana pasado?
  c) ¿Quién te llamó?
  d) ¿Cuál es tu dirección?
  e) ¿Cuál prefieres?
  f) ¿De quiénes son estos abrigos?

5 a) No quiero comprar esta falda — quiero comprar esa.
  b) Si quieres leer un libro, puedes leer aquel.

6 a) El tren **para** Madrid va a salir en diez minutos.
  b) Hice esta tarta **para** Melissa, porque es su cumpleaños.
  c) Gracias **por** el regalo.
  d) Pagué treinta euros **por** los zapatos.

7 a) Comió tres peras **y** dos piñas.
  b) Quiero dar un paseo **pero** está lloviendo.
  c) Yo cocinaba la cena **mientras** ellos iban al parque.
  d) Puedes hacerlo **si** quieres.

Page 137: Verbs in the Present Tense

1) bailo
2) bebemos
3) nadáis
4) corre
5) aprende
6) visitan
7) escribes
8) Vive aquí desde hace un año.

Page 138: Irregular Verbs in the Present Tense

1) Comienza
2) Vais
3) Queremos
4) Doy
5) Puedes
6) Sé

Page 139: 'Ser' and 'Estar' in the Present Tense

1) Está
2) Es
3) Somos
4) Estoy
5) es
6) es

Page 140: Quick Questions

1 a) tener
 b) querer
 c) vivir
 d) cantar
 e) escribir
 f) pensar

2 a) Sita y Raúl **escriben** muchas cartas.
 b) Alejandro, **¿escribes** una novela?
 c) Yo **escribo** cerca del mar.
 d) ¿Usted **escribe** mucho?

3 a) Como pollo todos los días.
 b) Vengo aquí desde hace cuatro años.
 c) Esperamos desde hace una hora.

4 a) Yo **pienso** que él tiene un perro.
 b) **Almuerzo** a las once.
 c) Correct
 d) Correct
 e) No duermo bien cuando **llueve**.

5 a) Sé que tiene una hermana.
 b) Cuando va al parque, juega al fútbol.
 c) Prefiero hacer mis deberes en seguida.

6 a) Daniel y yo **somos** griegos.
 b) Mi padre **es** bombero y mi madre **es** traductora.
 c) Boris y John **son** unos jóvenes muy inteligentes.
 d) Tú **eres** una persona muy amable.

7 a) El libro **está** en mi mochila.
 b) Estoy muy cansado/a hoy.
 c) Bilbao **está** en España.
 d) ¿**Estás** enfermo/a hoy?

8 a) ¡Hola! **Soy** George.
 b) No puedo venir a tu fiesta. Todavía **estoy** de vacaciones en Escocia.
 c) No **somos** de Valencia, sino de Málaga.
 d) Hannah **es** una persona bastante trabajadora.
 e) Ethan **está** triste porque ha perdido su dinero.

Page 141: Talking About the Past

1) lloraron
2) comimos
3) escribisteis
4) cené
5) diste
6) pude
7) hicisteis
8) puso
9) viniste
10) trajimos

Page 142: Talking About the Past

1) cantaba
2) éramos
3) aprendía
4) decía
5) volvían
6) seguíais
7) nadabas
8) iban

Page 143 Talking About the Past

1) hacía
2) volví
3) Fuiste
4) Iba; tuve

Page 144: Talking About the Past

1) Habían cantado.
2) Ha viajado.
3) Habéis aprendido.
4) Ha visto.
5) Había bebido.
6) Habíamos terminado.
7) Ha seguido.
8) Has vivido.

Page 145: Talking About the Future

1) voy a comer; comeré
2) vamos a tener; tendremos
3) va a bailar; bailará
4) voy a dar; daré
5) van a poner; pondrán
6) vais a jugar; jugaréis
7) vas a poder; podrás
8) va a cantar; cantará
9) vamos a querer; querremos
10) vais a vivir; viviréis

Page 146: Would, Could and Should

1) irías
2) cantaría
3) vendríamos
4) diríais
5) partiría
6) saldrían
7) hablaría
8) tendríamos

Pages 147-148: Quick Questions

1 a) lloró
 b) salimos
 c) suspendiste
 d) duró
 e) abrí
 f) escribimos
 g) comisteis
 h) aprobaron
 i) nació
 j) bebieron

2 a) Mercedes, ¿tú **fuiste** a la pescadería?
 b) Mis primos y yo **pusimos** la caja en el coche.
 c) Yo **traje** mis libros.
 d) Vosotras **vinisteis** al espectáculo.
 e) Luis **hizo** su maleta anteayer.
 f) Tus amigos te **dieron** un sombrero.
 g) Lia me **dijo** que Joe estaba triste.

3 a) Visitábamos a nuestra abuela.
 b) Eras cocinero/a.
 c) Veía películas los viernes.
 d) Cantaba en el coche.
 e) Nevaba en el campo.
 f) Iban a ese supermercado.
 g) Hablaba mucho.
 h) Comíais mucho chocolate.

4 a) cantabas
 b) fui
 c) cenábamos
 d) Hacíamos
 e) dijo
 f) era
 g) hizo
 h) Estaba

5 a) Cuando oí el ruido, estaba en casa.
 b) Hacía mucho frío y llovía también.
 c) Iban a York cuando vieron el gato.
 d) Tenía una chaqueta verde.

6 a) hablado
 b) pedido
 c) abierto
 d) visto
 e) puesto
 f) bebido
 g) escrito
 h) nadado
 i) dicho
 j) hecho
 k) vuelto
 l) roto

7 a) He comido una ración de tortilla.
 b) Lucía ha escrito una historia interesante.
 c) Hemos hecho un viaje a Londres.
 d) Has puesto las tazas en el lavaplatos.

8 a) El examen había empezado.
 b) Habías elegido estudiar arte dramático.
 c) Habían abierto el monedero.
 d) Había comprado el collar en una tienda.

9 a) You had broken the windows.
 b) Federico had already had lunch.
 c) We had seen that film.
 d) They had slept on the sofa.

10 a) aprenderemos   c) cantarás   e) mentirán

    b) traerá   d) Corregiré

11 a) Buscaré el libro mañana.

    b) Cenaremos en el restaurante de mi padre.

    c) Nos llamarán después del espectáculo.

    d) Pondréis los lápices en la mesa.

    e) Tendrá un paraguas.

12 a) Viajaría   c) Podría   e) Daría

    b) Tendría   d) Haría   f) Dejaría

13 a) Comería, pero no tiene hambre.

    b) Ayudaría, pero no puede conducir.

    c) ¿Podrías darme esa bufanda?

    d) Deberíamos visitar a Sergio.

    e) Compraría un recuerdo, pero no tengo dinero.

    f) No venderían su casa.

Page 149: Reflexive Verbs

1) me llamo; me he llamado

2) se levantan; se han levantado

3) se lava; se ha lavado

4) te acuestas; te has acostado

5) nos sentimos; nos hemos sentido

6) os vais; os habéis ido

7) se viste; se ha vestido

8) te despiertas; te has despertado

Page 150: Verbs with '-ing' and 'Just Done'

1) está cayendo; estaba cayendo; acaba de caer

2) estás abriendo; estabas abriendo; acabas de abrir

3) está saltando; estaba saltando; acaba de saltar

4) están diciendo; estaban diciendo; acaban de decir

5) estáis corriendo; estabais corriendo; acabáis de correr

6) estamos siguiendo; estábamos siguiendo; acabamos de seguir

7) estás dando; estabas dando; acabas de dar

8) estoy leyendo; estaba leyendo; acabo de leer

9) están sirviendo; estaban sirviendo; acaban de servir

10) estamos bailando; estábamos bailando; acabamos de bailar

Page 151: Negative Forms

1) No fui al cine.

2) Ya no vamos al gimnasio.

3) No vas ni a Oslo ni a Faro.

4) Sally no tiene ninguna manzana.

5) No hay nada aquí.

6) No hay nadie en el coche.

Page 152: The Passive and Impersonal Verbs

A) Sentences 2 and 3 are written in the passive voice.

B)   1) Se compra   2) Se comen

Page 153: The Subjunctive

1) saltes   3) limpiemos   5) venga   7) puedan

2) escuche   4) abran   6) hagamos   8) tengáis

Page 154: The Subjunctive

1) present subjunctive

2) imperfect subjunctive

3) present subjunctive

4) imperfect subjunctive

Page 155: Giving Orders

1) ¡Canta!; ¡No cantes!

2) ¡Bailen!; ¡No bailen!

3) ¡Ten!; ¡No tengas!

4) ¡Dé!; ¡No dé!

5) ¡Abrid!; ¡No abráis!

6) ¡Venid!; ¡No vengáis!

7) ¡Sea!; ¡No sea!

8) ¡Vayan!; ¡No vayan!

Page 156: Quick Questions

1 a) te llamas   e) se acuesta

   b) me siento   f) se van

   c) nos levantamos   g) nos despertamos

   d) os dormís   h) se pone

2 a) Estoy charlando con mis amigos.

   b) Está escuchando música en el salón.

   c) Estamos pidiendo unas bebidas.

   d) Estaba leyendo el periódico.

3 a) Joe ya no enseña química.

   b) No vamos nunca al parque.

   c) No llevo ni gafas ni un collar azul.

4 a) —   e) —

   b) fue fundada   f) —

   c) —   g) será llevado

   d) está pintado   h) fueron comprados

5 a) iii   b) i   c) ii   d) iv

6 a) deje   b) venga   c) esté

7 a) enviaras   b) fuera   c) tuviera

8 a) ¡Canta!   d) ¡Sé!   g) ¡Di!   j) ¡Miente!

   b) ¡Abre!   e) ¡Salta!   h) ¡Ven!   k) ¡Ten!

   c) ¡Haz!   f) ¡Pon!   i) ¡Corre!   l) ¡Sal!

9 a) Siga   b) Gire   c) tome

Practice Exam — Listening Paper

Question Number	Answer	Marks
1	Maths — P	[1 mark]
	Geography — N	[1 mark]
2	English — P+N	[1 mark]
	Business Studies — N	[1 mark]
3	History — P	[1 mark]
	Biology — P+N	[1 mark]
4	Spends time with her husband and children.	[1 mark]
5	two from: do some exercise; play tennis; stay at home and read books	[2 marks]
6	It's just opened. / It's in the plaza de San Juan.	[1 mark]
7	No, because she thought her boyfriend's starter was better / smelt delicious.	[2 marks]
8	She had eaten tuna the day before yesterday.	[1 mark]
9	There would be a more relaxed atmosphere.	[1 mark]
	There would be fewer children shouting and running.	[1 mark]
10	hot air coming from Africa / the Sahara desert.	[1 mark]
11	C	[1 mark]
12	lie down in a dark room	[1 mark]
	have a cold drink	[1 mark]
13	A + D	[2 marks]
14	B + E	[2 marks]
15	cultural visits / trips	[1 mark]
	they're expensive	[1 mark]
16	he wants to visit Asia	[1 mark]
	he intends to go to the USA (to spend time with his friend)	[1 mark]
17	you see the best parts of a country without getting bored	[1 mark]
	visiting the mosques in Turkey	[1 mark]
18	She failed most of her exams.	[1 mark]
19	They suggested she should redo the exams she did badly in.	[1 mark]
20	phone her / offer to help with her revision.	[1 mark]
21	C	[1 mark]
	They want to make a difference.	[1 mark]
22	B	[1 mark]
23	A	[1 mark]
24	A	[1 mark]
25	B	[1 mark]
	A	[1 mark]
26	C	[1 mark]
27	A	[1 mark]
28	Las empresas buscan a individuos que tengan buenas habilidades comunicativas.	[1 mark]
29	B	[1 mark]
	D	[1 mark]
30	C	[1 mark]
	E	[1 mark]
31	B	[1 mark]
	C	[1 mark]
32	A	[1 mark]
	D	[1 mark]

Total marks for Listening Paper: 50

Answers

You'll find mark schemes for the Speaking and Writing papers on p.219 & p.220.

Practice Exam — Speaking Paper

Role-play sample answer

1) Practico deporte dos veces a la semana.
2) Me gusta jugar en equipo porque es divertido y puedes jugar con tus amigos.
3) Me encantaba practicar deporte cuando era pequeño/a.
4) ¿Te gusta practicar deporte?
5) Podría beber más agua y comer menos caramelos para llevar una vida más sana.

Photo Card sample answer

1) En la foto hay una familia. Las personas están celebrando la Navidad juntas.
2) Sí, me gustaría pasar la Navidad en España porque me interesa la tradición de los Reyes Magos. Además, me gustaría probar el turrón.
3) La fiesta que más me gusta es la Nochevieja porque me encanta ver los fuegos artificiales. Siempre organizamos una fiesta y nos divertimos mucho.
4) Fui al cine con mis amigos y luego fuimos a un restaurante de comida italiana. Recibí muchos regalos y lo pasé fenomenal.
5) Creo que alguna gente gasta demasiado dinero en los regalos de cumpleaños y de Navidad. Los niños no necesitan treinta mil regalos. Sin embargo, me encanta preparar comida especial para las fiestas y eso cuesta dinero.

General Conversation sample answers

Local, national, international and global areas of interest

1) Mi casa es bastante moderna. Tiene seis habitaciones y un jardín bastante grande. Mi habitación preferida es la cocina, porque siempre huele a pan y hay una televisión muy grande.
2) En el futuro, me gustaría vivir en una gran ciudad multicultural como Londres. Habría más gente y más instalaciones de ocio. Me gustaría poder ir al teatro y a los mejores museos del país sin tener que viajar mucho.
3) El problema medioambiental que más me inquieta es el cambio climático. Algunos científicos creen que el cambio climático ha causado desastres naturales en algunos países.
4) Hay muchas organizaciones benéficas que ayudan a los sin techo. Podemos donar ropa o libros a una tienda solidaria. Además, podemos ayudar con la organización de campañas.
5) Ya me he ido de camping con mis amigos. Lo bueno de ir con amigos es que tienes más libertad que cuando vas de vacaciones con tus padres, pero claro, tienes que organizar y arreglar todo sin ayuda. No me gustaría irme de vacaciones largas con mis amigos porque creo que sería estresante.
6) El verano que viene iré a París con mi madre y mi hermana. Iremos a Francia en barco y luego alquilaremos un coche. Visitaremos a unos amigos que viven allí e iremos a varios museos. Probaremos la comida típica de Francia e intentaré hablar un poco de francés. ¿Tiene usted planes para el verano?

Current and future study and employment

1) Voy a un instituto mixto. Es bastante grande, ya que tiene unos mil alumnos. Generalmente, las instalaciones son muy buenas, pero el año que viene van a construir otra sala de profesores, porque de momento no hay suficiente espacio para los profesores y todos los libros que tienen.
2) Mi asignatura preferida es la biología porque me gusta aprender sobre el cuerpo humano y la naturaleza. Siempre me ha gustado el inglés, pero este año no me gusta tanto porque el profesor es un poco aburrido.
3) Pienso que hay algunas reglas muy buenas. Por ejemplo, no se puede correr en los pasillos y hay que llegar al colegio a tiempo. Sin embargo, odio el uniforme que tenemos que llevar porque es incómodo.
4) No, no me gustaría continuar con mis estudios, pero no sé exactamente lo que quiero hacer. A lo mejor buscaré experiencia laboral o empezaré a trabajar en la empresa de mi tío.
5) Cuando era pequeño/a, quería ser cocinero/a. Tenía una cocina de plástico y me gustaba vestirme de blanco y preparar cenas imaginarias para toda la familia. Todavía creo que sería un trabajo bastante interesante, pero lo malo es que hay que trabajar por la noche. ¿Cree que sería una buena opción?
6) Sí, creo que puede ser una buena idea tomar un año sabático porque te da tiempo para pensar en lo que quieres hacer. Mi primo se tomó un año libre, viajó por el mundo y lo pasó fenomenal. Aprendió mucho sobre el mundo y conoció a mucha gente.

Practice Exam — Writing Paper

Q1.1 — Sample answer

Trabajo en una tienda benéfica. La tienda vende ropa y muebles y da el dinero a los sin techo. Decidí trabajar allí porque tuve que realizar algún tipo de trabajo voluntario como parte del programa 'Duke of Edinburgh'. Es esencial que ayudemos a los demás. En mi opinión, hay mucha desigualdad social en mi ciudad y si no apoyamos a otra gente, la situación no puede mejorarse. Para contribuir a la sociedad podría ayudar en una residencia de ancianos. Creo que sería interesante hablar con la gente que vive allí y aprender sobre el pasado.

Q1.2 — Sample answer

Acabo de volver a casa después de pasar dos semanas estupendas en Cornwall con mi familia. Prefiero irme de vacaciones en verano porque suele hacer mejor tiempo. Además, en verano puedes estar en la playa hasta las diez de la noche sin tener frío. Generalmente me gusta ir de vacaciones con mi familia. Me llevo bien con mi hermano porque nos gusta hacer las mismas cosas y siempre nos divertimos juntos. En un mundo ideal, pasaría un mes de vacaciones en Australia. Visitaría el puente de Sídney y nadaría con los peces tropicales. ¡Serían unas vacaciones fenomenales!

Q2.1 — Sample answer

¡Hola! Ayer fui al cine para ver la película 'Tartas, por favor'. Se trata de una mujer, Mila, que se emborracha y decide abrir una pastelería con su amigo a pesar de que no saben nada sobre los pasteles. Yo creí que al final, aprenderían a hacer unas tartas riquísimas y que se enamorarían, pero no pasa nada así. En cambio, ella causa un incendio y la pastelería se destruye. Pierden todo su dinero y tienen que volver a sus vidas originales. La película me gustó mucho porque la trama me sorprendió. Además, las actuaciones fueron muy impresionantes. La actriz que tuvo el papel de Mila es una gran estrella y me gusta mucho. Lo único que cambiaría es la banda sonora. La música fue un poco aburrida y por eso no contribuyó mucho a la atmósfera. Te recomendaría esta película, creo que te gustaría mucho. Un saludo.

Q2.2 — Sample answer

¡Hola! Trabajo aquí en España desde hace una semana y hasta ahora, ha sido una experiencia fenomenal. Para mí, la ventaja de trabajar aquí es que gano dinero y consigo experiencia laboral mientras mejoro mi español y aprendo sobre otra cultura. Voy a gastar el dinero que he ganado en unas excursiones que quiero hacer el fin de semana que viene. Creo que vale la pena buscar experiencia laboral, porque si la tienes, es más fácil encontrar un trabajo en el futuro. Lo mejor es que mi nivel de español ya ha mejorado mucho. El septiembre que viene, volveré al instituto porque voy a hacer el bachillerato. Por fin, dejaré de estudiar las asignaturas que no me gustan como el dibujo y la historia. Luego me gustaría ir a la universidad porque me encantaría ser profesora de español. Además, me encantaría visitar algún país en Sudamérica, como Perú o Argentina. Seguro que lo pasaré fenomenal. ¡Hasta pronto!

Q3 — Sample answer

Me gusta reciclar. En casa, reciclamos botellas y papel. Pensaba que era aburrido, pero ahora pienso que es esencial. Creo que será más importante en el futuro porque si no reciclamos, habrá más basura en las calles. ¿Estás de acuerdo conmigo?

Practice Exam — Reading Paper

Question Number	Answer	Marks
1.1	10 minutes	[1 mark]
1.2	When you pass the fishmonger's	[1 mark]
1.3	police station / Post Office	[1 mark]
2.1	He prefers them because you can learn new things / He prefers them because they're about interesting topics.	[2 marks]
2.2	Sometimes there are jokes that the children don't understand. / Sometimes there are jokes that make the adults laugh.	[1 mark]
2.3	B	[1 mark]
3.1	B	[1 mark]
3.2	A	[1 mark]
3.3	A	[1 mark]
4.1	C + D	[2 marks]
4.2	So that everyone can take advantage of the benefits of yoga.	[1 mark]
5.1	C	[1 mark]
5.2	one of the most fun cities in Spain	[1 mark]
5.3	A	[1 mark]
6.1	B	[1 mark]
6.2	B	[1 mark]
6.3	C	[1 mark]
7.1	B	[1 mark]
7.2	C	[1 mark]
8.1	A	[1 mark]
8.2	A + P	[1 mark]
8.3	A + P	[1 mark]
8.4	P	[1 mark]
9.1	positive; incredible atmosphere / unique experience	[2 marks]
9.2	negative; described as a comedy but there are sad bits	[2 marks]
9.3	positive and negative; it's charming but disappointing (because there's no mention of what happened to the man's wife)	[2 marks]
10	E, G, D, A	[4 marks]
11.1	Ha trabajado durante todo el verano. / Ha ahorrado suficiente dinero.	[1 mark]
11.2	Juan ha comprado un móvil parecido.	[1 mark]
11.3	sacar fotos	[1 mark]
11.4	charlar (con la gente) cara a cara	[1 mark]
12.1	por Internet	[1 mark]
12.2	two from: la oportunidad de ser creativa / viajar por todo el mundo / conocer a personas interesantes	[2 marks]
12.3	Es casi imposible mantener amistades. / No sabe quién es un verdadero amigo.	[2 marks]
13.1	La generación que viene va a sufrir.	[1 mark]
13.2	el gobierno	[1 mark]
13.3	Es aburrido. / No es su problema.	[1 mark]
13.4	(Piensa que) hace suficiente.	[1 mark]
14.1	A	[1 mark]
14.2	C	[1 mark]
14.3	B	[1 mark]
15	We have just spent *[1 mark]* an incredible week in Granada. *[1 mark]* We stayed in a modern hotel in the city centre. *[1 mark]* The food was delicious and the room had an enormous balcony. *[1 mark]* If I could return to Granada tomorrow *[1 mark]* I would do it straight away, *[1 mark]* especially because we didn't have time *[1 mark]* to visit the cathedral. *[1 mark]* We will have to return next year! *[1 mark]*	[9 marks]

Total marks for Reading Paper: 60

Answers

Speaking Exam Mark Scheme

It's very difficult to mark the practice Speaking Exam yourself because there isn't one 'right' answer for most questions. To make it easier to mark, record it, and use a dictionary, or get a Spanish teacher, to mark how well you did. Use the mark schemes below to help you, but bear in mind that they're only a rough guide and that the mark schemes for your exam board might not be exactly like these ones.

Role-play (15 marks)

In the Role-play, you're marked separately on your communication and your use of language. There are 2 marks available for communication for each of the 5 bullet points (tasks) in the Role-play (10 marks in total), and then 5 marks are available for your use of language.

Marks	Communication (per task)
2	You complete the task clearly.
1	You complete part of the task clearly.
0	You don't complete the task correctly.

Marks	Knowledge and Use of Language (overall)
4-5	Your knowledge and use of vocabulary is good / very good.
2-3	Your knowledge and use of vocabulary is reasonable.
0-1	Your knowledge and use of vocabulary is very poor / poor.

Photo Card (15 marks)

You are scored out of 15 for the Photo Card, and the only criteria is the quality of your communication.

Marks	Communication
13-15	You reply clearly to all of the questions and develop most of your answers. You give and explain an opinion.
10-12	You reply clearly to all or most of the questions and develop some of your answers. You give and explain an opinion.
7-9	You give reasonable answers to most questions and develop one or more of your answers. You give an opinion.
4-6	You give reasonable answers to most questions, but some of your answers are short and / or a bit repetitive.
1-3	You reply to some of the questions, but your answers are short and / or repetitive.
0	You don't say anything that's relevant.

General Conversation (30 marks)

The General Conversation should last between five and seven minutes, and you are marked on four separate criteria.

Marks	Communication
9-10	You consistently give well-developed answers, present information clearly, and explain your opinions convincingly.
7-8	You regularly develop your answers, present information clearly, and give and explain your opinions.
5-6	You develop some of your answers, usually present information clearly, and often explain some of your opinions.
3-4	Your answers are generally short, but you present some information clearly and sometimes explain your opinions.
1-2	You give short answers, and there are some questions you can't answer or don't answer clearly. You give some opinions.
0	You don't say anything that's relevant to the questions.

You lose one mark for communication if you don't ask the examiner a question at some point during the General Conversation.

Marks	Range and Accuracy of Language
9-10	You use an excellent range of vocabulary and structures. You use the past, present and future tenses confidently and correctly. Any mistakes are small and only occur when you're attempting complex structures and / or vocabulary.
7-8	You use a good range of vocabulary and structures. You use past, present and future tenses correctly, with small mistakes.
5-6	Your vocabulary is good and you use some structures and tenses correctly. Your meaning is clear despite some mistakes.
3-4	You use simple vocabulary and structures well. You use some different tenses and your meaning is generally clear.
1-2	You use simple vocabulary and structures, with some repetition. Frequent mistakes can make your meaning unclear.
0	You don't say anything that makes sense or can be easily understood.

Marks	Pronunciation and Intonation
4-5	Your pronunciation and intonation are mostly / consistently good.
2-3	Your pronunciation and intonation are often good, but there are several mistakes.
1	Your pronunciation can generally be understood, and you attempt to use some intonation.
0	You don't pronounce anything clearly and you cannot be understood.

Marks	Spontaneity and Fluency
4-5	The conversation flows naturally and seems spontaneous. You answer promptly and your speech flows easily at times.
2-3	The conversation generally flows well, but at times it seems as though you're relying on pre-learnt answers. Sometimes you answer promptly, but you hesitate before answering some questions, and you may not be able to answer them all.
1	Lots of what you say seems as though it has been pre-learnt. You hesitate a lot and your answers don't flow.
0	You don't show any spontaneity and can't be easily understood.

Writing Exam Mark Scheme

Like the Speaking Exam, it's difficult to mark the writing exam yourself because there are no 'right' answers. Again, you ideally need a Spanish teacher who knows your exam board's mark schemes to mark your answers properly. Each of the writing tasks has a different mark scheme.

Question 1 (16 marks)

Marks	Content
9-10	You've completed the task fully, your meaning is always clear and you've expressed multiple opinions.
7-8	You've written a good answer covering all four bullet points. Your meaning is clear and you've used multiple opinions.
5-6	You've written a reasonable answer, covered most bullet points and given an opinion. Your meaning isn't always clear.
3-4	Your answer is quite basic, covering some of the bullet points. You've given an opinion, but your meaning can be unclear.
1-2	Your answer is limited, covering one or two bullet points. Your meaning is often unclear and you haven't given an opinion.
0	You haven't written anything relevant. If you score 0 for content, you automatically get 0 for the whole question.

Marks	Quality of Language
5-6	You've used a wide range of vocabulary, some complex sentences and structures, and at least three tenses. Errors are mostly minor, and any major errors occur only in complex sentences and structures, with the meaning remaining clear.
3-4	You've used a variety of vocabulary, some complex sentences and structures, and at least two tenses. There are frequent minor errors and some major errors, but the meaning is usually clear.
1-2	You've used a narrow range of vocabulary and your sentences are mainly short. There are frequent major errors.
0	You haven't written anything that's suitable for the task.

Question 2 (32 marks)

Marks	Content
13-15	You've written a relevant, detailed answer that clearly gives a lot of information, and you've justified your opinions.
10-12	Your answer is detailed, mostly relevant and it usually presents information clearly. You've justified your opinions.
7-9	Your answer is generally relevant and gives plenty of information. Some bits are unclear, but you have given opinions.
4-6	Your answer gives some relevant information, but at times your meaning is unclear. You have given an opinion.
1-3	Your answer is basic, contains limited relevant information and is often unclear. You may have given an opinion.
0	You haven't written anything relevant. If you score 0 for content, you automatically get 0 for the whole question.

Marks	Range of Language
10-12	You've used a wide range of vocabulary, some complex sentences and structures, and an appropriate style.
7-9	You've used a variety of vocabulary, attempted some complex sentences and structures, and used an appropriate style.
4-6	You've tried to use a variety of vocabulary and sentences. Your style of writing is not always appropriate for the task.
1-3	You've repeated some vocabulary, your sentences are mostly short and simple, and you haven't thought about your style.
0	You haven't written anything that's suitable for the task.

Marks	Accuracy
4-5	Your writing is mostly accurate and you've formed verbs and tenses correctly. There are only a few small errors.
2-3	Your writing is more accurate than inaccurate, and your verbs and tenses are mostly correct. There are some errors.
1	You have made some major errors, your verbs and tenses are often incorrect, and your meaning is not always clear.
0	You haven't written anything that makes sense or could be easily understood.

Question 3 (12 marks)

Marks	Conveying Key Messages
5-6	You've conveyed nearly all / all of the key messages in your translation.
3-4	You've conveyed most of the key messages in your translation.
1-2	You've conveyed very few / few of the key messages in your translation.
0	You haven't written anything relevant. If you score 0 here, you get 0 for the whole task.

Marks	Use of Grammar, Language and Structures
5-6	You've shown very good / excellent knowledge of vocabulary and structures, with very few mistakes.
3-4	You've shown a reasonable / good knowledge of vocabulary and structures, and the translation is more accurate than inaccurate.
1-2	You've displayed limited knowledge of vocabulary and structures, and there are lots of mistakes.
0	You haven't written anything that's suitable for the task.

Transcripts

Section One — General Stuff

Track 1 — p.3

E.g. **M1**: ¡Hola! Soy Carlos. Voy al gimnasio todos los días y los jueves juego al fútbol.

1) **F1**: ¡Buenos días! Me llamo Anabel. Celebré mi cumpleaños anteayer y fui a un restaurante con mi familia y mis amigos.

2) **F1**: Ayer, fuimos de compras a Londres, pero mañana por la mañana, iremos a Oxford. Me encantan las cafeterías en Oxford.

3) **F2**: ¡Hola! Me llamo Julia. Mañana voy a ir al cine con mis amigas, y el viernes vamos a ir al teatro.

Track 2 — p.10

E.g. **M1**: ¿Qué te gusta hacer los fines de semana, Carolina?

F1: Me encanta ir a la piscina.

1) **F1**: Y tú Antonio, ¿qué te gusta hacer los fines de semana?

M1: A mí me gusta ir de compras, pero no me gusta escuchar música.

2) **F1**: ¿Por qué te gusta ir de compras?

M1: Me gusta ir de compras porque es muy divertido y las tiendas en mi ciudad son estupendas. Alguna gente cree que ir de compras es para chicas, pero eso no es verdad.

3) **F1**: Ah, muy bien. Pero, ¿por qué no te gusta escuchar música?

M1: Mucha gente adora la música, pero a mí nunca me ha interesado. Prefiero leer. Acabo de terminar una novela fenomenal. Las novelas y los periódicos sí que son interesantes porque se puede aprender mucho. ¿Estás de acuerdo?

4) **F1**: Sí, estoy de acuerdo. Me encanta leer porque es relajante, pero me gusta escuchar música también.

5) **F1**: Prefiero los grupos de música pop porque la música pop me parece guay.

Track 3 — p.11

E.g. **F2**: A mí me encanta viajar por España. Hay tantas ciudades maravillosas, pero mi ciudad preferida es Madrid, sin duda. He visitado la ciudad seis veces.

1a) **F2**: ¿Te gusta viajar Carmen?

F1: Sí, lo encuentro muy interesante. Mi país preferido de los que he visitado es Irlanda. Fui por primera vez en 2003. El paisaje es tan pintoresco y la gente es muy agradable.

1b) **F2**: ¿Fuiste a Irlanda en avión? Siempre voy a Madrid en coche. Está a unos ciento noventa kilómetros de mi ciudad.

1c) **F1**: No, fuimos en barco. Cuando cumpla veintisiete años, espero volver a Irlanda.

Track 4 — p.11

2a) **M1**: Farah, ¿te gusta el café?

F2: Cuando era pequeña, no me gustaba para nada. Sin embargo, ahora me encanta el café. Lo bebo todos los días.

2b) **M1**: ¿Por la mañana?

F2: Sí, normalmente. Mi desayuno preferido es una taza de café y una tostada con mermelada. No me gustan los cereales.

2c) **M1**: Y, ¿qué piensas de las verduras?

F2: En general, me gustan las verduras, sobre todo los champiñones, pero odio las patatas. ¡Tienen un sabor horrible!

2d) **M1**: ¿Cuál es tu fruta preferida?

F2: Mi fruta preferida… me encantan las peras. Sin embargo, mi madre no las compra nunca porque no le gustan para nada.

2e) **M1**: ¿Y te gusta el chocolate?

F2: Sí, a mí me gusta el chocolate, ¡es delicioso!

Section Two — Me, My Family and Friends

Track 5 — p.18

1) **F2**: Esta persona parece bastante baja. Tiene el pelo liso y castaño, pero no lo tiene especialmente largo. Lleva unas gafas bastante grandes. Es una persona joven.

2) **M1**: Tiene el pelo negro, pero no es ni liso ni rizado. Creo que tiene los ojos marrones y que es una persona bastante alta. No lleva gafas.

3) **F2**: Esta persona no tiene ni barba ni bigote. Tiene el pelo largo y moreno, y creo que es bastante delgada. Lleva maquillaje y no tiene pecas.

4) **M1**: No es totalmente calvo, pero no tiene mucho pelo. Tiene el pelo gris, y tiene barba. No sé el color de sus ojos. No es joven — la verdad, parece bastante viejo.

Track 6 — p.25

E.g. **M1**: ¡Hola! Soy Luca. Tengo los ojos marrones, el pelo largo y rizado, y tengo una barba también.

1a) **F1**: Soy Beatriz. Tengo el pelo rubio. Cuando era pequeña, tenía el pelo cortísimo porque era más fácil y más práctico correr, pintar y jugar así. Ahora tengo el pelo largo. Necesito llevar gafas porque veo muy mal.

1b) **M2**: Soy Faisal. En el futuro, quiero tener una barba porque hoy en día está muy de moda. Mis padres tienen los ojos azules, pero yo tengo los ojos marrones. Tengo el pelo negro y rizado.

1c) **F2**: Mi nombre es Pilar. Soy de altura mediana. Acabo de cortarme el pelo. Lo tenía muy largo pero ahora lo tengo corto. Preferiría tener el pelo menos rizado porque los rizos me fastidian mucho.

Track 7 — p.25

2a) **F1**: ¡Hola Saúl! ¿Qué tal? ¿Cómo vais con los planes para la boda?

M1: Bien gracias, Inés. Tendrá lugar el 22 de junio.

F1: Fenomenal. ¿Dónde vais a celebrar la boda?

M1: Bueno, yo quería casarme por la iglesia, pero Alba no quería hacerlo así, así que vamos a casarnos en la playa.

F1: ¡Qué emocionante! ¿Vais a invitar a mucha gente, o solo a vuestras familias?

M1: Habrá muchísima gente y espero que haga buen tiempo.

F1: Espero que os vaya bien.

M1: Gracias.

2b) **M1**: ¿Te gustaría casarte algún día?

F1: No lo sé. Sería muy romántico. Me encantaría tener una fiesta y llevar un vestido blanco.

M1: Entonces, ¿por qué no?

F1: Pues mis padres no están casados, pero se llevan muy bien. Creo que es más importante hacer cosas juntos y pasarlo bien que tener una fiesta.

M1: Ya entiendo.

Section Three — Technology in Everyday Life

Track 8 — p.34

1a) **M2**: Bueno, Laura, ¿para qué usas Internet?

F2: En primer lugar, uso Internet para hacer mis deberes. Sin él, no podría buscar la información que necesito para estudiar.

M2: Sí, yo también uso la red para aprender. Es una herramienta muy útil. Sería muy difícil sin tener una conexión en casa.

1b) **M2**: ¿Usas la red para algo más, Laura?

F2: Sí, uso la red para hacer las compras. Es muy fácil elegir lo que quieres y lo mejor es que no tienes que salir de casa.

1c) **M2**: Pero, ¿no te preocupa la idea de comprar cosas por Internet? He leído unos artículos muy inquietantes sobre la seguridad.

F2: No. De hecho, uso Internet también para organizar mis cuentas bancarias. Es más conveniente que ir al banco, y tengo un buen servidor de seguridad.

1d) **M2**: No sé cómo puedes pagar así. Para mí, la desventaja más grande de Internet es que la gente puede robar tu información, incluso tus contraseñas.

1e) **F2**: No estoy de acuerdo. Para mí, lo más inquietante de la red no es el riesgo de fraude, sino que hay mucha gente peligrosa que te puede mentir.

Track 9 — p.34

2a) **F1**: Bueno, me llamo Azucena. Estoy aquí con mis compañeros de clase Sharif y Silvia y voy a empezar el debate. Según mi madre, las redes sociales crean un sinfín de problemas. Cuando tengo disputas con mis amigos, ella siempre echa la culpa a las redes sociales. Sin embargo, son muy importantes en mi vida. Desde mi punto de vista, no tienen ni una desventaja.

2b) **M2**: Muy interesante, Azucena. Sin embargo, a mi modo de ver, hay dos tipos muy diferentes de redes sociales. Por un lado, hay las salas de chat en las que hablas con la gente que no conoces y por otro lado, hay otros tipos de redes sociales en las que solo hablas con tus amigos. Debido a esta diferencia, las salas de chat son peligrosas, pero otras redes sociales pueden tener muchas ventajas.

2c) **M2**: ¿Qué opinas tú, Silvia?

F2: Cuando vamos a un restaurante, mis amigos hacen fotos de la comida y las cuelgan en seguida. No me gusta porque mis amigos no quieren ni hablar ni divertirse — solo quieren publicar cosas aburridas en sus muros. Creo que es de mala educación hacer eso.

Section Four — Free-Time Activities

Track 10 — p.40

E.g. **M1**: ¡Hola Marisol! ¿Cuál es el género de música más importante para ti?

F2: Diría que mi género preferido es la música rap porque creo que es la música más original y distinta. Me encanta la música clásica también porque es relajante. Sin embargo, según mi hermana menor, la música más importante para nuestra generación sería la música pop.

1) **M1**: ¿Tocas algún instrumento?

F2: Cuando era más joven, tocaba el piano, pero en este momento, no tengo suficiente tiempo para practicar. Me encantaría aprender a tocar el saxofón porque es un instrumento fenomenal y porque el jazz es un tipo de música que siempre me ha fascinado.

2) **M1**: ¿Cómo escuchas música, Marisol?

F2: Me gusta escuchar música por Internet, porque es muy rápido descargar canciones y cuesta menos que ir a una tienda para comprar un CD.

3) **F2**: Me encanta ir a conciertos también, porque la música en directo es siempre muy emocionante.

Track 11 — p.43

E.g. **M1**: ¡Hola! Soy Joaquín. Cuando era pequeño, me gustaba comer muchos caramelos y helados y odiaba las verduras. ¡No me importaba para nada la salud!

1) **M1**: Ahora como de todo — mariscos, legumbres y carne. Odio la comida basura porque no solo engorda, sino que suele llevar cantidades enormes de sal y azúcar. ¿Qué te gusta comer, Alejandra?

2) **F1**: Creo que comes mejor que yo, Joaquín. Si pudiera comer caramelos todos los días, lo haría. Sería mejor si comiera más fruta, pero no me gusta mucho. Mis padres me dicen que bebo demasiado café, así que ahora estoy intentando beber más agua.

3) **F2**: Me llamo Raquel. No como ni pescado ni carne — soy vegetariana. Normalmente es bastante fácil evitar la carne porque me gustan las legumbres. Sin embargo, cuando voy a restaurantes con mis amigos, es más difícil porque hay pocos platos sin carne. Por otro lado, los platos vegetarianos suelen ser más baratos que los que contienen carne o pescado.

Track 12 — p.47

1a) **F1**: ¡Buenas tardes señor! ¿En qué puedo servirle?

M1: Quisiera una limonada grande con hielo, por favor.

1b) **F1**: Muy bien. Y ¿quiere comer algo?

M1: No sé si prefiero unos calamares o un filete. ¿Qué me recomendaría?

F1: Los dos platos están siempre muy ricos, pero creo que el cocinero recomendaría el filete. Es muy sabroso y la carne viene de esta región.

1c) **M1**: Pues entonces pediré el filete con verduras y patatas fritas, por favor.

F1: Sí, claro. Y ¿postre también?

1d) **M1**: No debería tomar nada de postre, pero un poquito de helado no me haría ningún daño. Un helado de fresa, por favor.

F1: Muy bien, señor.

Track 13 — p.47

2a) **F1**: ¡Hola! Soy Mireia. A mí me gusta jugar al fútbol porque es muy divertido. Sin embargo, solo lo veo de vez en cuando porque para mí es menos entretenido verlo en la tele. En cuanto a los deportes que veo, tendría que decir que prefiero ver el tenis. Veo todos los partidos de Wimbledon y la dedicación de los jugadores siempre me parece fenomenal.

2b) **F1**: ¿Te gusta ver el tenis, Rahim?

M2: A mí no me gusta mucho porque los partidos duran hora tras hora. Me encantan los Juegos Olímpicos. Los deportes olímpicos que más me gustan son el atletismo y la natación. No sé mucho sobre esos deportes, pero me convierto en experto cada cuatro años.

2c) **M2**: Y a ti, Isabel, ¿te gusta ver el deporte en la televisión?

F2: Pues a mi hermano siempre le ha encantado ver el rugby todos los fines de semana. No podía evitarlo, entonces empecé a ver los partidos con él y ahora veo el rugby incluso cuando él no está en casa. Además, me gusta ver el fútbol y la natación.

Section Five — Customs and Festivals

Track 14 — p.54

1) **M1**: El premio es trece millones de euros y el número ganador es… ochenta mil seiscientos setenta y tres. ¡Felicitaciones a todos!

2) **F1**: ¡Hola! Soy Ana. Estoy contentísima porque gané 2.000.000 de euros en El Gordo. Voy a comprar un apartamento de lujo, y luego iré al Mediterráneo con mi novio tres semanas.

3) **F1**: Carla, ¿qué hiciste esta Navidad?

F2: En Navidad, me lo pasé fenomenal porque mis abuelos vinieron a quedarse con nosotros. Viven muy lejos de aquí, así que casi nunca los veo. En Nochebuena, mi madre preparó una cena deliciosa. Había mariscos, carne y varios postres, pero lo que más me gustó fue el turrón de chocolate.

4) **F2**: ¿Recibiste regalos, Diego?

M1: Sí, se me cayó el móvil el mes pasado, y por lo tanto, mis padres me dieron un móvil nuevo. Mi hermano había pedido unos juguetes pero le regalaron una bicicleta azul. Cuando la vio, estaba tan emocionado que ¡empezó a bailar por el salón!

Track 15 — p.55

1a) **M1:** ¡Bienvenidos a todos! Vamos a empezar esta visita guiada aquí. En esta pared, hay colgadas fotos de una fiesta muy tradicional que se celebra en México — el Día de los Muertos.

1b) **M1:** Las fotos más antiguas están a la izquierda y las más modernas están a la derecha, así que podrán entender cómo ha cambiado la manera de celebrar el Día de los Muertos a través de los años.

1c) **M1:** Como se puede ver, muchos mexicanos llevan maquillaje y se disfrazan de esqueletos. Además, las tiendas venden esqueletos y huesos hechos de azúcar.

1d) **M1:** También se puede ver imágenes de unos cementerios decorados por las familias de los muertos. Hay que recordar que a pesar de las celebraciones, el Día de los Muertos también es una fiesta seria en la que se recuerdan parientes difuntos.

1e) **M1:** El Día de los Muertos siempre tiene lugar el primer día de noviembre y es una de las fiestas más tradicionales e importantes de nuestra cultura.

Track 16 — p.55

2a) **F1:** Soy Clara. Mi padre es español y mi madre es de China, así que tenemos la suerte de celebrar el año nuevo dos veces — una vez el 1 de enero y luego otra vez en febrero con mis abuelos maternos. Si solo pudiera celebrar el año nuevo una vez, lo haría al estilo chino porque es más impresionante: hay procesiones larguísimas, dragones y todo el mundo se viste de rojo.

2b) **F1:** Sin embargo, lo que más me gusta en cuanto a las celebraciones del año nuevo en España es que cuando escuchas las campanadas de medianoche, tienes que comer doce uvas. Parece una tradición tonta, pero en realidad es muy divertida, tanto para los niños como para los adultos.

2c) **M2:** Mi nombre es Tariq, y ya que soy musulmán, durante el mes de Ramadán, no debo ni comer ni beber durante el día. Luego, al fin del mes, celebramos Eid al-Fitr. Me encanta porque llevamos ropa nueva y visitamos a nuestros parientes. Sin duda, lo mejor de las festividades es que comemos muchos platos tradicionales que no tenemos tiempo para preparar normalmente.

Section Six — Where You Live

Track 17 — p.64

E.g. **F2:** ¡Hola! Quiero hacer una tortilla española para una fiesta de cumpleaños y necesito unos ingredientes. ¿Me puede ayudar?

M1: Sí, claro. ¿Qué le hace falta?

1) **F2:** Pues primero, necesito un kilo de patatas. Y póngame también medio kilo de cebollas.

M1: Claro. ¿Algo más?

2) **F2:** Sí, deme seis huevos, pero no necesito sal, porque ya la tengo en casa.

M1: Aquí tiene.

3) **F2:** ¡Ay, casi se me ha olvidado! Necesito también una botella de aceite de oliva.

M1: Desafortunadamente, no tengo aceite de oliva. Acabo de vender la última botella.

4) **F2:** ¡Qué pena! Tendré que ir a otra tienda. ¿Cuánto cuesta todo?

M1: Cuesta seis euros cincuenta.

F2: Vale, gracias. Aquí tiene. ¡Adiós!

M1: Gracias. ¡Adiós!

Track 18 — p.65

E.g. **M1:** ¡Hola! Te voy a hablar de mi barrio. Es un barrio histórico, así que hay un castillo, un ayuntamiento y un teatro.

1) **M1:** El teatro está en la parte este del barrio donde también hay muchos restaurantes. Está al lado de un museo muy impresionante.

2) **M1:** En la plaza hay un bar que es muy popular tanto con los jóvenes como con los jubilados. Había tres supermercados hace un par de años, pero ahora solo hay uno.

3) **M1:** Se puede encontrar el supermercado al fondo de la calle San Felipe, enfrente de la comisaría.

4) **M1:** Luego, si sigues esa calle y tomas la segunda calle a la derecha, encontrarás la iglesia.

Track 19 — p.67

1a) **M2:** Háblame de tu casa, Emilia.

F1: Vivo con mis padres en una casa adosada en las afueras de la ciudad. Me encantaría vivir en una casa más grande, pero costaría demasiado dinero.

M2: Pero, ¿te gusta la casa, no?

F1: Sí, por lo menos está situada en un barrio muy popular y seguro. El interior de la casa es muy moderno y tenemos varios estilos de muebles.

1b) **F1:** ¿Dónde vives tú, Santiago?

M2: Alquilo un piso pequeño con mi primo. Compartimos un cuarto de baño y una cocina.

F1: ¿Te gusta vivir allí, Santiago?

M2: Lo malo es que nuestro piso se encuentra en la quinta planta, ¡pero no hay ascensor! Me fastidia tener que subir y bajar las escaleras, especialmente ya que las lavadoras están en el sótano. Quiero mudarme pronto.

Track 20 — p.67

2a) **F1:** ¿Qué haces para ayudar en casa, Juana?

F2: Pues mi madre es muy simpática y no me hace ayudar nunca en casa. ¡Ni siquiera sé poner el lavaplatos ni la lavadora! ¡No sé qué haré cuando vaya a la universidad el año que viene!

2b) **F1:** ¡No es justo! Tengo que ayudar mucho porque mi padre no vive en casa desde hace muchos años.

2c) **F2:** Dame un ejemplo de lo que tienes que hacer, Manuela.

F1: Durante la semana, debo quitar la mesa, arreglar mi dormitorio y a veces sacar la basura.

2d) **F2:** Y los fines de semana puedes relajarte, ¿no?

F1: No, los fines de semana tengo que preparar la cena para mi mamá y mi hermana menor.

Section Seven — Social and Global Issues

Track 21 — p.75

E.g. **F2:** Desafortunadamente, hay miles de personas sin techo en España.

1) **F2:** Debido a los problemas económicos que tenemos, muchas personas han perdido su trabajo y no tienen suficiente dinero para pagar el alquiler.

2) **F2:** Algunos pueden pedir ayuda a sus padres o amigos, pero otros acaban en la calle. Lo que todos tienen en común es que tienen una vida dificilísima.

3) **F2:** Sin embargo, lo peor es que frecuentemente son víctimas del prejuicio, lo que les puede dificultar la vida bastante.

4) **F2:** Este prejuicio existe porque mucha gente cree que los sin techo no pueden pagar su alquiler porque son perezosos.

5) **F2:** Si queremos cambiar la situación de estas personas, tenemos que trabajar juntos — es la única manera de hacerlo.

Track 22 — p.78

1a) **F1:** ¡Hola! Soy Briana. Vivo en el norte de España, donde hemos visto unas inundaciones terribles. Ha sido un gran problema para mucha gente. Por eso, a pesar de que hay sequías en otras partes del mundo, el problema medioambiental que más me preocupa es la amenaza de inundaciones.

1b) **M2:** Entiendo por qué dices eso, Briana. Yo soy Alberto y por mi parte, creo que hay muchos problemas inquietantes, entre ellos los desastres naturales y el cambio climático. Sin embargo, la deforestación me parece más preocupante porque los árboles nos ayudan mucho.

1c) **F2:** Muy interesante, Alberto. Mi nombre es Raquel y para mí, el problema que más me molesta tiene que ver con nosotros. Alguna gente es tan perezosa que en vez de buscar una papelera, tira su basura en la calle. ¡Qué asqueroso! Debemos reducir la cantidad de basura que producimos.

Track 23 — p.78

2a) **M2**: ¡Hola a todos! Yo soy Arturo y hoy vamos a hablar con una política que quiere transformar la vida en nuestra ciudad. ¡Hola, Señora Rodríguez!

F2: ¡Buenos días!

M2: Bueno, usted ya ha dicho que hay unos problemas que quiere solucionar. ¿Por dónde quiere empezar?

F2: Voy a empezar con el problema de la desigualdad social. Aquí los ricos son muy ricos y los pobres son muy pobres.

2b) **F2**: Me parece ridículo que haya gente que no tiene suficiente dinero para comprar comida y ropa para sus familias. Además, algunas personas pasan frío en sus casas porque no tienen dinero para gastar en calefacción.

2c) **M2**: Vale. ¿Hay algún otro problema que usted quiera mencionar?

F2: Sí. Debido a la desigualdad social, hay mucho prejuicio. Alguna gente cree que los pobres son perezosos.

2d) **F2**: A veces, este prejuicio acaba en violencia, sobre todo entre los jóvenes. Este es el último problema que me gustaría solucionar.

Section Eight — Lifestyle

Track 24 — p.86

1a) **M2**: Tenemos aquí a Julia. Julia acaba de lanzar una campaña para animar a la gente a desayunar de una manera más saludable. Julia, ¿por qué es importante que la gente desayune?

F1: Pues tengo dos hijas y hace unos años, noté que la menor había dejado de desayunar porque no quería engordarse. Me preocupó mucho porque yo siempre había considerado el desayuno como la comida más importante del día.

1b) **M2**: Entonces, ¿qué hizo usted?

F1: Empezamos a buscar información juntas sobre el tema del desayuno. Resulta que la gran mayoría de los científicos cree que es esencial desayunar debido a la relación bastante fuerte que hay entre la gente que desayuna todos los días y la gente que lleva una vida sana. Después de informarse un poco más, mi hija decidió que sería mejor no saltarse el desayuno.

1c) **M2**: ¿Qué deberíamos desayunar, entonces?

F1: Yo creo que lo más importante es desayunar lo más equilibrado y variado posible. Como dice la expresión, la variedad es la sal de la vida. Pero en serio, huevos, cereales y tostadas son opciones buenas y baratas. Lo único que hay que recordar es que algunos cereales contienen cantidades extraordinarias de azúcar, lo que puede afectar a los dientes.

M2: Muchas gracias, Julia.

Track 25 — p.86

2a) **F1**: ¿Qué piensas del consumo del alcohol, Tom?

M1: Desde mi punto de vista, creo que beber demasiado alcohol es peligroso. No me gusta cuando mis amigos beben demasiado.

2b) **F1**: ¿Crees que es la responsabilidad del gobierno limitar el consumo excesivo?

M1: Sí, sin duda. Podría limitar o incluso prohibir los anuncios publicitarios de alcohol para combatir el consumo excesivo.

2c) **F1**: ¿Y eres fumador?

M1: Yo no, pero mi novia sí. Odio el olor del humo. Me alegro de que ahora no se pueda fumar ni en bares ni en restaurantes.

2d) **F1**: ¿Quieres que tu novia deje de fumar?

M1: Sí, el tabaquismo es un problema grave. Me preocupan mucho los efectos negativos que tiene en la salud de mi novia. Los cigarrillos hacen mucho daño.

Section Nine — Travel and Tourism

Track 26 — p.92

1) **M1**: Los hoteles son regulares en general, contándose dos buenos.

2) **M1**: Los tres mejores que hay dentro de la ciudad son el de Pfaroux, el de las cuatro Naciones, y el de Europa.

Fuera de la ciudad, y en el camino de Botafogo, hay dos ingleses y uno francés: el mejor de todos, tanto de los de la ciudad, como de los de fuera, es el Hotel de los Extranjeros en la plaza de Catette.

3) **M1**: Es una gran casa, de moderna y elegante construcción, sólida, con anchas y magníficas habitaciones: un gran jardín al pie del mar, vistas admirables, comodidades muchas.

4) **M1**: El hotel todo está alumbrado por el gas: tiene baños, billares y grande capacidad: en el Hotel de los Extranjeros, viven la mayor parte de los individuos del Cuerpo Diplomático extranjero.

Track 27 — p.97

1a) **F1**: Hotel Cristal, buenos días.

M1: ¡Hola! ¿Es posible reservar una habitación doble para esta noche y mañana por la noche?

F1: Un momento… Sí, hay habitaciones disponibles.

M1: ¡Perfecto! Y, ¿es posible reservar una habitación que tenga vista a las montañas?

F1: Claro que sí.

M1: Finalmente, ¿a qué hora se cierra el restaurante en el hotel? Es que no vamos a llegar hasta las nueve y media.

F1: No se preocupe, señor. El restaurante se cierra a las once y media.

M1: Gracias.

1b) **F1**: Hotel Cristal, buenas tardes.

F2: Buenas tardes. Soy Paloma Beltrán. Tengo una reserva en el hotel esta noche. ¿Puede confirmar que tengo alojamiento de media pensión? No me acuerdo bien, ya que reservé la habitación hace cuatro meses.

F1: Sí, usted tiene alojamiento de media pensión.

F2: Estupendo. Y, ¿hay aparcamiento cerca del hotel? Es que tenemos un coche bastante grande.

F1: El aparcamiento más cercano está a unos cinco minutos del hotel.

F2: Fenomenal. Y, ¿el aparcamiento es seguro?

F1: Sí, hay unos guardias que vigilan los coches 24 horas al día.

F2: Muy bien. Muchas gracias.

Track 28 — p.97

2a) **M2**: ¡VaVaVacaciones! Buenos días, soy Javier. ¿Cómo puedo ayudarle?

F2: Hola. Quisiéramos reservar unas vacaciones. Todavía no hemos decidido adónde queremos ir, pero nos gustaría ir en febrero. ¿Puede usted aconsejarnos?

2b) **M2**: ¡Por supuesto! ¿Ustedes prefieren viajar lejos o visitar un país cercano?

F2: A mi marido no le gusta viajar lejos en avión, por eso diría un país cercano.

2c) **M2**: Muy bien. Y, ¿qué les importa más — el sol o la cultura?

F2: Las dos cosas. Mi marido prefiere broncearse en la playa, pero a mí me encanta visitar centros históricos.

2d) **M2**: Entonces les recomiendo Roma, la capital de Italia.

F2: No hemos estado nunca en Roma. ¿Cuánto cuesta?

2e) **M2**: El mejor precio sería €495 por persona, todo incluido.

F2: Lo reservaremos. ¡Muchas gracias!

Section Ten — Current and Future Study and Employment

Track 29 — p.103

1) **M1**: ¡Ay, Marta! Odio los lunes.

   F1: ¿Por qué?

   M1: ¿No es obvio? Tenemos matemáticas, comercio y después del recreo, inglés. Es horrible.

2) **F1**: Pero los martes son mejores, ¿no? Me gustan las ciencias y el dibujo.

   M1: ¿Y el francés?

   F1: No me emociona mucho. Prefiero las asignaturas más prácticas.

3) **M1**: Estoy de acuerdo. Yo prefiero los miércoles. Es una oportunidad para ser creativo. Por ejemplo, empezamos con los trabajos manuales. Después hay el español y a las diez y media, tenemos música. Es mi día preferido.

Track 30 — p.111

1a) **F1**: Soy Nuria. Quiero hablar sobre el acoso escolar. Por lo general, los alumnos en este colegio son simpáticos, pero hay algunos que intimidan a otros estudiantes. Me parece muy injusto. Creo que sería una buena idea tener un profesor dedicado al apoyo de las víctimas del acoso escolar.

1b) **M1**: Soy Syed. Para mí, el problema que más me afecta no es el acoso escolar, sino el número de reglas que hay. Creo que algunas reglas son importantes. Sin embargo, hay otras reglas que me fastidian porque las encuentro estúpidas. Por ejemplo, no nos dejan ir al baño durante las clases. Eso me parece muy injusto.

1c) **F2**: Soy Lucía. A mi modo de ver, nos dan demasiados deberes. Es importante hacer los deberes, pero creo que una hora cada día es suficiente.

1d) **F2**: Además, si tuviéramos menos deberes, tendríamos más tiempo para hacer deporte y relajarnos. Estaríamos menos estresados y probablemente las asignaturas nos parecerían más interesantes también.

Track 31 — p.111

2a) **F1**: ¡Hola! Soy Kyra y acabo de solicitar un puesto de abogada. Tuve que mandar mi currículum a la compañía y tendré que ir a una entrevista. Lo malo de este empleo es que sería bastante estresante. Sin embargo, soy una persona ambiciosa y me gustaría tener un sueldo bastante grande.

2b) **M2**: Soy Rafael y me gustaría ser contable. He estudiado matemáticas y me gustaría trabajar con los números. Creo que se puede encontrar por lo menos un inconveniente relacionado con cualquier empleo. En este caso, es que sería aburrido pasar todo el día en una oficina.

2c) **F2**: Mi nombre es Laura. Actualmente creo que me gustaría ser bombera. Es un empleo difícil porque tienes que trabajar por la noche y los fines de semana también. Pero por lo menos me daría la oportunidad de ayudar a otra gente, lo que resultaría muy gratificante.

Practice Exam — Listening Paper

Track 32 — p.163-172

1) **F1**: A mí me encantan las matemáticas porque las encuentro facilísimas. Además a veces puedo ayudar a mis amigos. Sin embargo, detesto la geografía porque es aburrida.

2) **F1**: ¿Qué piensas tú, Vanessa?

   F2: El año pasado, el inglés fue mi asignatura preferida, pero ahora tengo un nuevo profesor que nos da demasiados deberes así que no sé si me gusta o no. Este año, tengo que estudiar comercio, y no me gusta nada. Los profesores dicen que nos prepara para el futuro, pero creo que es poco útil.

3) **F2**: ¿Cuál es tu asignatura preferida, Francisco?

   M1: Desde mi punto de vista, es muy importante estudiar historia. Por lo tanto, escogería esta asignatura como mi preferida. Dicho esto, me gusta la biología ya que me da un conocimiento más profundo del mundo y de la naturaleza. Sin embargo, no consigo sacar buenas notas porque no entiendo algunos aspectos fundamentales, lo que me pone triste.

4) **F2**: Después de un día duro de trabajo, suelo terminar muy tarde. Para mí es muy importante ver a mi familia, así que siempre paso tiempo con mi marido y mis niños.

5) **F2**: Si tengo un poquito de tiempo libre, intento hacer un poco de ejercicio porque me hace sentir más tranquila. Los fines de semana, cuando no tengo las presiones del trabajo, me gusta jugar al tenis con mis amigos o quedarme en casa y leer novelas históricas.

6) **M1**: ¿Qué tal tu cumpleaños, Blanca? Fuisteis a un restaurante, ¿no?

   F1: Sí, lo pasé muy bien. Fuimos al restaurante que acaba de abrir en la plaza de San Juan.

7) **M1**: ¿Qué pediste?

   F1: De primer plato, pedí gambas fritas. Me gustaron, pero mi novio pidió calamares y creo que él eligió mejor que yo, porque olían riquísimos.

8) **M1**: Y ¿de segundo plato?

   F1: Pues la especialidad del cocinero es atún a la plancha, pero ya que había comido atún anteayer, pedí pimientos asados con champiñones y ajo. Los pimientos estaban muy dulces, pero lo malo del ajo es que el aliento te huele fatal después de comerlo.

   M1: Sí, sí, eso siempre es una desventaja.

9) **M1**: ¿Volveríais allí?

   F1: Creo que sí. Sin embargo, iría un poquito más tarde porque creo que habría un ambiente más relajado ya que no habría tantos niños gritando y corriendo por entre las mesas.

10) **M2**: ¡Alerta roja en Madrid! La capital está en alerta roja por temperaturas que podrían alcanzar los 40 grados. Debido al aire caliente que está llegando desde África, específicamente del desierto del Sáhara, las temperaturas subirán hasta un nivel peligroso mañana y se mantendrán hasta el sábado que viene.

11) **M2**: Ya que el centro de Madrid se convertirá en un horno, le ofrecemos unos breves consejos para que puedan evitar la insolación. En primer lugar, se recomienda tomar muchos líquidos. Además, no se debe hacer ejercicio físico durante las horas más calurosas del día. Finalmente, no es recomendable permanecer demasiado tiempo en lugares que no estén frescos.

12) **M2**: Es bastante común sufrir de un dolor de cabeza a causa del calor. En casos así, es aconsejable acostarse en una habitación oscura y tomar una bebida fría.

13) **F2**: Para tener una vida sana, te aconsejaría tres cosas. En primer lugar, evitar las bebidas alcohólicas porque contienen una cantidad enorme de azúcar. Las personas que beben más de lo recomendado suelen tener sobrepeso.

14) **F2**: En segundo lugar, hay que dejar de fumar. Los cigarrillos dañan los pulmones y pueden afectar a otros órganos del cuerpo. Finalmente, adopta una rutina más activa. Si hicieras ejercicio un mínimo de tres veces por semana, protegerías el corazón y tendrías más energía.

E.g. **F2**: Hola, Danilo, ¿sabes adónde vas de vacaciones este verano?

M1: Sí, mis padres y yo vamos a Nueva Zelanda. Me encanta viajar en avión. ¡No puedo esperar!

15) **M1**: ¿Y tú, Galia? Tu hermano me dijo que vas a Portugal con tus padres.

F2: De momento, no estoy segura. A mi padre le encantan las excursiones culturales, pero a mí no me interesan. Supongo que podría organizar algo con mis amigos, pero ¡las vacaciones cuestan mucho! Es posible que me quede aquí.

16) **F2**: ¿Adónde vas tú, Gorka?

M2: Pues mis tíos van a Nepal ya que mi tía ha organizado una excursión a las montañas. Generalmente no me interesa el alpinismo, pero tengo muchas ganas de viajar a Asia, así que me iré con ellos. Cuando vuelva, tengo la intención de viajar a los Estados Unidos para pasar tiempo con mi amigo Lionel.

17) **F2**: Irene, vas a organizar un viaje por Europa, ¿no?

F1: ¡Sí! Voy a viajar por todo el continente. Voy a visitar muchos países, pero solo voy a pasar unos pocos días en cada uno. Me gustan las visitas cortas porque puedes ver las mejores partes de cada país sin aburrirte. El último país que visitaré será Turquía. Tengo muchas ganas de ver las mezquitas maravillosas que hay allí. Sin duda, la mejor parte del viaje será visitarlas.

E.g. **F1**: Oye, ¿has oído lo que le pasó a Elena el año pasado?

F2: No.

F1: Fue muy triste. Durante el trimestre de verano sus padres se separaron.

F2: ¡Pobrecita!

F1: Sí, claro.

18) **F1**: Ha sido muy difícil para ella porque ha tenido que mudarse de casa y todo. Pero lo peor es que como consecuencia, suspendió la mayoría de sus exámenes.

19) **F2**: ¡Ay, qué horror! ¿Qué tuvo que hacer?

F1: Habló con su colegio y decidieron que haría de nuevo todos los exámenes en los cuales no había sacado buenas notas. Además, le han dado más apoyo con las ciencias porque las encuentra difíciles. Lo peor es que no está con sus amigos.

20) **F2**: ¡Qué desgracia! La llamaré mañana para preguntarle si la puedo ayudar en algo. Podría ayudarla con el repaso.

F1: Yo también. Buena idea. Como somos sus amigas la tenemos que apoyar.

21) **M1**: Trabajo en una tienda con fines benéficos. Hay una gran variedad de gente que suele visitarnos. De vez en cuando, vemos a adolescentes a quienes les gustan las cositas que vendemos. Lo bueno es que todos tienen la misma actitud. Quieren hacer una diferencia en el mundo con su solidaridad.

22) **M1**: Alguna gente es muy generosa con sus donaciones. La semana pasada, un hombre nos dio unos muebles que no quería más. Unos son de madera y los otros de cuero, y todos están en buen estado. Otra gente es generosa con sus gastos en la tienda, lo cual es bastante importante.

23) **F2**: A todo esto eran las tres de la tarde, y el tren para Madrid salía a las cinco. — ¡Demasiado sabíamos lo mucho que nos quedaba que ver! Salamanca encerraba todavía iglesias, palacios, colegios, casas históricas y otros monumentos, para cuyo examen se requería por lo menos una semana de continuo andar.

24) **F2**: Pero no podíamos disponer de más tiempo, y, además, estábamos tan rendidos, que teníamos que sentarnos a descansar en los trancos de las puertas, con gran asombro de los transeúntes. — ¡Habíamos andado tantísimo en dos días escasos!

25) **M2**: Si buscas una experiencia única en la cultura española, no mires más allá de Las Fallas de Valencia. Es un festival que data de la Edad Media, cuando los carpinteros tenían que usar lámparas de aceite para ver durante el invierno porque claro, todavía no había electricidad. Luego, encendían fuegos grandes para celebrar la llegada de la primavera.

26) **M2**: Ahora, Las Fallas se han convertido en una gran celebración y atraen a miles de turistas cada año. La ciudad se llena de figuras de cartón y papel maché que se llaman 'ninots' y que forman parte de los fuegos en las plazas y calles.

27) **F2**: Hoy día, vivimos en una sociedad conectada por los medios sociales. Sabemos todos lo importante que es comunicarnos con la gente a nuestro alrededor, pero puede ser que la comunicación por las redes sociales nos deje menos capaces de comunicarnos efectivamente en la vida real. De hecho, les recomendamos no usar los medios sociales más de dos o tres veces al día.

28) **F2**: Hay que recordar que un mensaje de texto no reemplaza la comunicación cara a cara. Las empresas buscan a individuos que tengan buenas habilidades comunicativas, así que es esencial saber hablar con otras personas.

29) **F1**: Bienvenidos a la hora cultural. Tenemos un invitado especial que va a informarnos sobre su último programa de televisión que busca a personas que tengan talento musical. Hola, Gerardo, ¿es verdad que en este tipo de programa ves a muchas personas sin talento?

M1: Pues vemos a concursantes que no tienen muchas habilidades musicales, pero, por otro lado, ¡los que las tienen, las tienen en abundancia!

F1: Y ¿es normal que los concursantes toquen algún instrumento?

M1: Todo depende de la persona. Hay unos que tienen una voz perfecta y también saben tocar el piano u otro instrumento a la perfección, pero hay otros que solo saben cantar.

30) **F1**: ¿Cómo es ser juez de un programa como este?

M1: A mí me encanta porque tengo la oportunidad de cambiar la vida de una persona. Eso me resulta muy gratificante. Sin embargo, hay momentos en que necesito tener cuidado con lo que digo ya que para algunos concursantes, cantar es la única cosa que quieren hacer — es su sueño.

31) **F2**: Elegir una carrera es una decisión que resulta muy difícil para muchas personas. Hay pocos jóvenes que saben a la edad de quince o dieciséis años qué les gustaría hacer después del colegio. Por eso, es imprescindible que habléis con vuestros padres o amigos adultos para informaros sobre sus carreras profesionales.

32) **F2**: Este miércoles por la tarde, podréis hablar con unos profesionales sobre sus carreras. Podréis preguntarles cómo es ser piloto, cocinera, abogado, o incluso cómo es ser médica. Será muy interesante, pero os quiero dar un consejo: no importa qué carrera seleccionéis. Lo importante es que utilicéis todo vuestro esfuerzo para sacar las mejores notas posibles. Un mundo de oportunidades y éxito os espera, y quiero que os preparéis lo mejor posible.

Index

Index